TOUGH LOVE SCREENWRITING

The Real Deal From A

Twenty-Year Pro

By

John Jarrell

Cover Design by Brian Kelsey -- bpkelsey.com

Author Portrait by Robert Staley -- robertstaley.com

Clearance and Copyright -- Donaldson + Callif

toughlovescreenwriting.com

TABLE OF CONTENTS

"Writing a book is a horrible, exhausting struggle, like a long bout with some painful illness. One would never undertake such a thing if one were not driven on by some demon whom one can neither resist nor understand."

-- George Orwell

"Not much cock... but look at those balls!"

-- Charles Bukowski

PREFACE

First and foremost, here's what this book is <u>not</u> --

Tough Love Screenwriting is not a book teaching you "how to write".

An individual's "style" or "voice" is extremely personal, and in my experience best developed by quality writers' groups and good ol' fashioned "woodshedding" -- honing your skills and working your ass off via hundreds upon thousands of hours *actually writing*. Good writing. Bad writing. Frankly, *any* writing will help get you there -- as long as you *are* writing. Hard work, not super sexy, I know. But think Malcolm Gladwell's "10,000 Hours Rule" here -- you practice anything long and hard enough, you're bound to get pretty damned good at it.

With all due respect to Blake (whom I shared agents with for a while), this book is also not his extremely popular and helpful *Save The Cat*. Nor is it *How To Write a Screenplay in Twelve Seconds*. Or *Ten Easy Steps to Becoming a Hollywood Script Zen Master*. Or any other well-marketed screenwriting hustle based on shortcuts, gimmicks, getting rich quick, smarmy "plug in your story" paradigms or the "what Hollywood wants" approach.

My friends, there are no shortcuts to great screenwriting. Gimmicks don't build legit writing careers. Getting lucky never lasts.

Anyone tells you otherwise is completely full of shit.

1

"Just add water" is for microwave mac and cheese. Want a magic bullet? Download a book of German folk legends.

Bottom line, for real-deal professionals and hopeful aspirants alike, there is only the hard work of writing. Of waking up day after day to face "the white elephant" (the blank page/screen), seeking to breathe sincere life into the movie you're dying to write, the story you simply have to tell -- despite the intense physical, emotional and financial sacrifices it may require along the way.

Tough Love is aimed squarely at the dedicated writer, the pragmatic dreamer who has pledged themselves to their craft, regardless of results, come Hell or high water, win lose or draw. The straight-shooting individual who understands the odds of becoming a successful screen or television writer are long, but certainly not impossible; and that superb storytelling and stellar writing are your best weapons when seeking to overrun Hollywood's unforgiving granite walls.

So... if you're one of those half-baked jokers banking on blind luck to succeed, hoping to pull a fast one, weasel your way in via some capricious hook-up or random Act of God... forget it, you don't have a prayer.

You're already dead, bro. You just don't know it yet.

Those books I name-checked? Surf on over to Amazon or your online library and DL yourself one. Because, with all due respect, I don't think *Tough Love* is gonna be a good fit for you.

Still with me? Unfazed? Not exactly pissing your skinny jeans at first blush of that "tough love" the cover so boldly promised?

2

Fantastic. Anybody with courage enough to man/woman-up, kick off the security blankets and trashcan tired excuses sounds like a writer after my own heart. Because believe me, homeboys and girls, you're gonna need to break some psychological eggs to get your screenwriting omelet fried up in this town.

* * * * *

So exactly what *is Tough Love*? I'd like to think of it as a screenwriter's version of Anne Dillard's *A Writing Life* or *Henry Miller on Writing*, with no pretension at being anywhere near as literate or groundbreaking as either of those wonderful guides to living one's life -- inside and out -- as a working writer.

Following ever-so-humbly in their footsteps, however, I'd like to create a version for the contemporary film writer that deals point-blank with the intangibles unique to building a serious, successful *career* for yourself as a paid professional. <u>There's a critical mass of street knowledge essential to any screenwriter's survival</u>, and that's *in addition to* the ball-shattering task of writing well -- yet precious few sources outside the Business seem interested in sharing the 411 or giving the fresh meat a fair warning heads-up.

Largely ignored by today's burgeoning clusterfuck of self-proclaimed (read: unproduced) "Screenplay Gurus" are vital boots on the ground topics ranging from the cerebral, esoteric and slightly self-absorbed (the writer's inherent isolation, creative strategies for self-discipline, surfing self-doubt and the inevitable haters) to the more practical/technical side of things (coping with bad notes, breaking down scripts, succeeding in WGA Credit Arbitration). Whether these other folks simply don't understand the mechanics involved or lack anything authentic to share on these subjects, it's still you, the aspiring writer, who's left dick-in-proverbial-hand with another hole in your PayPal account when you buy their "products".

Tough Love doesn't have that problem. This book actively seeks to arm its reader with pro-style strategies and pragmatic game plans, life-saving nuts-and-bolts tricks of the trade. It stresses craft elements I've found particularly important while sharing hard-earned lessons capable of mine-sweeping many of the nasty surprises awaiting most new writers.

But beware -- this book is not gluten-free. It doesn't nurture your heart chakra. You won't find branded spin-offs with glamour headshots lining Internet cybershelves like spiffy feminine hygiene products.

<u>And unlike 99% of the cottage industry classes, books and webinars I've checked out</u> -- 99% created by people who aren't writers and haven't sold a damned thing in the real-life Film Industry -- <u>what follows comes from the direct, firsthand experience of a produced professional with two-plus decades under his belt</u>. A working writer and member of the WGA Screen Credits Committee who's sold scripts, had a hit movie, been hired on numerous writing assignments, dealt with sadistic Studio deadlines and handled batshit-crazy producers, directors and actors at their most extreme (core sample -- Steven Segal, Elie Samaha, Marcus Nispel).

Yep. Been there, survived that. There's nothing "theoretical" about what I share in the following pages. Speculation is not a factor. I've been to the Big Show, played in the Super Bowl, tasted the Championship rounds (add your own dorky sports reference here). Even cooler? By persevering and blindly surfing all the obscene shenanigans, I managed to make a damned good living for myself and my family along the way.

Tough Love is my stab at creating a practical navigational guide for today's screenwriting hopeful; as much memoir as combat field manual and film scribes' Google Maps, regardless of what "level of success" the reader has achieved thus far. Fancy Pants Produced writer? Hillbilly Hayseed unknown? If I've done my job, there should be something of real value here for each of them, and every other writer in-between.

So John, why take time to write <u>Tough Love</u> *in the first place? Risk relentless cyberscorn from wannabes, haters and bitter old trolls, invite contrary rebukes from other produced writers and have to deal with dim-witted pseudo-Spielbergs Net-sniping from the safety of their parents' basements?*

That's easy. For the same reason I teach my labor-of-love class in Los Angeles. Because if someone had taken time to share these insights and intangibles with me after diving headfirst into screenwriting, it would've spared me needless collateral damage and made my own bloody quest a helluva lot easier. **End of the day, this is the book I wish someone had given <u>me</u>**. Because just a shrewd bit of *Tough Love*-style mentoring might've saved me *years* of blind, innocent, unsuccessful soldiering.

If there's one complaint I hear repeatedly from students, it's that <u>nobody will tell them the real shit</u>. The Industry-of-it-all nurtures this ongoing process of self-mystification; legit info about the mechanics of the Biz, an accurate idea of how things really roll "in the room" during meetings (and why) always seems to be hidden from plain sight, confined largely to word-of-mouth forum boards and the inner-circle of those fortunate enough to physically participate. Because of this, fresh fish starting out ice cold like Yours Truly are forced to learn the ropes the hard way; faking everything possible, tiptoeing through ridiculously high-stakes games of liar's poker and praying like hell you'll survive long enough to finally figure it all out on the fly.

My simple question is *why*? You wouldn't send a guy up in an F-18 without going to flight school. Why stuff an unprepared writer headfirst into the trickiest, most volatile and capricious creative/political meat grinder American business has ever known?

Alas, *Tough Love* should help serve as the playbook you were never given, the memo you never got; a sort of Freedom of Information Act for those forever on the outside looking in.

* * * * *

By and large, riveting highs and knee-buckling lows, the Film Business has been very, very good to me. It enabled me to buy my parents a house, then later buy myself one. Its continual opportunity, hard as hell to harness as it can sometimes be, has provided me with a fully-vested pension, some modest savings and an absurd amount of <u>fun</u>; all as a wondrous byproduct of having dedicated myself to the only job I ever really wanted -- writing movies.

Hollywood and Los Angeles are places which made possible all my fondest young dreams coming true. In that light, what the hell, why *not* give back to the eager and uninitiated? Test drive the theory that "no good deed goes unpunished" -- even in Iggy Pop's unbeloved "Butt Town"?

6

It's my profound hope that, however you got turned onto this book, you'll find *Tough Love* aims to be a cut above the ever-burgeoning avalanche of screenplay lit; a book you're glad to have stumbled upon and excited to refer back to as your career progresses. In short, that *Tough Love* possesses the difference in potency between a Virginia Slims and an unfiltered Lucky Strike; or sex with a condom versus sex without.

* * * * *

Lastly, a heartfelt word about... profanity.

If you have any moral, ethical or religious issues with profanity, foul language, crude and unkind references and/or seriously fucked up stories, this book is probably not for you. Please, do not buy, borrow, illegally download or otherwise acquire it. Don't DL to your Kindle or iPhone X then write an indignant Amazon review saying it's the Devil's work, it harms the simple minded or threatens National Security. You'd simply be wasting your time... and Jeff Bezos's costly server space.

Who knows? Perhaps there is a successful screenwriter out there who's made it without using profanity in real life or having characters cuss violently within the pages of their scripts -- but I certainly haven't met them yet.

THIS WRITER'S FIRST, GLORIOUS PAYDAY... AND A '66 BUG

Trust me -- nothing will ever quite match the crack-high of earning your first real money from screenwriting.

Single male writers, experienced this scenario yet? You and your bros crash some screening/party/Industry mixer. People (even women!) ask what you do. You admit that you're a (cough) screenwriter.

Great, they say. Wow, how cool. Anything I'd be familiar with?

Not yet, you explain, you're unproduced and, no, haven't sold anything... but Lionsgate is really, *really* excited about a project of yours, they're showing it to Howie Mandel for the romantic lead and it should be any day now...

And that's pretty much where the new girlfriend hunt ends.

Because other than credits and/or money, there are no standards by which civilians and Industry insiders alike can differentiate between those working hard to become legit screenwriters and the army of ass clowns out there just playing at it.

So... what's an aspiring screenwriter to do? How can we rid ourselves of this dreaded Wannabe Syndrome, shake the metaphorical monkeys clawing at our backs? Parents, classmates, landlords, loan collectors, the faux-hipster who spotted you twenty bucks at The Farmacy, and, most importantly, our own stratospheric expectations?

8

The answer's pretty straightforward.

Get paid for your screenwriting.

Bury a 50-foot putt. Knock the guy through the ropes. Or as DMX so succinctly puts it, "Break 'em off somethin'".

Because rightly or wrongly, the business of screenwriting ultimately comes down to convincing a *complete stranger* to give you *real money* for something you dreamed up and typed into Final Draft.

Actually, this is great news – that part about strangers paying money for scripts. Because they're still doing it, even in this downsized, post-crash, new-model economy. Which means *you* can still make an honest buck writing movies.

Yeah, sure, no shit, John. Love the concept. But where the hell does one even START in this godforsaken town? By what means do you actually propose to get this done?

Bottom line? <u>By any and all means necessary</u>. Hard work. Blind luck. Freak breaks. Perfect timing. Brute Force.

...At least that's what worked for me.

$$* * * * *$$

Before you can get paid, however, you need an agent or manager. Getting my first agent is one of those classic, bizarre, by-the-seat-of-your-pants Hollywood stories.

One summer in the '90's, my actor buddy Mike was cast in perhaps the most nonsensical martial arts movie of all-time -- <u>Bronze Throat</u> starring Bree Lee. Bree was actually from Sherman Oaks, not China or Japan, and shouldn't be confused with Bruce Lee, Bruce Le, Bruce Li, Dragon Lee, Bruce Dragon Li, or any other <u>Enter The Dragon</u> copycats or knock-offs of that era.

Shooting was in Oregon, and late one night Mike went to a wedding party at the Portland Marriot. The bash got *crazy* loud, completely out of hand. Two women came over from an adjoining suite to complain, but rather than turn the racket down, the Groom convinced them to stay and party instead.

One was a hot blonde, and my bro took a liquored shine to her. Mike's a pretty handsome guy (he became a network soap star years later) and so he followed Young MC's advice to the Pepsi Generation to just "bust a move". (Under 30? Google it.)

Small talk kicked up. "Where are you from?", "What do you do?", etc.

The Blonde tells Mike she's a literary agent in Los Angeles.

And Mike, bless his heart, blurts out -- "Wow. I know about *the best script!*"

Cue stylus scratching LP surface. This chick's looking at him like, "I'm on vacation, in *Portland fuckin' Oregon*, and I'm still getting scripts thrown at me!"

But he managed to keep her talking (like I said, Mike's pretty hot himself) and put it out there that I'd gone to NYU and, long story short, she told him this --

"If you're serious, leave a copy at the front desk and I'll have somebody in L.A. look at it. I fly out at 6 a.m. tomorrow."

Want to know if your best buddy is the real deal?
Here's the gold standard.

Mike hauled ass back to our hotel, got *the only copy of
the script within 3000 miles*, penned a quick note with
my contact info, then drove all the way back to the
Marriot *again*, at 3 a.m., and left my script for her.

Raises the bar pretty damned high, doesn't it? Saying
nothing of the fact he could've gotten *laid* if he hadn't
decided to hook me up instead. Now that's Special
Forces-level commitment, above and beyond the call of
duty.

Next morning, Mike hipped me to what happened, and I
was like, great man, thanks, really appreciate it... and
promptly forgot all about it. I'd already had my ass
kicked so many times pushing that script I'd given up all
hope. Shitty coverage, hostile agency rejection letters,
demoralizing notes from junior, junior, baby studio
execs, all that. A man can only eat so much shit in one
sitting, am I right?

But one week later I found a message on my answering
machine.

"Hi, I'm Susanne, from the New Talent Agency in Los
Angeles. Please call me back. I read your script and I
think it could be very, very big."

Completely blissed out and brimming with newfound
confidence, I drove down to L.A. in my '66 Bug with
$200 to my name, ready to take my rightful place
astride the Industry's brightest and best paid.

Susanne got me meetings *everywhere.* Scott Rudin,
Mace Neufeld, Warners, Paramount, Universal – all the
Town's heavy hitters. This was Ground Zero of the '90's

Big Spec Era. It was ridiculous back then, like a cartoon when compared to today's Business. Writers were selling dirty cocktail napkins sketched with story ideas for a million cash. As *Variety* and *The Hollywood Reporter* loudly confirmed each morning, with a decent high concept, anything and everything was possible.

When it came to my project, however, there was one little glitch.

Bad timing.

My script was essentially <u>Taxi Driver</u> meets <u>Romeo And Juliet</u>. Two tough Irish kids, living in the burned-out bowels of Jersey City, get in trouble with black gangstas and the local Mob, gunplay and tragedy quickly to ensue. People loved the gritty characters and action and it was the type of genre film studios were still interested in making back then.

But then <u>State of Grace</u> opened, just as I was taking all these meetings. I'm talking *same exact week*. Even though it boasted Sean Penn and Gary Oldman, the film completely cratered at the box office, helping sink its home studio, Orion, as well as turning Yours Truly into collateral damage.

Everybody agreed, our stories were COMPLETELY different. But they did share the same *world*, and quite literally overnight, all my hard work turned toxic, Fukushima'd by <u>State of Grace</u>'s collapse.

One veteran producer put it perfectly -- "It's a shame one big, dumb movie out there is going to kill your sale."

And that's exactly what happened.

My new agent had nothing for me after that. One unknown with one good *unsold* spec wasn't any more likely to get a studio writing assignment in those days than they are now. All she could suggest was to write another spec -- the last thing on Earth *any* aspiring screenwriter wants to hear after having come mere inches from success.

I got pissed. Mega-testosterone, 24-year-old white-boy pissed. I cursed the Film Gods for crushing my quick sale and the lifetime of Hollywood leisure sure to follow. Bitterly, I resolved to knuckle down and write that second goddamn script, vowing it would be so good that some stranger would be *forced* to give me money for it -- they simply wouldn't be able to stop themselves.

Mike moved down to L.A., and together we took shelter in a studio apartment on the top floor of a yellow brick 1930's beach hotel. Venice in those days was a violent shithole, not the bearded Hipster/social networking kale-fest it is now. Borrowing a PC, desk and chair from our dope-harvesting landlord, I barricaded myself inside our new place and went on a screenwriting killing spree.

Grinding day and night, punching out page after page, wearing nothing but a bottomless bowl of Cheerios on my lap, I summoned forth the gripping tale of a Brooklyn attorney who witnesses a murder committed by a Mafia client he himself got off in court. When the attorney threatens to testify, the Mob comes after him and his family, gunplay and tragedy hot on their heels.

Twenty-four days later, I chicken-pecked "The End". I entrusted my *magnum opus* to Mike, holding his new *Backstage* hostage until he read it. He finished, grinned and said -- "If someone doesn't buy *this*, I don't know what to say."

(The photo above is me during the actual real life events described in this story -- "*Will you please buy my script now, please?*")

Flushed with pride and riding the final, indignant fumes of my prior rejection, I pointed the '66 Bug down to my agent's place. I remember bulldozing into her office like I was storming the Bastille.

"Here it is, my new spec, exactly what you asked for," I stammered, thrusting it towards her like a broadsword. "I believe this is... The Big One."

"Okay, swell, thanks for driving in," she said, L.A. County ward nurse handling potential mental patient. "I'll call you the second I've read it."

Standing next to her desk was a stack of client scripts maybe twenty, twenty-five specs tall; a Xeroxed, two-bradded Leaning Tower of Pisa. In harrowing slow-motion, she took my newborn masterpiece and discarded it atop the pile. Number Twenty-Six.

Something about it just broke me.

In that dark instant I got my first, unfiltered snapshot of how infinitesimal my odds really were -- and it ruined me. Like they say, when you're walking a tightrope, never, *ever* look down...

Returning to Venice, I marched into my half of the hovel and hand-shred all my notes; stepsheet, page revisions, all of it. Then I staggered, crushed, to the Boardwalk, bought a pair of 22 oz. Sapporo's, found an empty bench and got ridiculously, pathetically, comically shithoused.

Like a little baby, I cried out there, a sloppy drunk six-foot-one, 190 lb. pity party. I balled my fuckin' eyes out among the hacky-sackers and forlorn homeless, casting my broken dreams atop the invisible, flaming bonfire of their own.

So this was the real Hollywood, I thought. The one every B-movie, TV show and Danielle Steele beach book warns you about. A financial and emotional Vietnam from which cherry young recruits like myself never returned.

Fuck me. How in the hell could I have thought selling a script would be that easy?

* * * * *

Alas, Dear Reader, I'd overreacted. Turns out, I had not been irrevocably voted off Screenwriter Island.

Susanne called three weeks later with the ol' good news/bad news.

Good News -- She liked my script and thought it could sell. You heard me -- *sell. For money.* Awesome, right?

15

Bad News -- She felt it needed an *entirely new* Third Act. Susanne wanted to throw out everything I had and rethink the whole thirty pages from square one.

Sooner or later every screenwriter's life reaches a crossroads where the whole of their career -- the full possibility of what they may or may not become -- comes to rest in their own fragile hands. In that brief, terrifying instant, there's nobody and nothing to rely on save your own gut instincts -- not unlike the process when any of us face the empty page. All the solemn risks and rewards abruptly rest on your slumped shoulders alone.

My own crossroads came very quickly. On this very call, in fact.

Susanne insisted on a new Third Act before she'd go out with it. Not only didn't I want to do the extra work, I honestly wasn't sure it was the right call creatively. I was exhausted, beaten down, my self-doubt was flaring up and the Imposter Syndrome had me by the throat. The concept of more time in isolation, the unique self-loathing only a writer knows, was simply too much to bear.

So, brain racing, I decided to sack up and pitch this --

Why not cherry-pick one of the many esteemed producers we'd met when I first hit town, slip the draft to them and get their opinion first?

It seemed the perfect solution. We could get an objective, world-class opinion without exposing the script and burning it around town. Further, the producer's take would serve as our tie breaker. If he/she agreed with Susanne, then I'd get to work on the third act straight away, without further whimpering or backsliding. Conversely, if the producer agreed with me that it was ship-shape and good to go, we'd fire things up and paper the town with it.

Susanne liked the idea. All that remained was to pick the producer.

We chose Larry Turman, the wise man who produced <u>The Graduate</u> among many others. Larry was a real straight-shooter with a ridiculous wealth of experience.

Susanne messengered my script (anyone remember *those* days?) over to Larry's office on the Warner Hollywood lot, and a few weeks later his assistant called saying Larry wanted me to drop by and have a talk about what I'd written.

* * * * *

The endless crawl up Fairfax that day was brutal. The Third Street intersection has always been a clusterfuck, long before The Grove arrived. Legions of ornery blue-hairs shot-gunning in and out of the prehistoric Vons parking lot gridlock that corner with a mind-boggling regularity.

Already running way late, tragedy struck. I stepped down on the clutch and SNAP! the clutch cable broke. I actually heard it shatter, like a little bone giving way, and the pedal plunged straight to the floor as useless as a severed limb.

No clutch, no drive car. Simple math. If *your* clutch goes AWOL in a newer car, it's game over. You pull over, Siri AAA and kiss your day goodbye.

But I still had one blue-collar/grease monkey trick up my sleeve. True fact -- you *can* drive an old VW without a clutch. Here's how. Turn the engine off, cram the gearshift into first, then restart it. Your Bug will lurch and whiplash horribly, then start grinding forward. If you match the RPM's *just right*, you can shift straight back into second, too -- top speed, 20 mph.

So that's what I did, said "fuck it" and snailed onward, my Bug's antiquity a sudden asset in my favor.

This went down at the apex of Third and Fairfax, Clusterfuck Central. Hazards on, I politely edged to the shoulder. But that did nothing to halt the oncoming bloodbath. Apoplectic motorists began HONKING AND CUSSING ME OUT as they passed. *Every single motorist* had their horn pinned down and/or were commanding me to forcibly insert my Bug into my own colon. *Welcome to L.A. motherfucker.* Zero mercy, despite having already surrendered and run up the white flag.

This ceaseless road-rape only encouraged my defiance. Smiling my best "fuck you, too", I continued surfing the glacial grind towards Warner Hollywood, steering the VW full into traffic.

* * * * *

I was shown into Larry's office a humiliating forty minutes late. Here I was, this Dickensian scrub, some hat-in-hand wannabe, accidently insulting the only ray of hope I had in Hollywood.

Besides being mortified, I also *looked* like shit now. Oil-smudged hands, pit stains pock-marking my only clean shirt, hair matted flat to my humid skull.

"Larry, I'm really, REALLY sorry. My sincerest apologies."

I'd blown it, and I totally accepted that. No doubt, it was a colossal bed-shitting, one I'd have to live with forever.

18

But Larry was legitimately one of the nicest guys I'd met since crossing over the River Styx -- hell, he'd actually taken time to read my script as a courtesy! -- so I felt it important he know my fucking up was not intentional.

"Believe it or not, I drive an old Bug, '66 actually, and the clutch broke. Those last two miles I had to baby her in, at, like, ten miles per hour."

Larry peered back. What sense he might make of these ramblings, I had no clue.

"Well, your car may not be working too well, but I know something else that is."

"Huh? What's that?"

"Your brain," Larry said. "You've written a really good script here... and I want to buy it."

I am Jack's completely blown mind.

"You're fuckin' with me, right?"

"Not at all, John. We've partnered with a venture capitalist, and I want to acquire your project with some of the development money we have."

By naïve force of will, what Orson Welles once called, "The Confidence of Ignorance", trusting my gut and a shit-ton of hard work, I'd fought my way onto the big board. I was now a *paid writer*.

* * * * *

Money changed hands, and that changed my life, forever.

I was working a $125-per P.A. gig at Magic Mountain when I got The Call. Over the payphone, Susanne confirmed the deal had closed. Tomorrow, I'd have a check for $25K in my pocket, with the promise of THREE HUNDRED THOUSAND MORE once we set it up.

Believe me, it felt EPIC. Something I pray every last person reading this experiences someday. Think Tiger Woods, '97 Masters, triumphant fist uppercutting Augusta sky, Barkley suplexing Shaq flat on his back, Hagler/Hearns with Marvelous alone left still standing.

Oh, and by the way, Susanne was right -- it *did* need a whole new third act. Five of them, in fact. And I started working them up Day One/Page One with Larry.

Looking back, who knows? Perhaps Susanne's approach would've been best. Maybe if I *had* rewritten the Third Act in-house, we'd have sold it for even *more* money; started a bidding war, landed a massive, splashy spec sale putting me squarely on top.

But for me in '91, there was no tomorrow. It was land this script, <u>now</u>, or beg my folks for airfare and crawl back to N.Y.C. busted apart. Many times, I've reflected about how not getting it done would've affected me, as both a writer and a man. Thank Baby Jesus, I never did find out.

Of course, here's the punch line, the part I had no idea about --

This was just the first, brutal step of my climb up Screenwriter Mountain. Game One of a seven game series that would eat up a full *decade*, with a thousand times the agony of this sweet little walk in the park.

Eventually, though, I'd pay off my student loans with a single check. Realize the Great American Dream and buy my parents a house, then grab a vintage Gibson SG I'd long fantasized about owning. But meeting after meeting, script after script, I kept driving my trusty '66 Bug as a reminder to keep my head on straight, come what may.

TOUGH SHIT

The simple, obvious, unavoidable truth is this --

Hollywood doesn't give a shit about your screenplay.

And there ain't a damned thing "fair" about it.

Bad-to-mediocre scripts get sold for a shit-ton of money, many of which go on to make even worse movies (think <u>White House Down</u>), while scripts commonly accepted as fantastic are lucky to claw their way onto the Blacklist... and often vanish without reaching the big screen.

Talented writers bust ass for *years* trying to get a break; living in shoebox Valley apartments, driving Craigslist cars, subsisting on a steady diet of tuna, Taco Bell and top ramen, the pressure of student loans pressed Glock-like to their foreheads. Meanwhile, the jolly daughters, sons and spouses of Hollywood's elite -- unproven, unworthy and not particularly gifted -- get the hookup on agents, open writing assignments, sweetheart options, even their own production companies.

Nepotism Kills. Hardly a secret for any working-class writer in this town.

Execs, Managers, Producers -- none return your respectful calls, even when referred by personal friends and legit long-time connections. Gmail inquiries are swallowed by a tomb-silent cyber void, Industry web sites kick your submissions back based on logline alone. From what you can tell, nobody seems to want to *read* anything in this godforsaken town unless it comes from a "branded" writer or some fucking comic book.

And all this in a business built entirely on storytelling and the written word.

Beyond that, let's face it -- nobody outside yourself really believes you're gonna make it. Nobody. Family, your best back-in-the-day crime partners, BF's, GF's, BFF's -- best of intentions, they try to stay positive, be helpful, saying vaguely encouraging things ("*How can they not buy your script with all the crap in theaters these days?*") to artificially boost your confidence.

You appreciate it, you really do. But patient as your loving peeps may be, behind those steadfast smiles and supportive fist-bumps, you sense other, more honest emotions. Concern about your health and well-being ("*Has she lost weight?*"), about "limiting yourself", dimming your bright future beyond repair before it's even begun. Naked fear that your writing career simply won't work out, and worse, that an epic fail while chasing this amorphous dream might beat you up real bad, provide the "what might have been" that sours the many good years of living you still have yet to do.

Everyone else who learns of your plan? Grand Central Hater, from former classmates now slaving kiss-ass nine-to-fives to other writers craving the exact same success you do. Half-joking, half-hostile and smarmy as hell, they'll collectively piss all over your playhouse hoping to build up their own. "Yeah, right." "Get real." "Dream on." "I've seen your pages, bro -- you'd better lay off the Sour Diesel." No slight will be too small to leave parked in the holster.

So yeah, there you stand -- *where so many of us have stood* -- staring point-blank into this vast, uncertain, demoralizing abyss known as the Film Business. This is your Hero's Journey, it's nut-cuttin' time and, strangely, neither Joseph Campbell nor Bill Moyers can be found.

It's a real pants-pisser, no doubt. Hollywood, like the Universe itself, turns out to be inexplicably cruel when not agonizingly indifferent. There's a killer line in Sam Peckinpah's WWII masterpiece <u>Cross of Iron</u> where James Coburn/Sgt. Steiner says, "I believe God is a sadist... but probably doesn't even know it."

IMHO he could've swapped out "God" for "Hollywood" and it would play just as well.

And yet...

Despite the complete insanity of all this... the devastating reality of unfathomable odds... the staring down a bat-shit crazy business in a city well-known as an emotional Vietnam... where most days Little Baby Jesus, Gandhi's Ghost and the collective Film Gods seem to stand steadfastly against you...

Despite all these harrowing obstacles, every screenwriter still has <u>one</u> <u>great</u> <u>equalizer</u> at hand. A single, remarkable tool well within their grasp. One killer Ace left up their sleeve left to play.

True shit. Every aspiring film and TV writer possesses an über weapon with the power to obliterate any and all obstacles standing between themselves and the goal of making a living with their words. Think Arthur's Excalibur. James Bonds' Golden Gun. Thor's mighty hammer, Mjolnir (okay, I Wikipedia'd that one to appease the Comic-Con crowd).

Upon hearing such promising news, you may have literally sharted yourself, Nexus/Kindle/iPhone quaking anxiously in your hands.

What in God's name is it?

The blank page, dummy.

An empty piece of 8 1/2 x 11 paper. A legal tablet. That vacant Final Draft 8 or 9 Doc crowding your Retina screen or the Writers App on your fanboy tablet. Ain't gotta be fancy. Truth be told, some of my best scenes are written in Sharpie on Hal's and Peet's and Cafe Brazil cocktail napkins. But wherever you find space enough for words, there's a winning Lotto ticket waiting to be inked in.

Ah yes, the timeless, democratic beauty of the blank page -- that "white elephant" I mentioned earlier -- is what levels your playing field in a hopelessly canted and cockeyed world. **This is the one truly amazing thing about screenwriting -- *anyone can work hard and succeed at it.*** Anyone and everyone -- regardless of class, creed, color, what school they went to, how much money they have, how good looking they are -- has a fighting chance to plant their feet, square their shoulders and take their best shot going for the proverbial gold.

How fucking awesome is that? To know every living soul reading this has an opportunity -- hell, an open invitation -- to roll the dice, say what they want to say, tell the story they have to tell, and perhaps even get (GASP!) *paid* to share that story -- *your story* -- with the entire world?

Fat chance? Far-fetched? Impossible? Absurd?

Not so much, I'm delighted to say, as my own twenty-year journey will provide proof positive in the coming pages.

So while becoming a working writer may seem like a drug-addled pipe-dream today, some surrealist Cinemax "After Dark" ("Small town boy/girl hitches to Tinseltown, fights off freaks, dodges shady agents, makes good and gets paid/laid at last"), believe me, homeboys and girls, it's not.

People pay real money for writing in this business.

It's an industry in constant need of product to fill theaters, cable channels, networks, VOD outlets, Netflix, Amazon Prime, Redbox and a million other coming delivery systems which haven't been invented yet. For chris'sake, folks are paying to watch <u>The Godfather</u> on their *phones* now. So know there's an insatiable, built-in hunger for content to fill this growing myriad of Net-era pipelines, which means constantly having to restock all those cybershelves with fresh entertainment and something brand new.

That's where you come in. Cue the heads-up aspiring writer. This same supply and demand dynamic is what provides you with an evergreen opportunity, one that ain't going away anytime soon -- the need for <u>self-generated</u> <u>material</u>. For writers looking to build careers, this new media landscape is steadily evolving into the gift that keeps on giving. Regardless of where tech ultimately goes or what gadget we end up consuming our media with, the hunger for fresh stories and those able to put them down on in black and white will *always* remain a constant.

Will most of it pay get-rich-quick Late '90's/Early 2000's money? No. The day of the one-punch knockout is long over. After the economic meltdown of 2008, that model of film biz development was permanently mothballed. Except for a brandable, contemporary short list, writer deals now pay less across the board, and long-established quotes have taken big haircuts, if they haven't been discarded altogether. But hey, work is still work, deals are still deals, and they still pay real money a writer can live on. Best of all, you're being paid to do what you love most -- <u>write</u>.

Being paid to write. Wow. Sick job, right? And like I just said, it's guaranteed somebody's gotta do it. Someone's gotta keep those pipelines filled year-in and year-out with cool new stuff.

Which begs the same question you probably brought to this book in the first place --

"Why shouldn't that somebody be <u>me</u>?"

Honest answer? There's absolutely no good reason it shouldn't -- and couldn't -- be you.

Of course, to ignite this wondrous alternative future for yourself and start grabbing up all that opportunity, you'll need to accomplish one tiny thing first.

You'll need to write a great script.

Not "pretty good". Not "kinda cool". Not "just as good as that big dumb spec which sold last week". And certainly not "put Brad Pitt in the lead, you can totally see the movie" (Put Mr. Pitt in *anything*, even a Restoration Hardware catalog, you can totally see the movie).

Great, fellas. G-R-E-A-T. World-class. Brass ring. Top of the heap. An undeniably fresh and entertaining story that stands above and beyond the Industry's latest lame-o copycat epic-fail blockbuster release last weekend. Miles beyond that VOD video game genre flick you illegally DL'd from iptorrents. No sir, you'll need a fantastic screenplay which is made or broken, stands or falls, entirely on its own merits.

I know, I know. WTF? If Hollywood doesn't hold *itself* to that lofty ideal, why in the hell should I? Check out BoxOfficeMojo, bro. Aiming low seems totally the way to go.

But you couldn't be more wrong.

There are *reasons* a lot of shit gets made, most of them far from satisfactory, few of them made entirely public. Like being forced to fulfill on-the-hook pay-or-play deals or no-brainer sequels for blind-luck hits. And let's not forget the dreaded star director or actor "passion project" (Funny People or Spanglish anyone?), near-guaranteed to crater in the absence of reasonable checks and balances. This list of cinematic war crimes such as these scrolls on and on, seemingly into infinity.

None of which concerns you, by the way. You, my friend, are the aspiring writer, the neophyte, the nobody, the yet-undiscovered woman or man with budding talent who's currently on all fours *begging* for any chance to become the bottom rung on the same dysfunctional food chain I'm talking about.

Sound harsh? Welcome to the NFL. Tighten up your panties, boy.

Do not count on the loopholes and exemptions of established writers. They do not apply to you. There are no free passes for trying to get over with the same aggressively mediocre cinematic kitty litter we've suffered through most our American lives in one format or another. Jock-riders and copycats die quick deaths 'round these parts. Millions of wannabes have already tried and died going backdoor with the lazy shit, big dreams of Hollywood left rotting under the anonymous Burbank, Culver City and Santa Monica sun.

Nope. No excuses. No way around it. You'll need to write a great script.

Something that keeps the most jaded script reader alive wide-awake when they were planning on *Game of Thrones* and calling it an early night -- and believe me, brother, that's an extremely high threshold. Yet nothing shy of it will suffice.

Not to get all crazy hardcore on you (little late, I know), but your shit needs to be straight-up superior to the teeming mass of unsold specs being written, PDF'd, registered and Mail Chimped every damned day by the unseen army of other writers you're competing with. Make no mistake, sensitive eco-friendly Emo reader -- this is a competition, as cutthroat an endeavor as any American kid is likely to undertake. If you're hoping for a hug somewhere along the way, best you put this book down right now and run, run away.

Think I'm exaggerating? Busting balls for effect? Let me sharp-focus you with a quick stat --

According to the WGA West (wgawregistry.org), the Guild registers over 70,000 pieces of material a year. That includes scripts, treatments, outlines, TV pilots, etc. -- and that's just the civilians and outliers with the presence of mind to officially protect their work. God only knows how many other folks never figure it out and make it into that head count. Five times that? Ten? Christ, you can't throw a hot dog in Dodger Stadium and not hit somebody writing a spec episode of How I Met Your Mother these days. Some writers prefer U.S. copyright registration, some already have legit representation, and a boatload of first-timers don't know how, where or why they should register in the first place.

Conservatively, let's figure there's a <u>couple</u> <u>hundred</u> <u>thousand</u> pieces of material floating around Hollywood any given year. Minimum.

I am Jack violently shitting himself.

Getting the message now in IMAX 3-D? **You must separate yourself from that ugly herd at all costs.** Push yourself. Raise the bar. Take it to the house. This isn't a friendly suggestion, it's a written-in-stone prerequisite. Knee-jerk assuming "it's good enough" will put you at a crippling disadvantage you'll likely never overcome.

Personally, back of my own neurotic writer's mind, I never forget that maybe twenty or thirty thousand folks with the same spiffy MacBook as me are out there *tonight*, in my hometown of L.A., working harder, later and with far more focus to get there first -- to beat my ass to available open gigs before I even get in the room.

Yes, it's that real, and serious as a stroke.

* * * * *

Twenty-plus years ago when I was at N.Y.U., veteran screenwriter Larry Marcus (<u>The Stuntman</u>) told me that if you have a great script it may take a week, a year, or even ten years, but if you've written something of undeniable quality, someone in the Industry will find it.

I was a brash young punk at the time (ya think?), and nice as Larry was, I remember thinking, "That's bullshit." But what Larry said turned out to be true, and I've seen the same dynamic play out with my friends and myself many times as we've pursued our careers over the years.

30

Why? Because contrary to prevailing wisdom, <u>there simply aren't that many great scripts out there</u>.

It's straight-up supply and demand. The very best scripts are *immediately* recognizable by even the most cynical, hard-boiled professional. And if *they* feel something real during the read, they can bet their asses their peers -- other execs, producers, studios -- felt something too. That's how bidding wars begin. Nothing validates a project like another producer being willing to put their own money into it.

Great scripts leap off the page, grab the reader by the throat, ignite the deep passion within producers, directors and studios which fuels spending three, four, five years of their lives and tens of millions of dollars to see that the <u>movie version</u> gets made. Despite the urban legend and dog-eared sob story recounted at every unsold writer's pity party, there are <u>not</u> a ton of great screenplays laying around unwanted and ignored by Hollywood. There is no <u>X-Files</u>-style conspiracy against quality material. Not only is this town not threatened by it, it outright embraces it. Give 'em twice as many projects with legit commercial potential, they'll buy twice as many. There is an infinite number of winning scripts they are eager and willing to buy.

Take a beat and eyeball this from the Industry side. The better script a company starts with, the better talent (stars, directors) they can attract, the bigger budget they can get, the better movie they can produce, which, in turn, gives them the best odds at having a box office hit and making a king's ransom. And money -- cold, hard, seductive cash -- is what makes the film biz go 'round in the first place. On this point, you'll find little debate.

Huge benefits await agents, execs, et al. who discover these platinum needles in the Hollywood haystack. A junior exec bringing their company a great script puts themselves in the mix, sees their stock jump through the ceiling. Baby managers or agents who score get fast-tracked, become perceived as a rising stars, young guns to keep an eye on. If there's a splashy sale alongside it, the same writer may become this rep's first real client, putting them both on the big board Industry-wide. The standard representation fee is 10% -- that's $100,000 on a million dollar sale. So as you see, there's plenty of motivation, both professionally and monetarily, for everyone involved to help get a great script where it's going.

Alas, a few tinkerers and weekend warriors pull something out of their asses, getting lucky now and then. Some thirteen year-old Malibu girl sells her talking carrot movie for a million bucks, and yeah, it hurts like a hollow-point to the heart of any serious scribe. Blind luck is a bitch, right? But like it or not, that's part of the Biz, too.

(I always flash on that hilarious exchange in <u>Barfly</u> where the wife-beater next door accidently gets stabbed -- "Nothing but dumb luck," he says. "Yeah," answers Mickey Rourke as Hank. "But that counts too.")

But for those of you interested in making a *career* of it, of becoming an employed professional with health and dental, able to consider buying a home, starting a family or traveling the world -- all while continuing to grow creatively -- freak one-offs like this are silly distractions. Treat 'em as such and laugh 'em off. You are <u>not</u> in competition with the 'tweener writing The Talking Carrot Trilogies. Never were. Different targets entirely. However lucrative it seems short-term, they're playing hopscotch and you're gunning for the Stanley Cup. Never the twain shall meet.

My friends, the real key for any aspiring writer, the simple fact that supersedes all the other bizarre, random bullshit involved along the way is this --

"It only takes one buyer."

My first agent told me that during Clinton's first term, and it's every bit as true today. You can hear a thousand "No's", have a million doors slammed in your face, online and in person, but just one simple, glorious "Yes" validates everything. EVERYTHING. Your script. Your sacrifice. Your dream. *You.*

As a writer, I've always found real strength and inspiration in that. You don't have to conquer Hollywood, you just need to find that <u>one</u> <u>buyer</u> out there who gets it. The one player willing to pull the trigger based on your words and ideas and the vision you've so carefully constructed with them. The bright producer or executive that, despite being a total stranger you have yet to meet, reads your pages and sees the same movie you do.

That's the good news, fellas. The silver lining in all of this.

For screenwriters, one "yes" can obliterate a lifetime of "no's".

SELLING OUT TO THE MAN

By now, it should be kinda obvious this book assumes you're writing or planning on writing something "commercially viable" -- meaning something you can sell, for money.

Being "commercial" is no crime for screenwriters, despite the salvo of erudite protests your black-bereted film-wonk friends may fire off. By definition, *all screenplays are commercial.* They are written with the expectation of being made into movies, which are then marketed and shown -- for profit -- all over the globe, in a million different formats.

Pulp Fiction? Boogie Nights? The Big Lebowski? Pan's Labyrinth? Mainstream as a motherfucker. Paid for by The Man, made by The Man, marketed by The Man, distributed by The Man.

Point of fact -- nobody writes a screenplay hoping nobody else ever sees it. Suggesting such a thing is so retarded on so many levels my head hurts even thinking about it. Film writing is a visual medium, scripts the structural skeletons awaiting an overlay of cinematic flesh and blood which brings them finally to life. Other than becoming movies, there's simply no other reason for them to exist.

So a friendly word to the wise for any Mumblecore wannabes or half-cocked Jean-Luc Godards (do Millennials even know who that was?) -- don't waste your time in Hollywood. Rent the Red Camera, borrow a Canon DV rig, hell, shoot your teary-eyed esoteric examination of some white kid's existential angst on your iPhone. Just please don't waste time trying to push that shit up the ranks here. Asymmetrical tone poems, visual haikus, one shot, six-hour black-and-white features consisting solely of someone shaving off their pubic hair are about as popular with financiers as Al-Qaeda and a new strain of Avian Flu.

Don't get me wrong. Personally, I love the sick, twisted, challenging, different and defiantly uncommercial. At twenty, I was number one in line for the very first American screening of Wings of Desire -- which I promptly watched twice, back to back. I've seen Baise Moi ten times and anxiously await a BluRay with the penis-hating hottie director's commentary. I intractably contend that ultra-low budget indie I Melt With You is the finest film about the male mid-life crisis ever made, although every single one of my friends HATES IT and remains furious at me for erasing that ninety minutes of their lives. Know also that I forked over $100 for a Region 5 copy of Last Exit To Brooklyn because I simply refused to wait ten years for a proper U.S. release.

But as a professional screenwriter -- a working commercial artist -- I'm experienced enough to know my business has a very specific target, one which regrettably seems to be growing a little smaller every day. My goal is not to reinvent what's sellable, it's to refine, deepen and/or give it a fresh twist. I'm completely content leaving the trailblazing to braver (and I expect more solvent) souls than my own -- I have a wicked mortgage, a monster Bengal cat who's eating me out of that same house and home, and aging parents threatening to sell off everything, buy Harleys and join an outlaw motorcycle club.

Or as a super-smarmy Harvard-educated exec I once knew put it, "The only award I'm interested in winning is the Bank of America award."

SCREENWRITING 101

Comes to craft, I'm continually amazed at how many writers -- bright, hard-working, some with real talent -- overlook the primary questions centering the core of any good screenplay.

Problems with non-starter, D.O.A. scripts can often be C.S.I.'d straight back to ground zero, where the writer didn't install a bulletproof foundation and begin building from a place of real strength. I'm not talking about story structure here. I'm addressing <u>the birth of your concept or premise itself</u>.

From the moment of inception, that first, glorious instant when you cook up a fantastic idea for a film, resolving with every ounce of determination to go all the way and write the hell out of it, you need to address the following fundamentals. Some of this may seem self-evident and rudimentary as hell, but like the rest of my advice in *Tough Love Screenwriting*, I urge you to consider it from a fresh perspective, as if hearing it for the first time.

Trust me when I say you ignore their impact at your own peril. Ignorance in these departments is assuredly not bliss, and some serious consideration here could save you months, even years, of inevitable rejection down the line.

1) "What's the Movie"?

This is perhaps the most common question posed to writers in Hollywood. More than just "what's it about", this asks you to specify <u>what's new, different or wholly unique about your story or concept</u>? What separates and elevates it above the millions of other films and scripts already out there? Further, who's the <u>potential audience</u> for your film? Kids under 20? Adults over 45? This line of questioning is a direct invitation to make it easy for Industry folks by identifying the awesome key concept or premise that will <u>sell</u> your film.

Why is this of such paramount importance? Because it points directly at the heart of a project's marketability; and if the Powers That Be can't figure out how to successfully *market* it, they sure as hell aren't going to *buy* the fucker in the first place.

Sorry if this is a brutal awakening, but the movie business is precisely that -- a <u>business</u>, first and foremost. Everything else is secondary, especially how profound or necessary or Tarantino-cool you think your screenplay is. In this game, Money Talks, Bullshit Walks. And the money people expect to see profit potential in your project or they simply won't waste their time.

Go ahead and get mad, rant and blog and text about how unjust and unfair this is, how it cripples "cinematic art" -- but it won't make the slightest damned difference. You're going to "come to Jesus" on this point sooner or later if you want to participate as a professional screenwriter. My advice? Might as well take your diapers off and enter the acceptance phase now. Don't waste a good six years huffing and puffing like I did as a baby writer. Begin thinking and creating like a professional now.

Does this mean there isn't room for true creativity, passion, meaning, etc. in contemporary screenwriting? Don't be dim. But what it does say is all that wonderful, contemplative, top-drawer stuff needs to be encapsulated *within* an entertaining, marketable movie or nobody's going to give it a shot. I like to call this the "aspirin in applesauce" approach, based on the old-school practice of fooling babies into swallowing their medicine by stashing it inside a spoonful of Gerber's.

Cases in point -- <u>American Beauty</u> and <u>Fight Club</u>. Both supremely entertaining while also making more profound statements than perhaps any other films of their era. So clearly, it can be done. But first and foremost, to the people who both pay to make them and pay to see them, movies are entertainment. Any lasting messages or deeper subtexts are on *you*, a bonus made possible by your superior writing and storytelling within those fairly broad constraints.

So, again... **What makes *your* story fresh and different from all the other scripts out there**? **Exactly whom is the potential buyer/audience for the movie you've written?**

What's fresh and different about Christopher Nolan's <u>Inception</u>?

Christ, what *isn't* fresh about <u>Inception</u>? A unique blending of both sci-fi and heist genres, it introduces a killer new concept -- that of corporate espionage taking place inside an individual's <u>subconscious</u>. The story plays out within multi-tiered, interconnected "dream spaces" -- somewhat like 3-D chess -- with actions on any given level having an immediate trickle-down effect on the others. Brilliant concept and brilliant storytelling which also ensured brilliant visuals.

Who's the potential audience? Pretty much *everyone* -- plenty of action for the 15-to-25 demographic, plenty of brain-power for the 25-and-over crowd.

What about <u>28 Days Later</u>? Alex Garland and Danny Boyle's take single-handedly reinvented and resuscitated the zombie flick. First, by introducing "turbo zombies" -- new creatures far more terrifying than any turtle-slow, blue-faced version having come before. Next, by visually examining the sheer physical <u>scope</u> of a society's collapse (utilizing the actual streets of London) and then more deeply personalizing it via an insane level of human detail (think the "missing persons" board filled with all those tragic hand-written notes).

This serious new take tracked how you would experience a post-apocalyptic world emotionally <u>and</u> gave you the sickest, most fucked-up zombies you'd ever seen. Classic cake-and-eat-it-too scenario. The audience? Any genre horror or action lover from ages 15 to 50.

My friends, you need to be able to verbalize these same specifics as they apply to <u>your</u> <u>own</u> <u>project</u> without hesitation, the instant anyone asks. If you haven't come up with slam dunk answers (or don't actually know yet) you'd best get busy and puzzle 'em out. You *will* be quizzed on this -- by agents, managers, execs, producers; basically anyone along the food chain in a position to help get your script where you want it to go.

Not to sound all Liam Neeson/<u>Taken</u> extreme about it (whoops, too late), but either start thinking and strategizing like a professional at the beginning or risk writing and pushing a stillborn screenplay with zero chance of survival.

2) <u>"What's The World?"</u>

All great movies take us into unique, uncommon worlds -- which is one of the many reasons we enjoy them so much. They gift us fascinating glimpses of awesome new vistas, from strange alien planets (Pitch Black), ancient civilizations (Apocalypto) and Dark Ages dungeons (Black Death), to the smaller, more intimate universes like retirement homes (Cocoon), Chinese restaurants (Eat Drink Man Woman), the inside of a coffin (Buried) or an ecstasy dealer's crib (Layer Cake)-- not to mention the racist statutory rapist neighbors' house right next door (Alan Ball's superb Towelhead).

Choosing your world is one of the few arenas in life where size really *isn't* everything, just as writing something with commercial appeal doesn't necessarily handcuff you to big-budget eye-candy and CG up the wazoo. Far from it. John Sayles' coal mining camp in Matewan is far more fascinating to this writer than S.H.I.E.L.D. headquarters in The Avengers. The claustrophobic apartment of an unstable, supercomputing math genius in Darren Aronofsky's Pi contains more compelling questions than all three (or is it four now?) Iron Man pictures -- and the Transformers series -- put together. **Turning everything up to "11" will not make a crappy script better.** Somnolescent slackers Man of Steel and Pacific Rim (among a myriad of others) offer abundant forensic evidence on this point.

You'll find that familiar worlds are endlessly re-presented in both film and television, for obvious reasons -- day-to-day life on Planet Earth is generally centered around commonplace occupations shared by everyday people. For folks living in, say, Los Angeles, these would include struggling actors, DMV workers, hair stylists, U.S. Postal Employees, power yoga instructors and massage therapists, etc. But just because these worlds are ordinary doesn't exempt them from needing unique portrayals.

<u>Make sure you come up with a fresh take guaranteed to intrigue the reader</u> -- no matter what the size or scope of the universe you're scripting, from startlingly broad and complex, to the small and sublime. Help your audience experience your setting through curious, newborn eyes. Make your choice captivating, even for the die-hard film-fanatic who's seen tens of thousands of movies by now.

Take cop shows and movies. Millions have been made over the past hundred years, the gangster/crime genre itself one of very first ever committed to celluloid. We're all so well-acquainted with these stock, paint-by-number worlds we're actually numb to them now. We blindly accept everything from police routines and procedures to the accuracy of the art direction in cinematic station houses based solely on faith -- even though most of us have never visited our local police station. Point being, the cinematic cop world is very familiar terrain for 21st century audiences, however realistic or unrealistic its portrayal may actually be.

But we're not looking for familiar, are we? Fresh and intriguing is the gold standard for aspiring writers.

Given that, what sets a film like <u>Training Day</u> apart in the world department? What makes it so much more bewitching and compelling than any of its police thriller peers?

For starters, much of it plays out within Alonzo's (Denzel Washington) "G-Ride" -- a pimped-out, late-model Monte Carlo. With a maximum of imagination, writer David Ayer fashions Zo's wheels as a perfect point of entry into his script's world -- that of a corrupt, mobile, undercover L.A.P.D. street narc.

Quite literally, the G-Ride itself becomes Hoyt's (Ethan Hawke) world for the length of his training day, and the vehicle by which he's ferried across a figurative River Styx, deep into the ugly and obscene inner workings of Rampart-style L.A. street policing he'd never imagined.

To my knowledge, we've never seen this particular take presented from quite this perspective before. Sure, partners riding in cruisers are shown in every dime-a-dozen cop film and TV show, especially those set in So Cal. But none of them so boldly refashioned the cruiser itself into the emotional epicenter for an epic battle of wills and worldviews between its two protagonists *and* an observational flashpoint through whose windshield we -- the audience, right alongside Hoyt -- process the brass-knuckles, no quarter/no condom, industrial-strength sights, sounds and throwdowns of L.A.'s street-level drug pushing.

Totally bad-assed, right? I mean, for all intents and purposes, Alonzo's G-Ride could be a flying saucer skimming Hoyt across the surface of an alien moon with all its bizarre lifeforms and hostile, unknown possibilities. It's that colorful and our experience that unexpected.

Now *that's* the shit I'm talking about, brothers and sisters. The kind of story choice that gives me massive screenwriter wood. Taking a familiar world we assumed we already knew inside out/upside down and completely *re-imagining and remaking it* into something undeniably intriguing, special and unique. Deep shit for film geeks like myself.

The big question becomes what choice you'll make for your new script's world. When cooking up your latest creation, what'll elevate and extend its reach far beyond what a jaded audience and the cynical reader are already expecting?

One of the best studio execs I ever worked with, Dan Levine, said something profound enough to stick with me through dozens of projects over the years --

"You've got to surprise people."

That's really the nut of it, short and sweet. Hell, yeah, it means more work. But if there's a time to expend that extra energy it's <u>now</u>, on the front end, while things can still be reworked organically -- not after you've wallpapered the town with your script only to come up goose eggs.

Let me strongly urge you to consider Dan's wise words when choosing your script's world... or prepare to pay the ultimate price for half-assing it and flying blind.

3) <u>"Who's Your Main Character?" a.k.a "Who's your Protagonist?"</u>

In many ways, what ultimately happens or doesn't happen with your project revolves around the interest in your Lead Character by "name" actors (a.k.a. movie stars) and financiers of all stripes.

Today's film business is far more of a "star-driven system" than the Hollywood Studios of the '30 and '40's ever were. With rare exception, you must have a name actor (or combination of name actors) involved who money people can market and sell your movie around, both domestically and overseas. Like Coach handbags and Apple computers, actors have become big commercial "brands" to loyal ticket-buying consumers. Seeing Angelina Jolie or Leonardo DiCaprio's name on a one-sheet can mean the difference between hundreds of millions in box office receipts and a paltry couple hundred thousand.

Eternally paranoid and obsessed about losing money, the movie industry has become even more risk-adverse in the aftermath of the '08 crash. The Business is inherently dicey, a hit-or-miss pop culture Las Vegas where every bet placed runs between $10 million and $250 million. Despite the Industry's best attempts -- NRG audience tracking surveys, focus groups, etc. -- there have *never* been any guarantees when it comes to predicting a movie's financial success. Think about it. *Who the fuck knows what might capture a global audience's imagination at any given moment?* The outcome is largely random and governed by fortuitous timing and blind luck as much as any corporate marketing strategy. As many filmmakers have learned the hard way, the fates of blockbusters ultimately reside in the fickle hands of the Movie Gods alone.

Just the same, studios and financiers like to hedge their bets as much as humanly possible. Which wraps us back around to those names. Big names provide the closest thing to an insurance policy you'll find in this game. For the excessive fees they command (anywhere from $10 to $20 million a picture for A-list talent like Jolie, DiCaprio etc.) they provide proven track records of being able to open huge movies with massive audiences and generate boffo global box office receipts in the process. Other attachments may also play a part -- name directors, producers, the rare "branded" writer -- but there's no real substitute for having a bona fide movie star acting wacky or standing sullen and heavily armed in the TV spot, YouTube trailer, IMDB banner and/or your Facebook page.

Following this prevailing logic, if a producer can attach any one of these names to their project -- an actor that "means something" or can "open a movie" -- then they've got themselves a go picture.

How does this little primer on the macro stuff impact you, the aspiring writer in a studio apt. who just Dropboxed a buddy's Final Draft to start a new screenplay?

It confirms that creating an intriguing protagonist of seriously compelling interest to big-league talent is pretty much essential. Or as every agent and manager in Hollywood will be happy to tell you --

"Movie stars want to play movie star parts."

Damn straight. Great actors seek out spectacular roles with the potential to make them legit *stars*, and established stars twice as big as that, into *icons*. Jack Nicholson's career provides the perfect case study. They want beautifully-crafted characters with the power to resonate on every screen, laptop and smartphone across the globe, regardless of whatever language they've looped the actor's lines with. Truly memorable parts which remain vividly etched in the imaginations of viewers for the rest of their adult lives.

But hey, no pressure.

Listen, don't get it twisted. I'm decidedly NOT suggesting to go cookie-cutter cardboard cut-out Lead Character here. Quite the opposite. Today we enjoy extremely entertaining, multifaceted shows like *Homeland*, *House of Cards* and *Game of Thrones* which delightfully explore the darker, richer, fundamentally flawed nature of human beings. Emotionally complex films that go heavy on the grayscale like Prisoners and Concussion are also out there -- satisfying actors' and audiences' creative needs as well as the bottom-line producer's economic ones.

So consider this your official warning -- as a contemporary writer, if you aim low and lazy and decide to center your film around some old-model, seen-it-done-better-a-billion-times-before Protagonist, you risk immediate irrelevance in the eyes of those you're hoping to interest most. It'd be like bringing a Motorola "brick" cellphone to the new Galaxy S6 release. Who the fuck wants old tech, Holmes? Forget about buying your movie, you'll never see the inside of a junior exec's office.

Although they still cast a long shadow, the late '80's and early '90's are over. Flag-waving One-D Family Values stereotypes with Desert Eagle .44's and mirrored trooper shades are about as attractive to A-list talent now as Lyme disease. The Stallone/Harrison Ford/Arnold-style blockbuster hero and the other era-specific clichéd characterizations no longer hold the Biz hostage, blanket handcuffing top-tier talent the way they once did.

(Guilty Pleasure Flashback to Ford's cornball, yuppie mid-life crisis President snarling in Air Force One -- "HE PUT A *GUN* IN MY WIFE'S *FACE!*")

Yet still, many of us, even veterans like myself, unconsciously regurgitate these stereotypes we had drummed into our brains growing up; the syndicated ABC shows we saw after school or on snow day TV, the endless flicks watched stoned on VHS, DVD and college dorm cable. For any good writer, it's a continual fight to keep this shit in check, to monitor ourselves and our instincts and ensure we're not just puking out the same cruddy characters force-fed to us once upon a time.

46

<u>Here's my general rule of thumb</u> -- if you've seen a character or characters doing, saying, acting or making the same story choices in the same way <u>your</u> Lead is, then it's already been done. Time to upgrade and reboot your Protagonist.

Consider this from a name actor's point of view. Why would intelligent, astute, well-versed, hard-working men and women at the very top of their games want to backpedal their way *down* the food chain? With all the ridiculously cool, forward-looking and thinking projects out there vying for their commitment, why play a retread? Something lacking in imagination? A copy of a copy of a copy? Especially with your career longevity often hanging in the balance every time you agree to do a film?

You wouldn't do this, and neither will they. These people are busy servicing a much larger creative ambition. Given today's reliance on the Name Game, top-tier talent has plenty of leverage to pick and choose their roles more selectively. *Everybody* needs them for every project in town, so it's not a question of *if* they'll work, it's a question of *which projects* they'll consider strong and intriguing enough to attach themselves to.

Obviously the studios will continue churning out lukewarm multiplex fare, and even get away with it profitably from time to time. No surprise, and absolutely nothing wrong with it far as I'm concerned. That's a wheelhouse they pioneered a century ago and it's been pleasing certain moviegoers for generations now. And yeah, terrific actors will sign on to some of these projects to pay for passion projects, paternity suits, beach house mortgages and already overstuffed 401(k)'s. But the obvious, lumbering, über-commercial blockbuster fodder is studio and large production company terrain, the lion's share now squarely focused

on pre-existing IP (Intellectual Property) of some sort --
books, graphic novels, branded remakes, remakes of
successful foreign films, etc. -- over speculative scripts
(specs) from young new screenwriters.

Which is fine. Because for the most part that's not your
target anyway. And, once again, without anything
backing you the standard you'll need to meet is much
higher and deeper than that.

Movie stars want to play movie star parts. Which means
their reps and studio creatives are continually on the
lookout for riveting, lively, <u>original</u> material in pretty
much every genre. The projects that make them *feel*
something -- not the projects endlessly spit from the
Industry's big-budget cinematic sausage factory.

Accordingly, your task could not be better defined --
cook up a character that totally blows their doors off. A
character so sublime and captivating that big name
talent is burning a hole in the carpet to get somebody to
write a check and lock your script down.

Obvious next question -- what exactly makes for a
movie star part?

In broad, sweeping, entirely unhelpful terms?
Something juicy. Something heroic. Something flush
with authenticity. Something that sizzles. A part laden
with universal truths, yet specific to this character, now,
during the highs and lows of their glorious widescreen
journey. A strong-willed portrayal which gives voice to
important issues -- personal or political -- which the
actor both identifies with and/or wants to publicly
represent. A unique role they can totally sink their
teeth into, allowing them to inhabit the very soul of
someone completely dissimilar from themselves --
however foul, brutal, harrowing and/or challenging that

character's interior landscape might be (Charlize Theron in <u>Monster</u> anyone? Woody Harrelson in <u>Out of The Furnace</u>?)

Something fun. Something they love. Something that gets them high from acting. Something epic -- with best-case potential of becoming *legendary*.

While spitballing a Lead for your new script, one useful exercise is to reference your own comparable favorites -- the characters and roles that get *you* high watching or reading them. Some serious mechanical study here, picking out <u>why</u> these parts resonate more deeply and <u>what about them</u> affects you in different, more striking ways is a great exercise to help prime the pump of your imagination.

For this writer, a few amazing portrayals pop immediately to mind. Ben Kingsley as ruthless Cockney psycho Ben Logan in <u>Sexy Beast</u> (an Oscar robbery if there ever was one). Jeff Bridges as early '90's stoner hippie "The Dude" in <u>The Big Lebowski</u>. Brad Pitt as anarchist dildo-stasher Tyler Durden in <u>Fight Club</u>. Ian McShane as the martini-dry homosexual mobster in <u>44-Inch Chest</u>. Edward Norton as smash-mouth Venice skinhead Derek Vineyard in <u>American History X</u>.

There's also the elegiac dignity of <u>Seven</u>'s Morgan Freeman fighting to make a difference despite what he knows is insurmountable evil. Helen Mirren's noble, promiscuous, semi-alcoholic Detective Chief Inspector Jane Tennison which spanned the <u>Prime Suspect</u> series -- one of the truly lasting female roles ever. And what man or woman can resist Matt Damon's amnesiac, action-ready everyman Jason Bourne in <u>The Bourne Identity</u>?

Again, size is not a factor here. Remember, "epic" doesn't have to mean razor-thin on character, just as "Indie" doesn't have to mean mumbling, self-absorbed and existential. I found Dominic Cooper's portrayal of Uday in <u>The Devil's Double</u> to be plenty epic, hell, beyond epic. Yet it was relatively low budget with something like 70% of the film taking place inside Saddam's palace.

An infinite number of ways exist for human beings, both big and small, to become heroic. The ensemble adult cast of Oscar-winner <u>Little Miss Sunshine</u> are all pretty much losers. Loveable, yes, but still losers. Yet, by the time their collective journey climaxes, every last one of them has shown tremendous courage and heroism very specific to whom each of them are emotionally, inside.

Each of the scripted creations listed above came into existence via some writer firing up his/her computer and working their asses off to 3-D them out and bring them vividly to life. Each of these writers' fictional characters also exposed me to fascinating folks in unexpected circumstances, unique individuals I could learn from, identify or empathize with and often catch brief reflections of *myself* and my own journey refracted through the truth of their actions, thoughts and words.

Because that's what great characters do, right? They win you over. They involve you *personally*. They access your humanity, pulling a home invasion on the most hardened adult heart. They make you believe.

Enough so that when a complete stranger experiences their magic on paper, they want to give you money so they can own them.

* * * * *

Well-written characters are obviously a challenging calliope of moving parts. But primary in the mix is <u>who the character is</u>; their backstory, their baggage, what makes them tick, what's hurt them, what gives them joy and, in the final accounting, what they <u>want</u> out of it all before the movie ends.

Syd Field's *Screenplay: The Foundations of Screenwriting* is the Rosetta Stone and Genesis point of all script lit, and it's still the only book needed to cover the craft fundamentals IMHO. (Yes, I'm telling you to buy it a.s.a.p. -- <u>http://www.amazon.com/Screenplay-Foundations-Screenwriting-Syd-Field-ebook/dp/B000S1LAYG/</u>).

Screenplay brilliantly spotlights the core concern whenever creating characters by asking --

"What does your main character want to win, gain, get or achieve during the course of your screenplay?"

You need to be able to answer this with a short, deft, airtight response. No mumbling run-ons or verbal novellas necessary. John McClane wants to save his wife in <u>Die Hard</u>. King George wants to quit stuttering and become a worthy monarch in <u>The King's Speech</u>. Leigh Anne Tuohy wants to save an impoverished young man so he can realize his potential playing football in <u>The Blind Side</u>. Jason Bourne wants to uncover his real identity in (wait for it) <u>The Bourne Identity</u>.

(What does Ethan Hunt want in <u>Mission Impossible</u>? No idea... a script that actually makes sense?)

Accordingly, the one thing every writer needs to crack before writing even a single line is who their

main character _is_ and what they _want_ to achieve by film's end.

If there's any part of script building you <u>DO</u> <u>NOT</u> want to rush, half-ass or phone in, it's putting together an iron-clad take on your protagonist. <u>Spend whatever time is necessary to get this done right</u>. If you're forced to go off the grid for a solid month, laser-focusing on developing your lead and nothing else -- ruthlessly examining and exhausting the potential roads for them to have traveled, the idiosyncratic ticks, tells, flaws and traits that breathe life into whomever we meet as your story begins -- then sack the fuck up and do it. Duh. Without question. Don't stop until your guy or gal is firmly in the pocket, until you hear all the tumblers lock into place and get _that feeling_, you know, that quiet, thrilling whisper in your gut letting you know shit is _right_.

When it comes to your lead character, **the ultimate goal for any aspiring screenwriter is to put their awesome new creation squarely in the strike zone for both talent and financiers**. As I've already explained, this doesn't mean to dumb 'em down or knock off all their edges, so don't latch onto that as some cop-out as to why <u>you</u> haven't come up with something first class. Just get your Hero in tip-top shape, however long it takes.

One of the key things creatives do when reading your script is put your protagonist under the microscope. Count on it. If your lead can't handle that withering level of professional scrutiny, you get drag-and-dropped straight into the trash.

4) "What other movies are like your movie?"

52

Don't bother leaving the house until you have a solid working knowledge of <u>other films</u> out there similar in concept, character and/or execution to what you're writing.

These can range from legit classics and movies produced some years ago, to those currently in theaters, to projects in development or production you might want to get the 411 on as well.

<u>Do your homework</u>. Watch these films. At the very worst (read: laziest), research and read detailed reviews of them. If you have Industry connects, hit them up for scripts in development that may impact your project. Educating yourself on whatever's out there, at whatever stage, is mandatory. That way, when you stumble upon similar concepts, characters, scenes, bits, gags, etc. you'll know to change, revise or better yours altogether.

Also consider this a pre-emptive strike against the ubiquitous scruffy lurker in meetings who delights in pointing out rip-offs and close calls. Sadly, that's how some of these low-level butt-sniffers get their developmental jollies trying to look good -- by publicly punching holes in whatever you're pitching and farting on it.

(And NO, backsliders, <u>it doesn't matter if you wrote yours first, or your version is much better and funnier</u> -- whomever's take makes it into the public consciousness first, wins. Without exception.)

So what educating yourself beforehand offers is <u>protection</u>. Covering this ground can keep your ass from getting straight-up suplexed by creatives of all stripes.

Say you spend a ton of sweat equity dialing in your project, score a meeting and proudly walk into pitch it. Inside two minutes some fifteen-year-old exec smugly informs you there's another film *identical to yours* about to be released.

Even worse? The little shit's right.

Whoops. Lights out. Bed shat. Game over.

I am Jack's turtled penis who can never show its shrinking glans in these same offices again.

But hey, say your project *isn't* exactly the same. Cool. You'll still need to pack a big stick that can both <u>defend</u> and more precisely <u>define</u> this for your interrogators; pointing out the specific differences and pushing your more creative elements in reference to any project they might bring up.

You're the writer. It's incumbent upon you to make a compelling case on the spot. Offer a strong take which steers your project away from any awkward, lingering suspicion it might be drafting in some other finished picture's wake -- whether monstrous hit or disastrous flop. Both carry baggage capable of turning your proud efforts into collateral damage.

But if you land it successfully, you've got no problems. Plus -- a tight, friendly rebuttal here also offers a nice running start into the rest of your pitch.

Nobody is going to invest in something that's been done or *appears* to have been done -- any glue-huffing Silverlake musician can tell you that. Try and force that square peg into a round hole and you'll get savagely nutted and pointed towards the door for your troubles.

Big thing to remember here -- should you get wind of something that *sounds like* it's a dead ringer for your project, don't jump cut to despair and assume it nukes your months of hard work. Do not panic. You'd be amazed at how often "identical projects" have *nothing* to do with each other. Loglines are just that -- loglines. Brief, broad descriptions of potential movies. Wait until you get under the hood and see what's really going on before getting crazy on yourself or anybody else.

Beyond that, take heart -- even if the two scripts were totally identical (which never happens, by the way), as long as your rival project hasn't gotten the greenlight, it's still all about may the best man or woman win.

* * * * *

No matter what new masterpiece you're holed up plotting with Unabomber-like intensity, there will always be, bare minimum, *one somewhat similar film* that predates and preconfigures your own; a cinematic ancestor of sorts. The <u>Rear Window</u> to <u>Disturbia</u> (ripped-off clear down to the poster!), the <u>Planes, Trains and Automobiles</u> to <u>Due Date</u>, the <u>High Noon</u> to <u>Outland</u>, the <u>Battle Royale</u> to <u>The Hunger Games</u>.

Not a big surprise. Western Civilization's only dealing with thirty-six plots to begin with, and Wikipedia lists a meager twenty-one genres that narrative stories are categorized under.

By the way? Having a successful forerunner is a good thing. It can really help strengthen your pitch.

"Comparison pitching" -- the mash-up of two well-known movie titles to frame your own -- is very commonplace. You know, the "this meets that" framing of what your script is, i.e. "It's like <u>Mrs. Doubtfire</u> meets <u>12 Years a Slave</u>."

My long-time friend and producer Marcy had these sage words of caution when we discussed Comparison Pitching --

"Mixing two titles is fraught with danger!

Idiots/Rookies mix structural references with tonal ones, or a plot reference with a world and then you have a mess on your hands.

Imagine -- <u>Sliding Doors</u> meets <u>Schindler's List</u>.

What? They caught the wrong train and ended up at Auschwitz? (Turns out the writer intended it to frame their WWII tale of missed opportunities.)

Imagine -- <u>Tootsie</u> meets <u>Chinatown</u>.

A guy in drag uncovers a major conspiracy? A soap opera cast gets caught up in a world of deceit and corruption? (It was actually a comedy about a famous superhero's assistant and how he always solves the crimes while living in the shadows of Metropolis.)

I tend to use <u>one</u> title and a qualifier --

It's <u>9 to 5</u> but with young dudes -- <u>Horrible Bosses</u>."

So given whatever your project is, Marcy's suggestion is to use the "<u>Die Hard</u> in the White House" (again, the infamous <u>White House Down</u>) style over the "<u>Die Hard</u> meets <u>The American President</u>" or the like. This is a good way to avoid any inadvertent miscommunication about what you're selling. Very simply, your goal is to pick whichever reference offers the very best framing for your project.

And here's a big common sense no-no from Yours Truly -- Never reference a box office bomb or controversial money-loser when constructing your mash-up or "this meets that". For example, saying "it's The Lone Ranger meets John Carter" is tantamount to pepper spraying a potential buyer right in the mouth. Positing "The Astronaut's Wife" meets Waterworld" can get your skinny ass tossed into a mental ward, and "Cutthroat Island meets The Adventures of Pluto Nash" becomes an outright crime against humanity.

Simple concept here every scribe needs to accept -- profit good, losses bad.

Obviously, this has nothing to do with the *quality* of the movies in the mix, or your personal feelings about them. It's simply a best-case box-office framework to help stimulate the profit-minded imaginations of folks you hope to do business with.

Viewed professionally, in any pitch meeting, The Hangover good. This is 40 bad. L.A. Confidential (Oscar-winner, critically revered, modest box office) good. Gangster Squad bad. When Harry Met Sally (genre high-watermark) good. Town and Country bad (very, very bad).

Go on. Live a little. Test-drive a few on your own. For the more erudite readers, it may feel a little naughty at first, but you brainy fuckers'll get the hang of it eventually. Simply chillax and have some fun with this. When you land on the right "this meets that" combo for your script, you'll know. It'll hit you in the gut, sound and feel organic when you pitch it, and you'll see its underlying accuracy reflected in peoples' reactions.

That's why having forerunners is a good thing. Successful cinematic big brothers and sisters provide you with easily understood selling points and proven structural paradigms able to bolster *your* project -- inviting a certain "success by association". If you can invoke the spirit of money-making monsters who've roamed the Earth before you -- while still remaining fresh and unbeholden -- more power to you. Movie Gods permitting, perhaps the lingering scent of those past grosses will halo your own project during a truly exceptional pitch.

* * * * *

One last point -- if you seriously rack your brain and can't come up with *a single movie* that bears a resemblance to yours, you're doing something really, really wrong.

This is decidedly <u>not</u> a good thing. Don't believe for a second you're blazing some brave new storytelling trail, "breaking on through to the other side" in the Lizard King sense. More likely you're shitting the bed, hopping the reservation and heading for crazy town at warp speed.

If a broad parallel doesn't exist, there's a *reason* -- because it's never been successfully cracked. We've had over 100 years of moviemaking now, so no matter how high your Wonderlic, SAT's, Stanford-Benet, etc. somebody obviously would've hit upon the same concept (perhaps decades prior to your becoming a microscopic zygote in your mammy's tum-tum) and gone to the rack if they could've figured out a way to land it.

Don't back yourself into this tragic no-man's land, sticking with something you know or have been told repeatedly is "neither fish nor fowl". Simply rectify your work within the rules of the game. As Jordan once said, "Nobody's bigger than the game." Even M.J., the best in history, played within the established rules. It's how he excelled *within the box* which allowed him to outplay his peer group and redefine the world's understanding of basketball excellence.

The Big Four are your friends for life, whether you completely understand the wisdom of them or not right now --

1) "What's the Movie?"

2) "What's the World?"

3) "Who's Your Main Character?" a.k.a "Who's your Protagonist?"

4) "What Other Movies Are Like Your Movie?"

Know the answers or pay the price, it's really that simple. As an adult, you can choose to embrace them and evolve, or ignore them and piss dead into a typhoon. May the Movie Gods have mercy on your soul.

IS IT (GULP) ANY GOOD?

If you've seen Neil LaBute's <u>Your Friends and Neighbors</u> you'll know the line "*Is it me?*" plays a particularly brutal and brilliant role in the film, coming from any number of distraught characters in any number of devastating situations.

And yet, even though everyone keeps asking "*Is it me?*" throughout the film, nobody *really* wants to hear to the answer. You get the feeling that "<u>YES</u>. IT <u>IS</u> YOU!" blaring from a S.W.A.T. bullhorn would still go unnoticed, characters fighting like hell to avoid the acceptance phase at all costs.

Screenwriters have our own special version of "*Is it me?*"

It's called -- "Is my script any good?"

Hardcore, right? Welcome to *Tough Love*. Perhaps the only questions more difficult are "Am I good in bed?" and/or "Am I (gulp) big enough?"

(Women may want to fill in that blank with something equally resonant but far more anatomically desirable.)

So yeah, popping ourselves this question is pretty fuckin' personal. Tantamount to launching a drone strike on F.O.B. Self-Confidence. A swirling avalanche of self-loathing and self-doubt immediately buries you. Real Life and the World Outside remain bright and filled with promise, gloriously presented in 16x9 DTS 5.1 Blu-ray. But inside? Dear Lord, inside is a terrible, unholy place -- a bad, sunburned mushroom trip on the beaches of Screenwriter Hell.

But *why*? Why should this one, simple inquiry have such a destabilizing effect on us, both sage veteran and total newbie alike?

Straight up? Because the answer -- the *real* answer -- means so damned much. At certain times in a writer's life, it can feel like it means *everything*.

In the space of a text message, a truthful verdict has the power to ennoble or obliterate our fondest dreams and most sacred aspirations. Basic concepts such as being able to pay the rent or buy yourself or your parents a home. Silly things from replacing your Craigslist '92 Toyota MR-2 to the fantasy of actually having health insurance and being able to get your fuckin' teeth cleaned. All these slim, beggarly hopes walk that slender tightrope between words like "good" and "bad", "yes" and "no", "they want to meet" or "they passed".

There's all that other heavy shit, too -- the *psychological*. Wanting to feel that we've "made something of ourselves", in spite of a merciless business and ridiculous odds; "that we were right all along", even after calling ourselves liars, 2 a.m., a fresh day's uncertainty lurking behind the coming dawn. And lastly, that perhaps *what we write and think does have some real value*.

That we're not just kidding ourselves.

So, logically, <u>yes</u> -- when we finally complete our bloody climb and plant our flag atop Script Mountain, forced to stand naked and needy before any friend-of-a-friend-of-a-friend connections (aspiring execs, junior agents, puppy producers) or straight-up cold calls we might have the balls to make, and then ask "<u>Is my script any good</u>?"...well, yeah, it's *SCARY*. This really means something to us, and via that single, heartfelt Final Draft

61

PDF we're risking an epic level of personal exposure and disappointment.

Which is precisely why asking that worrisome question "Is my script any good?" is absolutely essential <u>before</u> making any of those moves.

Because in the absence of hard, honest truths about your work -- most of which you're probably not going to dig -- how can any screenwriter get where they're striving to go?

* * * * *

Consider what I like to call the "psychology of the read" -- *whom* you're giving your script to and *why*. Put more directly, your precise motivation for putting pages in front of somebody and your clear-cut expectation of what you're hoping to gain by doing this.

Let's start with the folks you probably *shouldn't* be sharing with first.

Family -- Why in Christ's name are you giving your script to relatives? Are they paying for the draft? Can they hook you up in this town? Get you a blind deal at Sony? Because if they ain't major stars/directors/ studio heads or otherwise Industry-connected in some massively epic and meaningful way, the unequivocal answer is NO. They cannot help you.

Far worse from a motivational point of view, just by *asking* you've thrown open a zero-yield Pandora's Box, from whence nothing good seems to come. One offhand comment from Baby Sis or your dear ol' Grandpappy ("Why'd they blow the spaceship up in the first place? I didn't get it.") can shitcan both your mood and your writing mojo for a month.

I get it. Screenwriting can suck 90% of the time. It's isolated. It's lonely. It's largely thankless. (Did I mention it's lonely?) So shamelessly fishing for artificial confidence boosters on the home front is to be expected, I suppose -- however bush league it might be.

(I call this the "Mommy, Mommy, Look What I Did!" Syndrome. Unlike third grade, however, Hollywood doesn't put Hello Kitty stickers or gold stars on your title page validating your efforts.)

Listen, your peeps are *civilians* -- give 'em a break. They have no frame of reference to properly evaluate screenplays. Man/Woman up here and help insulate them from the inherent toxicity of your quest. Troubleshooting and/or jerking off your zombie movie isn't for them.

Or as Rilke put it so much more profoundly, "*...be confident and calm in front of them and don't torment them with your doubts and don't frighten them with faith or joy; which they wouldn't be able to comprehend.*"

Word.

Relationships -- In my vast and horrifying experience, asking husband/wife, boyfriend/girlfriend, friends-with-bens or trashy OKCupid hookups the question, "Is my script any good?" leads to an impending trainwreck, for a myriad of most obvious reasons.

Blending contradictory passions like love and Film Biz success is a lot like mixing Styrofoam packing peanuts with gasoline -- best case scenario, you've concocted kitchen napalm... which puts you one crappy mood, meltdown, panic attack or unappreciated story note away from scorching the ass off everyone.

Would a humiliating incident from my own screenwriting infancy help better illustrate this? Fine. Shitty day of writing, self-confidence in the toilet, I once barked "*YOU'RE NOT GOING TO STOP ME FROM REALIZING MY DREAM*!" at my girlfriend for begging me to power down. Why was my Dearest One urging me to take a break? We were already an hour late for my best friend's birthday party. Yet despite her irrefutable logic, I still doused my sweetheart with my inner darkness, as if somehow *she* were the enemy, right? Like *she* was the reason behind Hollywood not fully accepting (and generously rewarding, of course) my obvious and inarguable genius.

God bless that young woman for giving me a free pass, accepting my apology and dragging me off to get drunker than David Hasselhoff's cheeseburger video (Youtube it). When it comes to girlfriends, fellas -- Just Say No. Screenwriting crack is whack. You don't want 'em anywhere near the blast radius.

Terrible thought, I know, but what if your loved ones HATE IT? Would prefer blinding themselves to reading another line? Nobody who sincerely cares about you would risk that kind of honesty, violently defecating on the magnum opus you've slaved on and worried over for God knows how long -- nor should they.

Ever consider why so many writers get the stock "Oh, yeah, I really liked it!" or "Dude, it's awesome, don't change a thing."? Auto-pilot comments designed to A) give you vague support and B) surgically extract *themselves* from the situation, vowing never to read anyone's script again?

It's because the person didn't want to -- and shouldn't have been -- reading your script in the first place.

In every conceivable category, sharing your work with intimates is high risk, low yield. No worries. Easy fix here. Simply put the gun down and walk away.

Other Aspiring Screenwriters -- I'll leave this to your discretion, but it can be a tragically mixed bag. Hungry young writers' hearts often turn a hateful pitch black when threatened with a fellow unknown's success. The old Somerset Maugham adage "it's not enough that I should succeed, but others must also fail" has been embraced as Hollywood's ultimate tag line.

Not trying to be über cynical here. Your peers may be completely trustworthy and beyond reproach; they may have superb story skills and the open-minded objectivity of fresh eyes on a fresh read -- all very useful tools. On the other hand, they're also *human beings*; suggesting they're not immune to jealousy, fear, envy, competitiveness and a whole list of other emotional toxins that can muddy normally good people's blood under such cutthroat circumstances.

Backhanded compliments can hurt worse than full-frontal assaults. Snarky barbs from those entrusted with your pages can cut to the quick as fast as any razor blade. Shit simply ain't cute when you're locked in mortal combat with the writing process and your dwindling sense of self-worth.

I've found that avoiding peer-to-peer bullshit is simply a matter of self-preservation. Taking on unnecessary negativity during your crimson climb up Screenplay Mountain can become energetically lethal. Why risk opening such a trap door? Why invite the aggressively unconstructive willingly into your own head?

Needless to say, people have different takes on this subject, so make your own calls and proceed at your own peril. Just know this is a Biz where old pals totally have your back... until they don't. Unseen punches come from awkward angles and the cluster bombs will land without fair warning.

Another hundred potential readers should probably be avoided as well -- the Cool Hipster Fedora-Dude Barista at Insomnia, Intelligentsia, The Novel, etc... your Power Yoga instructor and/or massage therapist... some online Xboxing WoW cosplayer... and, of course, anybody working the Cannabis Club counter or bartending anywhere in the world.

Again, flash back to the psychology of the read -- <u>who are you giving your project to and why</u>? Can they help you creatively or professionally? Because if they can't play a substantial role in moving the chains forward, IMHO you're wasting both your times. "Compliment collecting" can easily increase your uncertainty and confusion as much as temp-boost your confidence. By avoiding unnecessary white noise, you work to preserve maximum focus on the serious business at hand.

Don't mistake the larger message here. This is NOT about becoming some overly paranoid Hollywood douchebag unable to trust friends. It's about you beginning to <u>think and act</u> like a professional writer to realistically advance your goals. About getting real with it, and, in the process, becoming real yourself.

<u>Brass tacks, I feel like 99% of the time writers give their scripts out not expecting -- nor necessarily wanting -- insightful or prescient notes</u>. They simply want somebody, even complete strangers, to pay them lip service and inject some positivity into the process, however lightweight it might be.

Thing is, this isn't somebody else's trip. It's yours. And hiding under a bedsheet of empty praise will <u>not</u> make your screenwriting boogie men go away.

* * * * *

Right now, you may (or may not) be thinking -- "Okay, John, I get it. Love the concepts. Protect yourself emotionally. Don't be a punk. Quit compliment collecting.

...So whom exactly <u>should</u> <u>I</u> give my script to then?"

Give your script to what I call a "good read".

A good read is someone you can trust to read your screenplay, give you an honest, knowledgeable assessment of its pros and cons, then work with you to brainstorm fixes and prescriptive changes for whatever issues exist.

Ideally, this is someone who both has your back <u>and</u> knows their shit -- enough so they'll give it to you straight, sans sugarcoating, love it or hate it, like it or not.

A good read doesn't stroke you; stroking is meaningless to an aspiring professional. But they sure as hell don't beat you down and bust your confidence up, either. Think of them as your screenwriting Switzerland; an ego-free zone maintaining maximum objectivity in the most subjective, self-obsessed and opinionated business in the world.

Where exactly do you find <u>your</u> good read? One of these wildly insightful bastards able to give you that prescriptive dose of honesty without totally eviscerating (read: fucking up) what's already good about your script?

67

No magic potions here. Admittedly, it's not an easy task.

These guys and gals take some effort to find. Like everything else in Hollywood, a wicked amount of luck attends it all, and you can't dial in right place/right time on an iPhone app. Finding the perfect crime partner and then building a creative alliance is something you'll have to work at. Don't be surprised if you end up kissing a few frogs along the way.

One hand, fingers to spare, I can count my own good reads, and I'm extremely fortunate to have counted perhaps the most successful producer of my generation among them. Of course, when I first met this cinematic Boy Genius, he was a lowly unknown, making copies and doing coverage, yet to begin his heroic (and incredibly lucrative) ascent to the top. But his monster brain for storytelling and structure was already evident to the lowly, unknown Me from the moment we struck up a snarky conversation about The Flintstones having 52 writers (yes, it's true. More about that later).

...And therein lies a starting point for any aspiring writer. Search with eyes wide open for someone on the come, like yourself, with the skills and dreams and a fierce determination to match your own.

For example, underling assistants are cool because they evolve into agents and CE's and VP's, etc. Four guys I met late '90s working desks for $300 a week are now among Hollywood's most powerful manager/producers. This vaguely creepy, chain-smoking *Portlandia* type in the Venice bungalow next to mine has grown up to become a *Hollywood Reporter* Top 50 Powerbroker. Puppy producers and Peter Stark grads are good calls, too, as many have a decent eye for material and are often putting what little money they have on the line to make their own breaks and participate in this business.

Just consider producer Lawrence Bender discussing the now-legendary Quentin Tarantino/<u>Reservoir Dogs</u> of it all --

"We were both outsiders. We both were trying to fight our way into the system. And we just started talking about, 'Let's make a movie together.'"

Sound familiar? That's pretty much how a lot of great things get going -- kindred spirits joining forces with tenacious souls. So start putting the word out. Whenever you're done writing for the day, make and effort to get out of the house. Network Film Biz parties and events, as punishing and morally abhorrent as they can be. Join a few Hollywood tracking boards, spitball over vapo rips with friends-of-industry-friends, do a few shots with the kid from the UTA mailroom, *whatever.*

Seems like a long shot, sure, but were <u>Reservoir Dogs</u> and a myriad of other now-beloved scripts and films any different?

* * * * *

I simply can't exit the subject of feedback and whom to give your script to without saying something about the cottage industry "Notes for Hire" racket that's blanketed the Net like a pandemic of tertiary syphilis.

These days everybody and their French bulldog are offering paid "script and story consultations" -- despite not having *any* tangible real-life success in the Business with their own writing at all.

Call me old-fashioned, but optioning one Talking Dog script to an Bulgarian foreign sales agent or winning "Best Experimental Short Video" at the 1995 Fort

Wayne Film Festival does <u>not</u> a screenwriting expert make. Despite this, much like "life coach" and "massage therapist", it seems no legit qualifications are required to proclaim oneself a "story consultant" and hang out a shingle... other than liking movies, having read a few scripts and figuring out how to buy a domain name from GoDaddy.

Frankly, I'd say 90-plus percent of the notes-for-hire services I've surfed are absurd. I mean, seriously, let's get some real life perspective here. Can you call yourself an "NFL Quarterbacks Coach" if the closest you've gotten to pro football was watching NFL Sunday Ticket? Is it fair to offer your "expertise" as an architect if you've never designed, built and sold a building in your entire life?

And the prices? Don't get me started. This gaggle of WordPress warriors charge anywhere from $300 to $1000 *starting*, and often all those figures buy you is a paltry handful of <u>non-professional</u> notes. Many sites offer four pages in the neighborhood of $500 <u>or</u> six pages for a ballpark $750. So how does that work, exactly? Does that mean the more expensive notes are an additional 50% *better* -- implying they don't put as much thought into the cheaper version? Or do you just get 50% *more* of the average notes they didn't give you in the first place?

For realz, bro? You're kidding me with this shit, right?

Next level up are the well-branded $3K to $5K "Private Seminars" or "Weekend Retreats"; Google AdWords-advertised with pensive, soft focus, sepia-toned website portraits of the lecturer staring off into the writing cosmos, lost deep in staged contemplation. **In my professional opinion -- by which I mean being someone who has <u>made</u> <u>a</u> <u>living</u> with nothing but my**

screenwriting for twenty-plus years -- having the balls to charge this kind of bread is utterly cynical, taking the "a fool and his/her money" proverb to an outrageous new level of premeditation.

Three-thousand dollars? Shit, honky, you gotta be rich to think like that in the first place. Last time I checked, the object was to *make money* with your writing, not *spend money* listening to **unproduced non-professionals** talk about it.

(FYI -- did you know some of these goofballs have apparel for sale?!? WTF? How does selling somebody a branded baseball cap help their *writing*?)

Not to be a totally reductive twat (whoops, too late), but doesn't anyone wonder why these self-proclaimed gurus haven't sold ten blockbusters each by now? They've "mastered" story and structure well enough to charge you a couple grand with a straight face, right? Come to think of it, many of these folks have been lecturing about it for longer than I've been writing.

So why haven't they made millions writing and selling their own movies?

Where are the tangible results of all their massive, shrewdly branded and franchised "expertise"? And why should their long-running *lack* of professional successes inspire confidence in potential students? Shouldn't it be completely opposite? **Shouldn't aspiring writers be seeking out well-documented winners, not well-documented losers**?

Hate to be a buzz-kill, but this whole self-anointed "script guru" trip smacks of "Those who can't do give expensive three-day seminars". Like bad psychotherapists, they keep force-feeding the "I'm OK -

You're OK" racket. Me? I'd rather quit the Business than bullshit you.

Hold your horses, haters. Let me be very clear -- **I'm not saying there aren't experienced people doing legit consulting and teaching out there**. If an aspiring writer feels they're getting their money's worth from *any* program, so be it, that's ultimately all that counts. Baby Jesus works in mysterious ways, and <u>anything</u> that gets and keeps you writing is a fantastic thing. So if you feel like you're making legit progress with whomever you've entrusted, by whatever methods, at whatever cost, by all means, continue onward.

Please just be sure their consulting is objectively upping your game -- meaning <u>other</u> <u>people</u> and <u>professionals</u> have noticed your improvement, not just the smiling face you're writing checks to. Make certain your teacher or consultant's notes and ideas translate to the page, as well as the business of filmmaking and financing as practiced out in the real world. Otherwise, this is simply a cyber-era version of "The Emperor's New Clothes", with you paying real cash money for an invisible screenwriting suit nobody else can see.

Obviously, I have VERY STRONG opinions on the subject (ya think?), and frankly, you may not share them. No worries. That's what makes it a horse race. Regardless, my personal reaction to this sprawling cottage industry clusterfuck was to take the law into my own hands and do something positive in response to it.

I started Tough Love Screenwriting (originally called Tweak Class) completely out of pocket, a giving-back labor of love. The concept was simply to give struggling writers completely outside the Business (a.k.a. "civilians") an accurate, meat rack understanding of what it takes to both succeed creatively and survive emotionally as a screenwriter.

My first class was held in a Westside dance studio and offered (GASP!) for free -- blowing many a class vulture's mind here in Butt Town. I posted on my buddy Jeff Gund's entertainment industry site infolist.com and got 250 emailed applications in a week. From the writing samples, I cherry-picked nine students. Two years have passed since that first class, and my ever-evolving roster of students (whom I lovingly call "Tweakers") has been thriving -- without them having to plunge deeper in debt, take out a home mortgage line of credit or cash-out their 401(k)'s.

But hey, enough of my bitching -- the choice is ultimately yours. Keep paying max money to jerk yourself off with screenwriting snake oil or say "enough is enough" and start asking why none of these guys selling magic bullets have ever fired one themselves.

LOSE THE POETRY

Back in 1995, I wrote a Horror spec called <u>The Willies</u>. It was essentially <u>Carrie</u> with evil twins. People are constantly abusing and shitting on these orphans, until at last, after making a pact with the devil, they take their bloody revenge.

My agent went out with it and immediately got a shamelessly low-ball pre-emptive bid from a smaller studio in town. By that point in my life, my dream of becoming a legitimate screenwriter was nearing extinction. I'd been struggling in L.A. for four years, was stone-cold broke, about to lose my apartment, and my girlfriend and I were subsisting solely on the 49-cent value menu at Taco Bell. Facing even more of that ugliness, I did what struggling young writers have to do sometimes -- I sucked it up and took the dogshit money, simply glad to survive and hopeful I would live to fight another day.

First day working, I go into a story meeting with the company's "Creative" VP and Head of Development. We dug in and spent several hours doing notes starting Page One -- discussing what they thought worked, what didn't, and what I'd need to address in my rewrite.

At one point, the VP looks up at me and says, "Wow, John. This description on page 52 is really good writing. Would you mind reading it out loud?"

Flattery will get you <u>everywhere</u> with a screenwriter, and I'm sure I flushed slightly with pride as I found the page and paused to clear my throat.

The set up was simple -- a grieving daughter (our protagonist) looking through her deceased mother's belongings, which have all been boxed up and stored in the attic. The beat offered a brief respite from all the genre action, gave us a further glimpse into her character, and prompted her discovery of an important clue at the end.

This was the description I wrote, verbatim --

"She rifles several of the boxes, finding little more than old letters and checkbook stubs, key chains and their forgotten keys. The meaningless remnants of our too brief lives."

There was a long pause after I finished. The VP and Head of Development were nodding their heads in synchronized approval. Then the VP says --

"Yeah, it's really great. Great stuff."

(HARD BEAT)

"Lose the poetry, John, cut it all out. It's slowing down the script."

I'd never been quite so close to publicly crapping my pants. Did he just say LOSE... THE... POETRY? a.k.a. LOSE THE GOOD WRITING? Wantonly kill off two short sentences -- two sentences he actually *likes* -- which perfectly sell the moment? And replace them with what, Mr. Hemingway? "She opens her dead mom's shit and finds a mysterious clue!"

Like every indignant scribe during the century before me, I sat masked in a queasy half-smile, cerebral cortex locking up. Surely "development" couldn't be like this *everywhere*? Surely this exec must be a nutter, a lone gunman of sorts, some soulless script assassin who didn't value lightweight artistry over the groan-inducing stock lines which had stupefied readers for decades?

Nope. He wasn't the slightest bit insane. In fact, Mr. Company VP was the Gold Standard -- an Industry veteran and Number Two guy at the whole company. And if I didn't "lose the poetry" voluntarily, believe me, he would have no qualms hiring another low-ball writer to lose it for me.

Way back at NYU, an older studio vet had once shared a bit of sage wisdom with me -- "It's better for you to fuck up your script the way they want, than have 'em hire somebody else to fuck it up for you."

As baffling and counter-intuitive as this advice had seemed, now I went ahead and took it. I labored at "losing the poetry", beat after tight beat, good scene after good scene. For nine agonizing months, they "developed" the script this way. Any nugget of goodness was ruthlessly ferreted out, any clever turn of phrase or interesting character tic was quickly sandblasted into beige. My reward, such as it was, was being kept onboard as sole writer.

In the Industry, this process is commonly referred to as "Development Hell".

Finally, they were ready to go out with it. And they did. And in a matter of three short weeks, the company blew a sure-thing co-financing deal, flatlined similar offers via ego and absurd distribution demands, and then shelved the project out of self-loathing and shame, never to see daylight again. It also left The Big Question still looming -- Had sacrificing all my poetry to the Commercial Film Gods made my script better... or worse? Now, tragically, there was no way I'd ever know for sure.

Instead of my project -- and I'm totally NOT kidding here -- the company produced the urban side-splitter <u>Don't Be A Menace to South Central While Drinking Your Juice in the Hood</u> in its place. That film survived three embarrassing weekends before being euthanized and laid to rest in the VHS checkstand displays at Rite Aid and Ralph's.

During what I thought a poignant last ditch appeal, before all the lights had been turned out, I'd made the case to the company that horror was an American genre mainstay, essentially a license to print money when well executed, and this is what the same VP told me --

"Horror's dead, John. Nobody wants horror anymore. It's all about the urban audience."

<u>Scream</u> opened that same December and made $173,046,663.00 worldwide. In its wake, an uninterrupted avalanche of extremely profitable low-budget horror flicks dominated the coming decade.

And me? Exactly one year after the sale, my girlfriend and I found ourselves back at Taco Bell.

UNNECESSARY EVILS

Those first professional cuts for any young writer are excruciating. Everything about your script -- every flat character, every lousy throwaway line, every unneeded parenthetical -- feels personal and inviolate, gifted from the heavens and written in stone, somewhat on the order of Moses' holy tablets.

"Change something? Why? It was plenty good enough for you to buy it in the first place, wasn't it?"

Some version of this is what the working writer yearns to bark in his developers (read: torturers) faces. If you loved it enough to put real money behind it, why in the fuck do you want to change every last thing about it now? Where's the logic in dating a tall, skinny brunette if you really wanted a short, squat redhead?

This mentality is, of course, totally understandable. The script is quite literally your baby, your winning Powerball ticket, the lone vehicle by which you hope and pray to escape the nagging self-doubt and just-getting-by poverty of a middle class kid with a mountain of student loans. This is your shot -- perhaps the one and only shot you're gonna get -- and if it's mishandled somehow, if somebody shits the bed and drops the ball, you and you alone are the one who'll pay the ultimate price.

On the other hand... there are a couple big problems that come with sticking by your guns *every* time. One, without question, you'll be replaced as soon as your steps are up, and most likely won't work for that company or any of those people again. Producers largely dislike writers as it is. Certainly nobody wants to work with a "difficult" one, thumbs jammed in his/her ears, not listening and refusing to consider needed changes.

Two, and this can be a tough one for us writers to swallow, what if all these developmental numbskulls are actually <u>right</u>??? What if a few of those "shitty notes" you keep bad-mouthing to friends turn out to be gems, pure gold, BIG IDEAS that help take your script to that hallowed "next level"? Some writers are so busy saying "no" that they're throwing away the very ideas that can dramatically increase their odds of success... and survival.

So John, you ask, how in the hell do I know *when* to do *what*? How do I discern between the gold and the gravel, the shit and the pony? How can I ensure I do the right thing creatively while traversing such treacherous Industry tundra?

That, my friends, is the eternal question every writer faces, every time they book a gig. Because there *aren't* any right answers 100% of the time. The whole endeavor is entirely subjective, a complete crapshoot, with the looming possibility of some ravenous tiger waiting to bite your head off behind every door.

Your creative action -- or inaction -- affects not only this project, but the possibility of the many unseen projects yet to come. Of prominent producers and execs putting in a good word, greasing the skids for a full-freight first draft at 100% of your quote... or not. Of you being able to pay off those loans, take care of your hard-working parents, buy yourself something nice and live the creative lifestyle you've always dreamt of and suffered so damned much trying to actualize.

Being a writer is about <u>making</u> <u>choices</u>. Peel everything else away, that's where it nets out, and that's what's expected by the people who employ you. Often it requires the skill of a surgeon to juggle your honest creative instincts, the daunting politics of the situation and the challenging personalities involved.

Any time a writer's blood starts to boil and they become hell-bent on "taking a stand" or raising hell over something script-wise, I would urge them to inhale through their noses/exhale through their mouths a few times (a seven count is usually good), and make sure beyond doubt it's over an issue of critical concern.

Don't burn whatever script cred you may have whinging like an amateur over the silly shit -- stupid throwaway lines, meaningless location or costuming changes, near-invisible "subtleties" or "finesse points" that nobody outside you will ever discern as missing from the final product.

<u>Keep some perspective about what's being changed</u>. Go DEFCON Three on a host of non-factors or points easily remedied, you'll quickly paint yourself in as Mr. Shitty Pants. Barking "*I'm The Writer Of This Goddamn Project!*" at your D-Team may *sound* like a fantastic idea at the time... but it never yields the game-changing catharsis frustrated writers hope it will.

Pretty decent rule of thumb? <u>Make sure you *actually* care on any given point commensurate to the amount of noise you're prepared to make</u>. An easy measurement that should help temper any knee-jerk outbursts the darker, more insecure angels of your nature are inclined to trick you into.

* * * * *

In my entire twenty-plus years in the Business, I have never, ever, under any circumstances (frontal lobotomy, crack addiction, etc.) met a writer who *liked* getting notes.

After weeks, months or (God forbid) years of working on a project, pouring one's life's blood into it, no writer who's remained even halfway sane is going to bust out a joyful moonwalk across the conference table when some Candy Crush-distracted Exec insists they "like it a lot"... but that it needs major work, perhaps even a Page One. That somehow you "missed it" or "misunderstood the movie we were going for"... even though you're clutching their own in-house document delineating *exactly* what everyone agreed on you executing -- which is, of course, everything they absolutely *hate* now.

Venomous comebacks shotgun through a writer's mind -- "Did you even *read* it?" (rookie stuff), "Are you fuckin' mentally stunted or something?" (pushing it), "Do you jokers not *recognize* great writing and superlative storytelling when you see it, or do you simply not *understand* it?" (I'll be moving back into my parents' basement as soon as this meeting's over).

If only. But we don't dare Rambo down that road -- at least not if we're hoping to stay on the project. Lord knows, if screenwriters went all Tourettes and <u>Liar, Liar</u> with it, unshackling their darkest thoughts during certain story meetings, well, notes sessions would have to be sanctioned by Dana White and the UFC. Accordingly, the violence of any writer's first blush reaction must be quickly contained and damped back down, like radiation or contaminated drinking water. Kept from plain public view at all costs, lest one be forever branded as "difficult" or "uncooperative" -- career killers if ever there were ones.

As previously mentioned, complicating all this (whether we'll admit it or not) is the fact that most writers think of their work as essentially perfect *exactly the way it is*; an enchanting, inviolate whole delivered in the spirit of the Ten Commandments.

Dear Mr./Ms. Development Exec -- you wouldn't ask Moses to "chip off some stone" because the tablets feel "too big", would you? Have him trim the last two commandments (false witness, thou shall not covet) over running time concerns? Hell, no, you would not. So why would you sit there calmly expecting me to hack away at my work of art?

Been there myself, my friends. In one cringe-worthy burst of late '90's hubris I invoked (I shit you not) *Orson Welles* in my own defense on some silly story point -- made even more bizarre considering it was a buddy cop script. (Looking back, I thank Little Baby Jesus that Youtube and Twitter hadn't taken over yet.)

Back of every writer's mind or crowding the cerebral cortex right up front, most of us are pretty damned confident we've totally aced it by the time we turn in our pages. Slam dunked it. Obliterated it. Took it to the House. Made it squeal louder than Ned Beatty in the backwoods.

How could we not?

We just spent between <u>TWO</u> <u>AND</u> <u>THREE</u> <u>HUNDRED</u> <u>HOURS</u> constructing our masterpiece, scene by complex scene, quip by trailer-friendly quip. Previously unthinkable lows were easily surpassed in finishing this draft -- starting obscene and emotionally nonsensical brawls with girlfriends/boyfriends/husbands/ wives... crassly relegating rent-paying relatives to voice-mail... refusing to eat vegetables of any kind. We've gobbled

Spring Street ephedra, beer-bonged cold McDonald's lattes, snorted Adderall off empty tampon boxes... all to ensure each B-story was bulletproof, that every last scene tracked and twisted and landed appropriately, and that our lead character remained dark-and-edgy-yet-entirely-sympathetic-and-heroic -- someone who's pure shining gold in scenes with his wisecracking SAG actor 5-year-old son.

And now, after that soul-withering march through Satan's lair, you want to give me... *notes*?

Do you jokers not *recognize* great writing and superlative storytelling when you see it? Or do you simply not *understand* it?

* * * * *

Notes can rattle you pretty good. Quickly they become demonic gatekeepers throwing wide the daunting doors to Development Hell.

During the first shockwave of notes on a script (the "set" of revisions), I always feel my stomach windmill and my face flirt with crimson; some call this "butterflies" but mine feel more like big-eared Mexican bats. Far end of the conference table, witnessed-boxed all by yourself as the Inquisition begins, I get a very specific sinking feeling; maybe 50% indignation ("No, I *don't know* why you've stopped me, officer.") and 50% Imposter Syndrome (Wikipedia it). It's the anxiety-ridden build-up to a fresh root canal, only what they're drilling is your grey matter, and it's gonna hurt a lot more for much, much longer.

After stripping everything else away, what's truly maddening about notes is that they're entirely SUBJECTIVE. Who actually *knows* what's best for any given scene or line or character on any given page at any given moment? Is that one joke you added seriously funny or simply stupid? Does it play like magic or sit there reeking of flop sweat? Is it cool the Protagonist stows away under the Villain's Ferrari at 80 m.p.h. (clutching nothing but twirling drive-shaft) or is it as cornball and remedial as the baby's eyes at the end of <u>Angel Heart</u>?

Hell, Roman Polanski and Robert Towne went silent-treatment for twenty-plus over the ending of Chinatown (Polanski was right, it was better that Evelyn died, which Towne finally admitted).

All this can drive you nuts, and debates over these elements remain largely abstract and unsettled until your work faces a paying audience -- which most never do and by which time nothing could be done about it anyway.

When working with someone like Jeffrey Katzenberg, who's crossed the $100 Million Dollar line countless times, yes, the odds are pretty fuckin' good he'll have a better sense of what works and what doesn't coming from his direct personal experience. In this type situation, you'd be wise to pull back, dummy up, listen and *learn* (at least that's what I did working with him).

But hey, not every producer or executive is Jeffrey Katzenberg.

Many have yet to make a single movie -- and some won't make a film at all. Snazzy business cards and studio parking spaces don't guarantee any great skill with material. Execs may be proud Harvard grads, with dreams of becoming big-time Industry shot-callers, but do they have an Ivy League education in the very specific style of cinematic storytelling which underpins our Business? Browsing *Save The Cat* on your Kindle at the Lakers game just ain't gonna get it done in this dept. And with 99.9% of suits never having written a professional screenplay (or anything real at all, to be honest), they can't entirely empathize with standing in your Sketchers on the creative side, either.

But wait, there's more! Often you find the lion's share of notes aren't <u>prescriptive</u> in any tangible way. Translation -- they lack *specific ideas* capable of helping troubleshoot and improve your project. Doesn't take a Nobel Laureate to recognize logic holes and dialogue that needs to be punched up, scenes that don't quite land yet, etc. The cobwebbed developmental chestnuts "You're the writer, you figure it out" and "That's what we're paying *you* for" are about as helpful as non-secreting testicles and a club foot. By this point, it's the Executives' project, too, so you'd expect a modicum of teamwork come time to crack and fix; but sadly, that may or may not be the case.

Much of it comes down to whomever you're working with, luck of the draw. Like world-class doctors, great producers and execs are hard to find and worth their weight in platinum once you finally do.

* * * * *

Having sat in probably a hundred or so story meetings, I thought I'd share a few survival strategies I've worked up to keep myself from going berserk. To each their own, take 'em with a grain of salt, YMMV, YOLO and all that other online bullshit. Point being, if *any* of these tips helps keep just one writer out there fired up and in the game, I expect I've done my good deed for the day.

<u>That Initial Shockwave</u> -- After passing out the free Fiji water and wrapping up last weekend's box office gossip,

85

it's pretty much nut-cutting time. The D-Team may lubricate you before insertion with throw-away compliments ("The characters' voices feel much stronger now" or "Couple really solid new scenes here"), or they may jump right in and begin Turkish gangbanging you like a <u>Midnight Express</u> day player. Either way, I have but five words of advice --

Stay cool and surf it.

Do <u>not</u> let this initial barrage throw you off your game. Simply settle in and pay attention to what's being said. That's all you need do. Why? **Because at this point, none of what you're hearing is really *real* yet**. Get it? Some of it will stick, some won't; some will be flipped, bettered, modified or entirely forgotten long before picking up your parking validation stickers at the front desk. So this is the *perfect* time for you to lay back, take notes and listen. That's right, <u>listen</u> -- that weird thing we writers do on the rare occasions we're not chatter-boxing warp-speed like meth heads.

Because here's the thing -- one red-faced, hornet's nest reaction from a writer, a single microsecond of blanching-and-looking-ready-to-puke, can both set, and destroy, the tone of the entire meeting. Hell, sometimes the entire *project*. It can cause execs to lose confidence in you, i.e. "Christ, one tap on the chin this guy's legs go all wobbly? Forget about production, he won't last two drafts."

Make no mistake -- the people who hired you are expert at reading rooms, and they'll scrutinize your reactions with x-ray vision. Before the meeting's even set, they know you're not going to dig a lot of what they have to say -- no writer ever does. So what's actually on the table here is *how you deal with it*, how you deal with *change*, as much as whatever fixes you eventually land

86

on. Entirely reasonable from a business perspective, isn't it? Screenwriters can be epic pains in the ass, from well-meaning malcontents to the straight-up Rikers whack jobs.

Figuring out what kind of man or woman they're dealing with -- in addition to what kind of writer -- is a huge non-verbal part of the development process.

During an Aztec blood-letting on a project, the rookie producers couldn't throw my pages (and me) under the bus fast enough, accusing Yours Truly of ruining everything. Not that it matters, but this disaster came about by my painstakingly executing their detailed notes... against my better judgment.

Sure, I could've spazzed out, gotten indignant, pointed fingers, called my agent or threatened to walk the project like so many bitch-assed writers pulling guaranteed paychecks do. But I didn't. Instead, I calmed the waters by simply asking for a week to make good and promising I'd fix all their concerns. Most savage, soul-wrenching seven days of my life, sure, but I pulled it off -- and regained their confidence and trust moving forward. In the cozy aftermath, lattes proffered and order restored, I remember the Studio V.P. saying to me, "You handled that with great aplomb." (Still one of my favorite compliments I've received in this Business.)

On rare occasion, specific execs may appear to be baiting you, on purpose. Trying to get under your skin from the start. Why? Maybe they want to look sharp in front of their bosses, justify expense accounts, etc. Maybe they want *somebody else* for the project, and the sooner your steps are bulldozed through, the sooner they can make that new writer a reality. Maybe they legitimately don't like your writing. Maybe they legitimately don't like you. Who knows? *Who the fuck cares?*

The bullet point here is not to give 'em the satisfaction by taking the chump bait. Handle things with great aplomb. Stand tall in your saddle, the Screenwriter With No Name, confident in your work and that, worse case, whatever the issues, they can be fixed. After that, let the game come to you. You're two minutes into the first quarter, my friends, which leaves a helluva lot of basketball still to play. Shit is only personal if you decide to see it that way.

Or as Ice Cube and Das EFX advised many moons ago, "Check yo' self before you wreck yo' self."

* * * * *

Still, Screenwriting Zen Warrior or not, some of what they hit you with is going to suck. Big-time suck. Script-killing notes you *know* (with God as your witness) are harmful and wrong and capable of undoing months of passionate, precise storytelling. We're talking worst of the worst here, absolute bottom-of-the-barrel developmental dogshit, the stuff that sooner or later -- like jury duty, porn pop-ups and WGA dues -- every writer encounters.

Believe me, folks, I've eaten plenty of blue-ribbon turds myself, pulled straight-out of somebody's ass and pitched at me with dare-you-to-say-something smiles. Sometimes they're naive and well-intentioned... sometimes, well, not so much.

During pre-production of my first feature, I got faxed a list of surrealist "proposed changes" from our Taiwanese financiers which almost caused me to crap my baby writer pants. This came at the eleventh hour, and since it was *their money* paying for the film, I had no choice but to take it seriously. Point-blank the U.S. producer informed me the Taiwanese wouldn't fund any escrow accounts until their "story concerns" had been dealt with.

In Producer/Financier-speak that translates to "*DO THE FUCKIN' NOTES OR ELSE*". As most writers who manage to survive eventually find out, it ain't much of a "creative dialogue" when one guy has a loaded .45 in the other guy's mouth.

On first inspection, some of the changes were nitpicky and ultimately wouldn't matter one way or the other. If insisting the Male Bad Guy (a very macho Euro TV star) "wear black suits and smoke expensive cigars" in explicit scene description helped them feel better about making my movie, by all means, bring on the Montecristos.

On the more disturbing side, however, were instructions like those involving p. 43 (yep -- still have the original. Like any smart writer, I save *everything*).

This note explicitly called for the Male Bad Guy to surprise one of his victims dressed as her best friend, the Protagonist's <u>wife</u>. That's right, they were telling me to put the toughest guy in the whole picture in full drag --

"*Sharon turns and there's Tommy standing DISGUISED AS LISA with a wig (to fool witnesses) -- dressed to kill -- shock! (maybe there's even nail varnish on his finger pressing the door buzzer in the first place.)*"

Not only did they want Tommy dressed like a chick, these Asian kinksters wanted him to *look fabulous*, too.

"*Maybe even nail varnish*". Thank God no specific brand or color palette was being demanded of me as well.

Being as this was my first film entering production, I found zero humor in the situation. On a dime, I halted a new assignment and began masterminding an urgent five-page "Stay of Execution" for our Taiwanese friends, begging them, on metaphorical hands and knees, not to force me to Barbie up the Bad Guy as a smokin' hot tranny during a crucial sequence of suspense.

For a bold young fucker going balls-out like myself, this was a pretty risky strategy. No producer from *any* nation welcomes a formal written response every time they send some low-budget, twenty-something screenwriter notes. Regardless, compelled by a naive film wonk nutsack brimming with the gooey passion of youth, I chucked caution to the wind and wrote that sucker with the ferocity of an innocent Death Row inmate inking his final Supreme Court appeal. Here's a verbatim taste of how it read --

> "*P. 48* -- *Executing this change is a bad idea for two big reasons --*
>
> *First, the audience will BUST OUT LAUGHING at Tommy when they see this whack vision of him wearing a Chanel dress and Revlon "Revolutionary Color" nail polish -- and brothers, they'll be laughing at him, not with him. It's totally inconsistent in tone and intent with the rest of the film and, what's worse, whomever is playing Tommy will never live the scene down. Its campy, misguided vision will dog his career for the rest of his days.*
>
> *Secondly, it doesn't make any sense. There is no motivation for an organization as powerful and well-organized as the Mob to send some freak in drag to a*

*woman's front door to grab her in broad daylight.
The henchmen are simply going to slip right in and do
their business -- as quietly and <u>professionally</u> as
possible.*

*You need to start thinking BIG, SMART AND
SUSPENSEFUL for the Bad Guys in this movie. Stay
away from the gratuitous low-budget movie clichés
and you'll end up with stronger, more interesting
villains."*

Mind you, there were *five pages* of this -- me
sermonizing and unrepentantly biting the hand that
feeds mere *days* from shooting. Still not sure whether it
was the bravest or dumbest move possible for me to
make.

By the grace of God, they got it and... backed off. Or
simply forgot about it. Or never really gave a shit in the
first place, having fired off hasty, half-baked notes on
the way to lunch. Never did find out which, which
means I can't take any credit and certainly wouldn't
recommend this gonzo tone to any sane writer that
wants to stay employed.

This other time (at band camp) a Senior Exec became
completely obsessed with a specific kill in the horror
project we were developing. By design, the scene was
stock and straightforward -- a potential victim (the
story's bad guy) pulls into his garage late one night,
lowers the door and suddenly the lights go out.
Headlights flash on by themselves, dramatically
spotlighting THE EVIL GHOST that's been murdering
everybody in the movie (pure fuckin' Tolstoy, I know).
The bad guy's engine begins to rev and redline wildly,
car gassing the place with lethal clouds of carbon
dioxide. You can probably guess the rest. Victim can't
get his windows up, toxic gas billows inside to choke

him and the last thing he sees before dying is The Evil Ghost laughing maniacally in the headlights.

(Whew. Thank God *that's* over.)

So... as we're discussing punching this up with alternatives, the project's VP completely spazzes out, hushing the room.

"Wait, wait, everyone! *I'VE GOT IT!*"

All heads dutifully turned to hear El Capitan's brainstorm (his first and last of the project, I might add).

"What if... the engine's roaring, gassing the place up... this poor guy looks out to see the Ghost... and suddenly the exhaust pipe S-T-R-E-T-C-H-E-S out and extends... wrapping around the car and then <u>BAAAMMM</u>! Smashes right through the window... <u>AND INTO HIS MOUTH</u>!"

<u>Dead</u> silence. Crickets. Mouths agape. Poor fucker had literally acted this out -- lassoing his arm overhead and landing his cupped hand smack against his lips to imitate the imaginary tail pipe.

Bro, I didn't know *what* the fuck to say.

Luckily, the Director of Development bailed everybody out. She simply went right back to where she'd been in conversation and carried on like it never happened. We followed her lead and that was that. It went away. It didn't exist.

Maybe five minutes later, discussing an entirely different scene, the VP bolts upright again -- "Wait, wait -- I've got it!"

And pitches the exact same shitty idea <u>again</u>. Verbatim. Same exhaust pipe S-T-R-E-T-C-H-I-N-G out... wrapping around... and BAAAMMM! Smashes right through the window... <u>AND</u> <u>INTO</u> <u>HIS</u> <u>MOUTH</u>!" He just would not let it die.

No ducking it this time. I *was* the fucking writer after all.

Standing on the lip of this treacherous precipice, a tack sprang up that came to serve my career well over the coming years. Here's what I said --

"You know, Raj, let me put my brain on it and see if I can make it work."

Done. Simple as pie. I'd gone on record, acknowledged his note, and now collectively we could move forward with the script.

Back home, on my own time, I would in fact see if I could come up with something better -- because really, *that's all he was getting at in the first place*. The specifics in this setting were essentially unimportant; Senior Exec just wanted something <u>different</u> and <u>better</u>, only he didn't have the slightest idea what that might look like. And for the good money they were paying me, I was plenty happy to give it a rethink. Figuring that kinda shit out is what you're there for in the first place, right? That's your job.

So that's the big lesson. <u>Clinch</u> when you're rattled, like any good boxer. Take responsibility and politely defer. Buy yourself some time. Just like the U.S. Congress, send it to committee and live to fight another day -- *when it actually matters*. No need to Tea Party yourself, ideologically bogging down the proceedings, sidetracking your own progress and/or turning some studio player into a lifelong enemy.

Just tell 'em you'll put your big brain on it and move on. Couple days later, after an ample cooling off period -- no longer emotional or feeling threatened -- give it another stab. With a clear head you'll have a much better shot at figuring out how to make it work... or how to work around it... or whatever you decide to do.

What ultimately came of the dreaded Stretchy-Exhaust-Pipe-In-The-Mouth Brainstorm?

Next meeting, nobody brought it up. Not a peep. It was like the conversation never happened. Senior Exec never mentioned it again.

As I mentioned earlier, some notes will stick, some won't. You'd be amazed how many contentious life-or-death brawls go down over shaky notes, only to have these same points vanish without so much as a whisper by the next meeting.

Don't misunderstand me -- I'm <u>not</u> greenlighting writers simply ignoring bad notes in the first place. Not on your life. You *still* need to work out a fresh fix and/or interesting alternative to the beat in question. There's no telling what people in development will remember or become irrationally fixated on, so play it smart and fully prepare yourself on the off chance you are called back to the witness stand. Who knows? Perhaps during this process you'll come with something even *you* like better. Imagine that. Now everybody comes out on top.

Ultimately, the pro's goal is to do what <u>they</u> want, <u>your</u> way.

Wanna save yourself an ulcer, ten cases of J&B and a couple tons of Tylenol? Satisfactorily address the D-Team's concerns while simultaneously creating something you dig as well -- or at least something you can live with. It may be annoying, but spinning developmental dogshit into gold creates a win-win for everybody. Your stock will skyrocket and you'll have seized an opportunity to improve your script even more.

I want to be super clear on one last point -- I'm definitely not suggesting any writer swallow chud creatively as a matter of habit, rolling over with a welcoming ass in the air every story meeting. That doesn't help anybody, because the people paying you certainly don't want that either.

This from a Warner Bros. VP -- "*If we could do what you do, John, we would. But we can't. We need you here.*"

So it's good to keep in mind that you're not there by accident. You belong. Those are your hands on the wheel, and the people who hired you put them there. They do need all your skill, perspective and insight to get the project where it's going. In fact, they're counting on it -- which is why they're paying you, dummy. If they could do what you do, they would... but they can't.

So start spinning, my friend. You're gonna have a big batch of gold to make.

BETTER

While serving my screenwriting life-sentence, I've become a complete believer in the concept that everything can always be better.

Bad scripts can be boosted to sample-worthy -- say "B" instead of "F". Good can be refashioned into Great, "Pass" upgraded to "Consider". And the Great? The Great can be elevated to the Even Greater Still.

This legendary Shunryu Suzuki quote I heard via Pema Chodron perfectly sells the conceit --

"Each of you is perfect exactly the way you are... and you can each use a little improvement."

And so it goes for Hollywood screenplays as well.

One of my favorite examples of making great things even greater is from Brian Helgeland and Curtis Hanson's L.A. Confidential (I'm going to pray like hell that even the most clueless among you have seen the film. If not, see it a.s.a.p. -- as in, tonight.).

Take a look at that outrageously good first scene between Officer Bud White (Russell Crowe) and high-class call girl Lynn Bracken (Kim Basinger) at her home. Bud knocks to find Lynn and an Older Gentleman doing their thing with This Gun For Hire screening in background. When Bud tells the older trick to leave, the guy fronts like the tough guy character in the film --

BUD -- Hit the road, gramps.

96

Bud enters. The Older Gentleman strikes a pose. He still thinks he's Alan Ladd.

OLDER GENTLEMAN -- Maybe I will, maybe I won't.

BUD -- (flips badge) L.A.P.D. shitbird. Get the fuck out of here or I'll call your wife to come get you.

Sputtering, the Older Gentleman exits with his clothes in hand.

And that's where the scene in my draft ends.

However -- when watching the film, you'll notice a tiny tweak was made. The addition of two meager <u>new</u> <u>lines</u> tagging this exchange which elevates the encounter to another level entirely --

BUD -- (flips badge) L.A.P.D. shitbird. Get the fuck out of here or I'll call your wife to come get you.

Sputtering, the Older Gentleman exits with his clothes in hand.

OLDER GENTLEMAN -- Officer.

BUD -- Councilman.

Earlier pass, the guy was just some random John, could've been anybody. Which is fine and totally works. But by surgically adding those two lines -- the right two *words*, actually -- Helgeland and Hanson underscored the darker subtext informing their entire film; the relentless corruption saturating every strata of Los Angeles, down to its deepest roots.

Two words. Pretty fuckin' good, right? One of the many, many reasons these guys get paid the big bucks.

97

(You'll also notice they double their money later, giving this same new "Councilman" a quick scene reversing his vote on the highway project -- the swing vote which allows it to pass -- and all because Pierce Patchett has been keeping evidence of his carnal indiscretions with girls like Lynn.)

So -- was this small but essential tweak made in a later draft? I'm not sure, but I have the final shooting script and don't remember seeing any evidence of it. Perhaps Hanson and Helgeland added it on set? Always a possibility. Or perhaps Russell Crowe and the actor playing the Councilman simply ad-libbed it during the scene. Who knows? I suppose you'd probably have to ask someone who was there when they shot it.

However it came about, the key point is this -- Hanson, Helgeland and Co. didn't stop spitballing and settle for merely great. There was no resting on their proverbial laurels. They kept on pushing and challenging themselves to take it to that next level, to find even sharper, stronger layers and fixes.

Oh, yeah -- they won an Oscar for their troubles.

Key to your own evolution as a screenwriter is accepting the premise that whatever you've written, however good it may appear at first blush, however strong the coverage or feedback, whatever you may make selling it, your script can always be made better. Simple fact, my friends. Paul Schrader's famous comment that "Screenwriting is rewriting" is every bit as prescient now as in his Taxi Driver days.

Everything can always be better. No writer breaking into this biz is exempt from the continual need for improvement. Writing "Final Draft" on your title page won't fool a soul; no such animal exists for writers developing material. Whether paid for or purely speculative, should you fail to take the initiative, count on somebody else in the mix demanding it of you.

There are no free passes in this department -- nor should there be.

* * * * *

Let's flash back to that earlier curveball I brought up. The reality that sometimes the notes you get are actually good. Really good. Even spectacular.

Despite all frantic expectations to the contrary, every screenwriter's innate fears of their story getting fucked up, of its integrity being defiled, its "message" diluted, sometimes your producers and/or execs come through in a big way.

The key here is making sure you're receptive to that possibility -- and that you can actually *recognize it* if and when they do.

This is what I like to call "The Five Brains Effect".

My purchased inch-by-bloody-inch approach to Hollywood development is this -- <u>five brains are better than one</u>. This simply means that paid adult professionals bringing extra energy, thought and enthusiasm to the project can always be a good thing.

Get a grip on yourself, Dear Reader. Stop that psychotic screaming and hear me out.

Your brain bucket in communion with the grey matter of four execs/producers (grand total = five brains) brings five times the education, five times the life experience, five times the knowledge of films, five times the vision, five times the *ideas.* That's the computing

99

power of <u>five</u> <u>Film Biz</u> <u>CPU's</u> to help crack, restructure, re-strategize and/or troubleshoot any unseen fault lines that threaten to derail your script. Five Lotto tickets instead of your lonely one, substantially raising your odds of winning the developmental jackpot.

Did I mention you get all this help free? Yep. It's on the house. Because best-case, that's a big part of what quality D-people do. *They help the writer bulletproof the story.* It's a big part of their job descriptions.

Despite how it may feel (and ignoring any lingering scars from the odd traumatic experience), your fashionable, freshly spa'd allies aren't sitting in those Aeron chairs drawing a sweet salary with some bold studio mandate to slow things down and/or fuck 'em up. They want things to succeed.

Sure, you cynical bastards, five brains can bring five times the hassle as well. Their ideas can lick balls a lot of the time -- as can any of ours. Shit happens and "wrong place/wrong time/wrong company" always plays a factor. But if just *one* of them comes up with <u>one monster idea</u> over a dozen story meetings, it's still one more monster idea than you started with, right?

Free good ideas? Sign me up. Sounds pretty righteous.

Nudge this concept one step further. Suppose this brainstorm (one of Henry Miller's hallowed "happy accidents") is so sublime and spectacular it becomes a total game-changer, illuminating your pathway to the promised land. Say it reinspires all involved, catapulting the project towards "we-gotta-fast-track-this-fucker" status? (Hey, bitches, it happens. Not every damned day, but a lot more than you'd think. Such is the power of One Big Idea.)

Know the best part of this?

<u>You</u> get all the credit for it.

You're the writer. You do all the heavy lifting, and by rights the fruit of shared brainstorming belongs to you. When people see the rewrites or (God willing) the movie itself, believe me, all they'll see is *your name* inking the title page or lasering the one-sheet. It's one of the few real benefits writers get. The sum total of developmental genius gathered during the process gets stuffed into your stocking.

There are no monopolies on good ideas. They can come from anyone at anytime, completely out of the blue. *Anybody* onboard your project -- Producer/EP/VP/Director of Development/Junior Exec or the halfwit Hipster Intern in the scanner room -- is capable of nailing the killer crack that saves your story. A single off-the-cuff, unsolicited quip may push your script squarely over the hump into the kill zone.

Ironically, some writers seem to have just as tough a time accepting good notes as they do crappy ones.

Pride, ego, *whatever* -- be sure to gut-check yourself on this going in. There's no shame in folks pitching in to get things firing on all cylinders, and there's absolutely no need to get shitty or territorial about it. **Screenwriting is a team sport, after all**. Group participation is expected, hell, *required* in this game. Some of the best scribes in Hollywood history, Academy Award winners even, have encountered this dynamic -- and embraced it -- along their storied journeys.

Let me go you one better. <u>Never be afraid to issue a team *mea culpa* once you realize you were wrong about some point</u>. That's right, suck it up and openly acknowledge the better answer or idea, no matter whom or where it came from. In a world this heavily 'roided on egotism, it takes a big man or woman to own things, especially having dug in and fought passionately for a different idea the first go 'round. Not only will stepping up grow your writer cred, it'll reinforce story meetings as a "safe space" for sharing, while giving your execs a well-earned (and much appreciated) tip o' the hat to boot.

Take a second to rejoice, my friends. Good ideas are *everywhere*. No one writer can possibly hope to have or harness them all. My take is to let the Movie Gods assist you whenever and however they're willing. Why waste the power of a "happy accident" falling into your lap because you're too busy not listening or deciding you hate something you haven't fully considered yet?

Wrapping all this up, a brief word of caution. Never forget the concept that every screenwriter "chooses their hills to die on". If you're thinking of taking a stand and going apeshit over something script-wise, make sure it's absolutely essential and that you care commensurate to the amount of noise you're prepared to make.

Become rigid on damn-near everything, you'll find any accumulated goodwill evaporating right alongside your creative credibility. You only get to play those cards a couple times before you become The Boy Who Cried Wolf, Mr. Pain In The Balls, the difficult little twat who doesn't get it and refuses to make changes.

NUTS AND BOLTS

To aspiring writers outside the circle, spending some serious thought about how your screenplay *looks* as well as what it *says* may seem pretty silly . As any weekend warrior will rush to testify, it's all about the characters and story and shit, dumbass. Stuff like formatting and margins and how many lines are used in description become irrelevant the moment these Hollywood jokers realize how goddamn good your script is.

Well, hell, brother. You wanna get all theoretical and "perfect world" about it, I suppose this could be true -- in the same way it's a fact somebody wins the Powerball jackpot now and again. If you're packing a script of undeniable value and power (say Prisoners or The Sixth Sense), I suppose you could hand-write it in Jazzberry Jam Crayola and get over to a point; provided a perfect storm of blind luck, good timing and the ever-fickle blessings of the Movie Gods.

Problem is, 99.9% of you *aren't* packing The Sixth Sense in your Dropboxes -- just like the vast majority of us won't win at Powerball. All potential readers will see and remember about your script is the semi-psychotic fuchsia crayon marks.

My take is that presentation is key in the screenwriting game, very much like many other high-end businesses.

When you dine Three-Star Michelin, you expect your meal to look straight off a Pinterest page and taste fuckin' amazing. That same supper comes out with a dirty thumbprint in your risotto and some poo-smeared plum sauce, yeah, you're gonna have issues no matter how good it tastes -- especially at those prices.

When you waltz into the Rodeo Drive Louis Vuitton to purchase one of the world's finest handbags, twelve-foot high hardwood shelving greets you, every clutch and shoulder bag immaculately showcased in all its leathery glory. For $3K a pop *minimum*, would finding those same bags picked over in a sloppy heap mess with your high a little? Make you wonder if that *Selene MM* was actually worth a major bite out of your bank account?

In short, sloppy presentation would undermine your confidence in not only the product, but the management as well.

I believe any screenplay plays by the exact same rules.

Correct presentation is essential because it instills *immediate confidence* in whomever's reading your script. Straight out the gate, it says *you know what you're doing,* that you're sharp enough and cared enough to ace the simplest step in the whole process -- getting the formatting and other rules right.

Of equal importance, proper appearance eliminates any possible <u>distraction</u> from the essential business at hand -- getting the reader to give your pages an honest, open-minded and dedicated reading.

Want Execs marveling at the sheer distorted audacity it took to go 18-point Copperplate Gothic Bold for your text... or you want 'em actually paying attention to the words/thoughts/ideas you spent hundred of hours so carefully crafting to make your project the very best it could be?

Many would say the very instant a writer even *chose* 18-Point Copperplate Gothic Bold they were doomed; that tragic act alone an admission they never had the right stuff to begin with. Just this once, however, I'm going to abstain from judging and posit that perhaps all such a writer needed was a quick heads-up to the folly of such ways. Consider this that heads-up and take it to heart.

Call it shallow, call it stupid, call it whatever you want -- the slightest reason for dislike or prejudice can ruin the outcome of your read and what the coverage says about your script.

"Coverage" is a logline, synopsis and comments section stamping an official final grade on your project -- Excellent/Good/Fair/Poor in one section, then Recommend/Consider/Pass in another. It serves as the film biz Cliff Notes for the multitude of screenplays being sent out, considered or developed. Ubiquitous within the Industry, once in the system it pretty much follows you the rest of your life. You'd have better luck ridding yourself of genital herpes from a Tijuana T.G.I.Friday's toilet seat than purging coverage from Hollywood's collective memory banks.

Point of fact -- <u>producers, studio heads, top-shelf VP's, etc. rarely read your script themselves.</u> That's just the way the cookie crumbles, kids, despite what your reps or anyone else assures you. These folks don't have the *time* to read every damned script circulating out there -- especially from green unknowns like yourselves. These are Hollywood's legit movers and shakers, and they're crazy busy doing super important stuff, like, say, having their gluten levels checked or getting healing body massages from blind Nepalese children.

"Reading stuff" is what their <u>development teams</u> do. They're the hard-working, largely unappreciated folks backstage that actually read your script, pay attention and write the appropriate coverage.

Should your project gain traction, get some big league heat behind it, hell, yes -- the proud peeps atop the food chain will probably glance at some pages. Until then, stay cool and don't crap your Underoos gang-texting everyone that Ridley Scott is reading your screenplay. *He's not.* Trust me. Mr. Scott's people are. When things get *really* real -- when your project has *earned* that level of attention -- then (and only then) Mr. Scott himself might take a peek.

Just for kicks, I had a friend at Sony do a coverage search for an ancient project of mine, the first script I'd written some fifteen years earlier. Freeze-frame my jaw smacking the floor when it took her all of five minutes to find it, easy as pie. Christ, there hadn't been a physical draft of my script on that lot for *decades*, but the coverage was still right there, ageless and daisy-fresh -- making it the default judgment on my screenplay for the rest of my natural life.

Perhaps now you're understanding why I'm such a stickler for correct presentation and getting shit right the first time. Very clearly, the last possible thing you want is to invite the inadvertent scorn or disdain (read: hate/judging) of some unknown reader and have it translate into the Official Word on your project.

Consider it from the developmental P.O.V. These people's *jobs* are to wade through dozens of scripts each week, hundreds each month, the plain majority awful at best. Reading bad scripts en masse will give you a headache unlike any other. Your brain is literally being forced to host *other people's shitty ideas* for the one or two hours it takes to read, make sense of and then write

106

coverage for them. Think <u>Marathon Man,</u> dentist's chair. Pretty much nails the sensation.

When any human being is force-fed that bulk of bad material, it becomes super easy to make snap judgments. And you know what? Ninety-plus percent of the time those snap judgments are <u>right</u>. If a writer can't handle the most elemental rules of the game -- i.e. how their script should look and read -- what are the odds they're insightful, self-aware and/or talented enough to have written a killer draft beyond that. <u>ACTION</u> <u>IS</u> <u>CHARACTER</u> as every screenwriting book in the history of Mankind will tell you. This is a prime example of that.

What? You included your own *full-color laser-printed storyboards and costume designs* with your script? Bye-bye, fucktard. Welcome to Darwinian Fitness, script game-style.

When you boil it all down, doing things "differently" risks singling yourself out -- in a bad way. Hard-working D-people are looking for any excuse to lighten their loads, any reason not to take your script seriously. Hard to blame 'em? Please don't make eliminating your project that easy for them.

You'd be stunned how many bright people fuck this up, the easiest part. And what's really, REALLY silly is how easy it is to follow simple Industry-standard guidelines. In fact, being the incredibly helpful bastard I am, let me share some of those guidelines with your ass right now...

Format/Style Concerns

The following are to be used with ZERO EXCEPTIONS. Yes, this means <u>you</u>, Mr. Smart Ass Reader. Per <u>Fight</u>

107

Club -- "You are not special. You are not a beautiful or unique snowflake. You're the same decaying organic matter as everything else."

Got it? Fantastic. Please commence paying attention.

Document size -- 8.5 x 11.

Font -- Twelve point Courier/Courier Final Draft. That's it. Leave your Hello Kitty, Disco '70's or Avengers fonts in the holster, rookie.

Standard Industry Margins -- Final Draft software gives you an array of pre-fab script templates to choose from for writing feature films, so there's some leeway here. Personally, I chose to put together a customized template modeled on the hallowed Warner Bros. production draft. My version is different from Final Draft's WB Template, painstakingly duplicated from actual hardcopies of famous WB scripts I have. (Dyed-in-the-wool Film Wonk anyone?)

Here are the settings/measurements for what I use, and you're welcome to them. But hey, if you find some other template which works or feels better for you, by all means, use it. Just make sure it's Final Draft standard or comes from the blueprint of an authentic, professional script source.

(Ed Note: I still use FD 7.0 during first drafts because I prefer the look of Courier fonts on my aging MacBook screen over either 8.0 or 9.0. Yes, they do look different. File Under -- Nutty, Neurotic Screenwriter Shit.)

Final Draft V. 7 -- Under Format >Elements > Paragraph --

Alignment/Left -- Spacing/One -- Spacing Before/One

108

General (Paragraph) -- Left, 1, 0. Indents -- Left 1.50, Right 7.75

Scene Heading (Paragraph) -- Left, 1, 1. Indents -- Left 1.50, Right 7.75

Action (Paragraph) -- Left, 1, 1. Indents -- Left 1.50, Right 7.12

Character (Paragraph) -- Left, 1, 1. Indents -- Left 3.87, Right 6.75

Parenthetical -- Left, 1, 0. Indents -- Left 3.25, Right 5.75

Dialogue -- Left, 1, 0. Indents -- Left 2.50, Right 5.87

Transition -- Right, 1, 1. Left 4.25, Right 7.75

(Both SCENE HEADING and TRANSITION should be ALL CAPS by default under Elements > Font)

Under Document > Page Layout > Margins

Text Margins -- Top 0.75, Bottom 1.00

Header Margin 0.75, Footer Margin 0.75

Under Options, Line Spacing Tight.

That should pretty much get you started...

General Rules of Thumb for Formatting --

Never go longer than stock with your margins -- long margins kill.

Never increase your font size above 12 point.

Never drop your font size below 12 point.

These are three painfully obvious attempts at changing a script's length -- either by making it look longer (higher page count) or jamming more content inside an acceptable number of pages. Friends, you're only fooling yourselves, pros have x-ray eyes when it comes to this novice shit.

Script's too short? That means you're probably missing scenes you need but didn't think up in the first place. Simply go through and flesh out the story more. Script's too long? Cut it down, goofball. Find some fat -- yes, there's *always* plenty of fat in early drafts -- and take that shit out.

Script length is one of the few accurate diagnostics a writer has. That's why you want everything standardized -- so you can make sense of what your project's length is trying to tell you. Placement of plot points, the midpoint, act breaks, etc. belong within certain general ranges. Discovering they're off tells you the larger structure is off as well and needs to be tweaked or recalibrated.

Believe it or not, there's a reason screenplays have a predetermined length -- **every one page of script equals one minute of screen time.** For example, 100 pages means your movie runs approximately 100 minutes. If you begin distorting that measure through page manipulation, you won't know the movie's length with any accuracy, what budget is required, etc. Your "90 pages" may actually film at 70 minutes -- not long enough for a U.S. theatrical release. Conversely, 90 pages may film at 120 minutes -- meaning the budget may fall short. If you're lucky enough to get anywhere near the precipice of production, producers will call you on this shit anyway. Real money's involved and an accurate length is needed to physically make the movie.

Here's my question -- why risk looking like an amateur douchebag in the first place? You may want to work with these folks again someday and not be remembered as The Boy With The Fischer-Price Screenplay.

Never use any color pages but white, even including your title page. White, motherfucker, white. Nothing else.

Never, EVER include scanned photographs, drawings, storyboards or the like. This ain't film school and nobody cares how well you draw.

Never put your WGA Registration Number or Copyright info on the title page. Two reasons: 1) If Hollywood actually was trying to steal your script (which they aren't) giving them the number would theoretically make it even easier to poach and 2) Only rookies, goofballs and cross-eyed bumpkins put this shit on title pages to begin with. Talk about giving yourself away as a noob. Heed my warning -- "Registered WGA" or "Copyright *Your Name Here*" is all you need.

As long as we're talking Title Pages, here's a big one -- **Always make sure to fill in your Final Draft Title Page**. Using Final Draft 7.0 or 8.0, you'll find it under Document>Title Page (Haven't played around with Final Draft 9.0 yet, so I'm not sure if it's the same). It's mind-boggling how many writers forget to do this -- or don't even know about this feature in the first place. And nothing looks more amateur when opening a script to find the factory default "SCRIPT TITLE, Written by, Name of First Writer, Based On, If Any" and nothing else.

Title and Author's name should be centered top/middle of the page.

Contact Info (phone number and email only) bottom right of page, Draft Date bottom left, or vice-versa. If you feel the need, put "Registered WGA" on the left side as well -- but again, don't put down your actual Registration Number.

Less is always more when it comes to your title page. Keeping it clean and uncluttered makes it look far more professional. Here's the title page of a big movie written by one the best in the Business to give you an idea how the real pros do it --

Page Count -- After glancing at the title, the very first thing any reader looks at is page count. Trust me on this. Expect an immediate scroll or flip to the last page to see what kind of beast they're dealing with.

Never exceed 120 pages max. You're not writing Goodfellas or Lawrence of Arabia here. One page of screenplay equals one minute of screen time. One hundred and twenty pages means two full hours.

Even better, if you absolutely must go long, 118 pages should be your limit. Silly as it sounds, you'd be amazed what a huge psychological difference it makes for a reader to see a "1-1-8" on that last page over a "1-2-0".

In today's Hollywood, there's a sense that 110 pages is optimum for features. Every script can be tightened up to save pages, and producers start weed-whacking the moment you get into development. Why not make your script look nice and tight by trimming what *you* want before outsiders even see it? Get her down to fighting weight in advance of actually climbing in the ring?

I know -- all this focus on page length seems absurd. Shouldn't readers be more interested in what a script *says* than how long it is? Perhaps. But do you want your script to become the icebreaker on this? Some freedom fighter "statement" against the unfairness of "page-length prejudice"? Highly doubtful. But look, if you feel that strongly about it, go ahead and use the screenplay you're banking all your future hopes on as a guinea pig. Sacrifice the fucker, feed it right into the meat grinder. Maybe someone will name a street after you someday... but probably not.

Bottom line, if you keep your draft tight and somewhere between 110 and 118 pages, you should be in good shape.

Kill any descriptive lines that aren't absolutely necessary. Combine/thin out descriptive lines and action whenever possible. I see this all the time in my classes -- people tend to use five lines where two or three will do. From a writer's point of view, this is totally understandable -- you want to ensure you've sold a certain action or character description with a maximum of cleverness and color. Problem is, when you keep hammering away at it and adding on, you generally end up with four or five lines that basically say the *exact same thing*, inadvertently muting the impact of any individual stand-out along the way.

However, overwriting can become a very constructive part of your process. Here's what I mean. Go ahead and write the four or five (or six) lines you just have to get out of your system, then cherry-pick them down to the one/two that best say what you're going for or Frankenstein the winning parts of each into just one/two killer sentences.

More words don't equate with being more descriptive. Conversely, it's a process of addition *by subtraction*. It's always preferable to be short and oh-so-sweet than bloated and left overstaying your welcome.

Do NOT use Transitions (CUT TO, FADE OUT, SLOW DISSOLVE TO, ETC.) unless absolutely critical to impart the pacing/tone of the sequence. If needed, what I try and do is tack these directions onto your last line of description above to see if they'll work there, saving you at least three lines each time you do this.

So instead of --

"Tommy runs like hell to get out of there.

                                                  DISSOLVE
TO:"

Try doing it this way --

**"Tommy runs like hell to get out of there. DISSOLVE
TO -- "**

Every writer has their own style. This is something I've
found helps keep a script from feeling flabby while still
getting clear instructions across. Take it with a grain of
salt, use it or don't, up to you. Regardless, the main
point here is to use Transitions only when essential.

The real kiss of death for newbie scripts in this arena is
the use of **"CUT TO"**.

Christ, sometimes I even see it used on its own, like a
Slug Line, with a blank line above and below. Fellas,
please, DON'T DO THIS.

"CUT TO" is unnecessary in contemporary
screenwriting. You're writing a *movie.* By definition,
every time you go to a new scene or slug, a CUT takes
place. That's how movies work -- both on-screen and
on the page. So "CUT TO" is redundant, something
already assumed to exist. Nothing says "puppy writer"
like barking "CUT TO" at the reader page after page
after page.

Another tip -- always try and cheat a line, description,
etc. onto the bottom of the previous page if there's any
room for it. Because of Final Draft's formatting process,
eliminating just one unnecessary line space may pull the
next element up to the page before it -- thereby
shortening your overall length, sometimes as much as a
full page.

The Big Picture Look Of Your Page -- Great writers know how to shape a page so it keeps a reader flying along. Again, Tony Gilroy's The Bourne Identity has one of the most brilliantly styled first pages I've seen. His use of slugs and sentence length, of blank lines and tempo is perfect for building the drama of the read from the very start.

Here's a vague, entirely fictional and completely unintelligible facsimile of that first page using gibberish so you can see in macro how the presentation works its magic (and so I don't have to get corporate clearance to show you a single page of a screenplay) --

Notice how the flow of words is funneled downward, helping you to read *faster*, then stops on a dime with the shortest and most important line on the page -- "A dead body." (Well, that's what it would say if this were the actual script).

Of course, the body's not actually dead, it's an unconscious Jason Bourne. But the moment we see that naked body floating facedown in the ocean, we wonder <u>who</u> <u>it</u> <u>is</u> -- which perfectly establishes and echoes the film's major overriding question: "Who is Jason Bourne?"

Ask yourself this -- Who can resist turning to the next page after the first ends with "a dead body"? Nobody, that's who. It's a great device to capture the reader's attention and get them involved -- the very definition of a "page turner" Of course, it's a huge plus that everything written before it is spectacular as well.

(What about the use of "CUT TO" on this page, John? Didn't you just tell us <u>never</u> to use that?

Yes, I did. And when you reach Tony Gilroy status, you can tell me to go blow myself. Get as good as Mr. Gilroy, write the staggering number of special films he has, and I'll be happy to give you the greenlight.)

You think I'm totally cuckoo, don't you? That I've totally hopped the reservation with this whole crazy concept of "designing" (or at least paying attention to) the way a page looks?

Maybe you're right. Maybe Mr. Gilroy *himself* would say I'm totally full of shit (he wouldn't be the first on that list, by the way). That any underlying design is completely unintentional and that Mr. Gilroy didn't consider the structuring and presentation of <u>The Bourne Identity</u>'s first page for a nanosecond.

But being as incredible a writer as he is, I'd find that pretty hard to believe.

Intended or not, it's the same difference anyway -- it totally works. The page functions exactly as I'm pointing out, and lands precisely where it needs to land.

So... Am I mentally ill enough to suggest you spend hours primping and prepping each page into some hypnotic Rorschach blot capable of ensorcelling even the most jaded Hollywood reader? Don't be silly, my back-seating brainiacs. The most perfectly formatted and visually engineered script in the world *still* isn't going to sell if it sucks ass. Clearly (duh), how well scripts are written and what they have to say are always top priorities for any writer.

What I <u>am</u> saying very definitely is that paying attention to how your pages look is extremely important. If you can take it to the platinum genius level of <u>The Bourne Identity</u>, by all means, get it done. But at the bare minimum you can always sharpen/tighten your pages up and create a flow which helps <u>lead</u> <u>the</u> <u>eye</u>. Newspapers made an art form of this in decades past and so did magazines. Why not use this subtle trick of the trade to your advantage whenever possible?

File all this under one of my most harped-upon corollaries -- "<u>Help the reader embrace reading your script with as much positivity and enthusiasm as possible</u>". Little touches play as much a part in achieving that as big touches do.

See here's the thing -- **half-assed page layout and the dreaded patches of heavy black totally buzz-kill a**

reader big-time. Don't do it. Down to the last man and woman pulling a paycheck, readers and execs HATE this shit. It buys you an immediate death sentence. Nothing will get your screenplay shit-canned faster than pages that look like this --

Mind-bending monstrosities like this from new writers will NOT get read -- nor should they be. Even <u>Gone With The Wind</u> didn't look that dense and foreboding (I know because I have a draft).

Get off your ass and fix 'em, you self-indulgent bastards! You're neither Dostoevsky nor Thomas Pynchon. Mercilessly break up thick passages of description.

Don't use twenty lazy words trying to say what the perfect five will.

One place to start is by inserting necessary lines of <u>dialogue</u> between longer patches of action to help break them up. Note I said *necessary*. Don't just throw in a "Run, Tommy, RUN!" or "No... <u>NOOOOOO</u>!!!" trying to bail yourself out. You've got some serious downsizing ahead of you, and little cheats like adding throwaway lines do not a quality revision make.

You ain't writing a novel here, princess. Short, lean, precise, staccato style is everything -- more so in today's Net-induced ADHD world than ever before.

THE HONEST, SNARKY TRUTH

During the holidays last year, I was contacted online by an older female writer in Vancouver. She'd written a horror spec and was seeking an honest consultation on its prospects. Being "older" myself (in Millennial years, 40 is the new 70) I'm especially sensitive to these writers' plights. Many have families, homes and kids to pay for. Odds are they've been working straight jobs they're not particularly pumped about just to pay the bills. Real life can be a real bitch, and the day-to-day of it all conspires against hopeful older writers mustering their courage to finally take their shot.

Believe me, younger readers, as you age, it gets harder and harder to swallow feeling creatively stifled and further justify deferring one's lifetime dream. There's nothing quite so thunderous as the ticking clock of middle age.

So I said yes. Told Vancouver Writer to go ahead and send me the script, and that I'd make the necessary time to go over it.

One thing did worry me. This tiny red warning beacon (a quiet bit of "foreshadowing" in scriptwriter lingo) tucked into her last email. It came in the form of a single throwaway line --

"No need for any introductory statement -- this screenplay is NOT my first effort, nor is this the first draft of it."

Twenty-plus years hard time has learned me a few things. Here's a big one. Writers -- especially struggling writers -- are lousy at hiding even the slightest hint of annoyance or displeasure. Seriously, they're the absolute worst, worse than even actors. Industry folk can see a writer's stink face coming a mile away. It's this transparent, wounded mask of hangdog emotions for all the film universe to see, cycling through entitlement, irritation, indignation, anger, desperation, only to land tragically on despair.

Brothers and sisters, a quick word of caution. Your literary stink face opens the doors to only two things: an embarrassing bout of self-immolation and/or impending unemployment.

Secondly, any time a writer informs me that "this isn't their first rodeo" or "they already know it's good" or any other self-protective preface of this kind, I know *immediately* there are gonna be problems. You can get all New Age Tao Te Ching with this concept -- "*That which calls itself the Tao is not the true Tao*" -- or you can keep it blue collar and accept that struggling writers are very much like drunks -- before they can get better they have to admit they have a problem. Until then, expect relapse after relapse, blackout after blackout, DUI after DUI.

How can I speak with such authority on this?

Because "the Devil recognizes his own."

As a working writer, I've been guilty of this shit a ridiculous number of times. It can take *years* of growth and practice to develop a professional-writer poker face, to damp down the involuntarily bile accompanying each suggested overhaul and unexpected criticism. It took Yours Truly damn-near a decade (file under -- slow learner). Meantime, until you learn how to roll with it, you're hurting nobody except yourself... so try and suck it up once in a while.

Regardless, ignoring my tingling Spidey Sense, I shrugged this last email off and went back to work.

Couple days later, I began reading Vancouver Writer's script.

Straight out of the gate, there were massive problems. The über stock horror premise was as clichéd as they come. Stop me if you've heard this one before -- young people encounter scary, violent times inside an abandoned house out in the dark, foreboding woods.

Yes, it had the sullen, brutish and inexplicably hostile Hillbilly locals. Yes, it had the hick roadside tavern going silent when the kids walk in. Yes, there was a one-eyed man with a scarred face -- hell, he may have even been the bartender. Yes, there was a non-believer hayseed Sheriff and his smart-assed/aw-sucks Deputy. And no, none of the five twenty-somethings had a single smartphone or tablet between them -- which everyone alive knows is an impossibility. Lastly, of course, their car's GPS didn't work either.

Listen, if we could time-machine it back to 1972 when Deliverance was first released and films like Texas Chainsaw Massacres, The Hills Have Eyes, and a bazillion other subsequent rip-offs didn't exist yet, maybe -- and I stress *maybe* -- this script might have gotten looked at by a few low-budget companies. Maybe.

Unfortunately, it's 2014, and they *do* exist. Not only are these the Rosetta stone classics of the horror genre, they're established big money "brands" that have been marketed across the globe for FOUR DECADES. They've been sequeled and prequeled and origin-storied to death. To put it in perspective, in the past ten years alone, they've made THREE <u>Texas Chainsaw's</u> -- and <u>Chainsaw 4</u> is in pre-production as I type this.

Which brings us right back to those essential Screenplay 101 questions at the beginning -- **what's new, different or unique about your story**? What makes it fresh and contemporary when stacked against the ocean of clichéd copycat scripts already out there? And again, just as importantly, what's going to motivate potential <u>buyers</u> -- the money folks -- to take an active interest? Why would they put money into your lesser, regurgitated version of a branded product with a built-in audience that *already exists*?

Readers, seriously, ask yourselves -- would you put *your own money* into a project like that?

Not a snowball's chance. Shy of a production company serving as a money laundering operation, neither will financiers.

Bad script got worse. Characterizations were X-Acto blade thin, without any convincing backstories or motivations at all. Dialogue was completely expository (a.k.a. "on the nose") and the characters' voices were all identical. Worse, these kids didn't *sound* anything like real twenty year-olds do today; a surefire tip-off to readers and producers that it was scripted by an older writer -- not exactly something you want to advertise in today's youth-obsessed Hollywood. Sad to say, it only went cannonballing further downhill from there. By page 40 it was toast, irrevocably D.O.A., a compendium of all screenwriting's cardinal sins in one sloppy, migraine-inducing package.

So yeah, the news wasn't great. The script didn't need a band-aid, it needed a blood transfusion. It would take a helluva lot of heavy lifting to fix, no doubt, but still, even then, it wasn't impossible to reboot by any stretch.

Believe me, *nobody* likes hearing their project is fucked up. Think I'm any different? So to help buffer the initial shockwave of despair that hits every writer, I wrote thirteen pages of detailed notes. *Thirteen pages.* I gripped the bit between my teeth and went berserk breaking down scenes, trouble-shooting structure, suggesting plausible motivations and alternative storylines. I did everything possible to stress that, while the project wasn't working now, all hope was not lost. What the writer needed to do was steady themselves, take a deep breath and begin objectively considering the logic behind what needed to change. In the final accounting, once the smoke had cleared, this would be a good thing.

I Gmailed these notes and prepared for our scheduled follow-up call the next day.

The call never happened. Instead, I got a nasty reply that started something like this --

"I understand this is not any easy business. However, you are not an Oscar-winning producer nor head of a major Hollywood studio. You're a writer who's supposed to help and encourage others! Your notes are snarky and mean-spirited and the only person that benefits from that is you!"

Additionally, Vancouver Writer was upset I hadn't read the "whole thing" -- and asked that I refund half the fee if I was only going to read half the script. Essentially, that's like telling a coroner you want him to examine the toe-nails for signs of life even though the corpse's head was blown off.

Believe me, Dear Readers, I could not Paypal her a refund fast enough.

Sure, the concept of having given up two days of *my* writing week to cook up prescriptive, entirely unappreciated notes on a bad script stuck in my craw some. But hey, I'm a big boy, been around the block, and I fully accept that sometimes "no good deed goes unpunished" where dreams, egos and the commercial arts are concerned. Okay, A LOT of times.

But beyond that, there's the simple, self-evident truth that **scripts don't suddenly get better after forty lousy pages**. **Ever**. Nobody sprouts great storytelling skills a full third of the way in and begins banging out the best movie of all time. Even if the End of Days and/or some other demonic intervention allowed this to take place, it *still* wouldn't matter. Why? Because there wouldn't be anyone left reading it to find that out.

Ten pages. That's how long you get to hook your reader before they trashcan your script. *Ten fucking pages.* Brutal, right? That's the Industry standard. Sometimes readers new to the job will give bad projects the full First Act twenty-five out of pity alone... and *then* drag-and-drop it into oblivion.

Free passes for forty shitty pages? Forget it. Never happen in any of our lifetimes. You'd have better odds of getting Justin Bieber appointed to the Supreme Court.

Yet interestingly, neither of these things is what really bothered me.

What really killed? *That the writer totally missed the point of having a professional look at your script to begin with.*

126

You have sudden chest pains. You see a renown heart specialist. She gives you an electrocardiogram. The results ain't good. So lousy, in fact, she insists on doing open heart surgery immediately to save your life

And you respond by telling her... your feelings are hurt? That she wasn't "encouraging" enough?

Say whaaaat???

Why on Earth would you seek out a professional and pay good money only to get miffed by their opinion?

Seriously, as adult writers, what should you expect when having qualified, working professionals read your script? That the reader will be awestruck, dumbfounded, have their doors blown off? That they'll fire back an urgent, glowing email saying how perfect it was? How it didn't need even a single revision and how surprised they were it hadn't already been produced, Palme D'Or'd and enshrined in the Library of Congress?

Or... if we're keeping it real, is this actually some not-so-sly backdoor fishing expedition for confirmation of what you've not-so-secretly been hoping for all along -- official word that your work is undeniably brilliant and you're a bona fide genius after all?

It's okay, you can admit it. Thought that way myself, once upon a time. So I'd like to refer you to Uncle Junior's shrewd Season One *The Sopranos* quip regarding the odds of that -- "I want to fuck Angie Dickinson. Let's see who gets lucky first."

Real-deal screenwriters don't expect best-case scenarios every time they send a project out. Besides being vainglorious and delusional, it's unrealistic and completely unproductive. It's emotional suicide, an approach that can destroy you creatively as much as spiritually.

Real-deal screenwriters also learn to protect themselves emotionally. To accept that writing for film and TV is a relentless process of reworking and improving and reimagining -- way past your original pain threshold. Real-deal screenwriters understand this is not a quick munchies run to 7-Eleven, but an Apollo mission to the moon. Hot-to-trot noobs counting on walk-off homers and hundred-yard kick returns are either legit bipolar or as flat-out nuts as Sarah Palin thinking she would be Vice President some day.

See, this is a huge thing less-experienced screenwriters forget -- nobody else expects your early drafts to be perfect. That's just your own white noise, needless additional pressure you're putting on *yourself.* Forget about hole-in-ones, just lay that first tee shot squarely in the middle of the fairway. Screenwriting is about revising and rewriting... and then revising and rewriting some more. Only two times you're ever "finished" on a script -- when you get fired or when the completed film is locked and can't be physically changed again. That's it. Meantime, expect to keep working to the point you wish you'd never heard of movies or wanted to write screenplays in the first place.

Writing is a process. Always has been. From the inception of the written word, all of your favorite writers have gone through some version of it. Take heart from this. Let it deepen your faith in what you're doing. Get off your own backs. Give yourselves a break. No need to get angry or embarrassed, nor waste time lashing out or feigning superiority. It's hard for any writer to move forward when they're exhausting all their energy contending what clearly doesn't work actually does. You're fooling nobody save yourself.

Simply acknowledge that your script isn't there -- yet.
But hey, no worries, you're on your way, and fielding
and incorporating objective, quality feedback is a key
part of that journey.

For Chris'sake, could this be any easier? *Let the healing
begin already.*

Make sure you understand the key point of this story,
and it's definitely <u>not</u> that Vancouver Writer's script
sucked. **What's of lasting importance is <u>the writer's
wounded reaction to it sucking</u>.** It provides the
perfect cautionary tale for every writer out there,
blueprinting that crossroads moment you'll eventually
face between growing up and getting better or staying
immersed in self-deception and stunting your skills.
Between taking your prescribed medicine and getting
well, or stubbornly refusing and flushing your pills
down the toilet.

Look, if you honestly believe you know more than
everybody else, especially people with years and years
of paid professional experience, go right ahead, stuff
your fingers in your ears and play deaf. But if, like the
rest of us, you grasp that *every idea* should be seriously
considered, good or bad -- whether you choose to go
with it or not -- then stow the fuckin' attitude and start
paying attention.

You never know. Someone good out there just might be
trying to help you.

Making a living writing movies is a <u>privilege</u>, something
that'll come hard-earned, if at all. Hollywood doesn't
need you, doesn't give a shit whether you live or die,
and nobody -- and I mean NOBODY -- is gonna cry if
your Tinseltown dreams don't come true.

Remember that money line in <u>American History X</u> where Dr. Sweeney sees Derek/Edward Norton in prison and asks -- "*Has anything you've done made your life better?*"

When it comes to screenwriting, I believe we can (and should) ask ourselves a version of this with near-identical intent -- "Is how I'm approaching my craft making my writing career better? Are there any objective, tangible signs that what I'm doing is working?"

The answer may be "no". This might hurt like a motherfucker. But until we can look these issues dead in the eye, there's no hope of making real progress.

HOW TO BECOME A PINK BELT

A good friend of mine opened a martial arts school in
Long Beach. We're not talking some wannabe MMA
gym trying to get over -- my buddy was and is the real
deal, a legit bad-ass. He fought competitively, was
nationally ranked in Sanshou and lived in Thailand for
two years studying Muy Thai from the hardcore eighty
year-olds who practically invented it.

In short, as should be pretty obvious, my friend took his
craft very, very seriously. Seriously enough to spend his
entire adult life studying it. For now, let's just call him
Larry.

One sunny day, a local Soccer Mom bulldozes into
Larry's studio, dragging her sixth grader along hostage.

"Are you the owner?"

"Yes, ma'am." Larry replied.

"Well, I was just at the Tae Kwon Do studio down the
street? You know, Yong's Power Kick-Fu? In the strip
mall next to Pinkberry?"

Larry nodded politely. But he'd never heard of it.

"Well anyway, the *Sensay* there said my son Toby could
earn his purple belt in less than a month and his black
belt within two years," she paused to let the apparent
gravity of this sink in. "So -- how long would it take my
son to earn his black belt in *your* school?"

My homeboy Larry wasn't into the whole colored belt
scene. He understood perfectly well that's the cash

hustle in today's martial arts -- upselling pink, purple, orange, sage and fuchsia belts to the kids like flavored Popsicles is what keeps studios open and the serious greenbacks rolling in. About the only thing colored belts are good for is helping convince parents their progeny are making progress easily translatable to private school transcripts and the like... even if they aren't, well, making progress.

Because of this marketing-first approach, many martial arts schools in the U.S. have become largely toothless extracurriculars, about as bad-assed as scuba, yearbook (do they still have that?) and volleyball.

But here's the thing --

Traditionally, martial arts only have <u>two</u> belts -- white and black. What stands between them is a shitload of disciplined learning and hard work -- a.k.a. "sacrifice". Nope, not a damned thing sexy about it. No touch-screens or Twitter feeds. But come showtime, all that diligent study ensures you'll *actually know what you're doing.* So while this rainbow coalition of Crayola cotton may be all the rage, it's purely a gimmick, brought to you by the same folks that market the Easter Bunny and Santa Claus.

So... back to Soccer Mom's question.

"How long would it take my son to earn his black belt in *your* school?"

As you might expect, Larry's a real straight-shooter. He fixed the woman right in the eye, adult to adult, and gave it to her straight --

"When your son can protect himself against a full-grown man, he can have a black belt."

132

Time stopped. Soccer Mom daggered Larry like he'd just called her a crackhead and her son a fag. She jerked little Toby out of that studio with enough velocity to dislocate the kid's shoulder, neither of them to ever be seen again. Shortly thereafter, this same nitwit poisoned the well with other local Tiger Moms and Trophy Wives by spreading the word Larry was a child-hating caveman, and his younger enrollment suffered big-time because of it.

Personally? I thought his answer was brilliant. In the strictest and purest sense, Larry made clear he was looking out for her son -- *by trying to protect him.* Which is precisely what people like myself pray for with any instructor of anything who works with kids.

Soccer Mom asked for the truth, and, a la Jack in <u>A Few Good Men</u>, she couldn't handle the truth. Was it my buddy's fault she didn't get it? Larry's a *businessman*, for Chris'sake. He knew up front that pushing honesty instead of sleazing the upsell could cost him customers. But he remained content to cockblock this woman's mindless transcript-padding agenda with a dose of old fashioned integrity.

Know why? Because this is where it all nets out -- colored belts may *look* cool on Snapchat and Instagram and in prep school transcripts, but they <u>DO</u> <u>NOT</u> keep your ass from getting kicked. Only the ability to actually defend yourself does.

In Real Life, right outside Soccer Mom's Sienna (a.k.a. the Swagger Wagon) door, strutting around in a dry-cleaned *gi* with a Creamsicle-colored belt basically guarantees the school bully jamming his foot up your kid's butt in record time. Your poor son will be wearing that belt as a fuckin' tail by the time the bigger kids get done gangbanging him.

And it's at that precise instant -- lil' Toby's brain bucket slow-motion smacking into sidewalk -- that Mom's big hurry to buy him a black belt begins bearing its tragic fruit.

* * * * *

Okay, John, what in the name of Christ does this long metaphor or morality tale or whatever the fuck it is have to do with <u>screenwriting</u>?

Just this --

As aspiring screenwriters, we all have to ask ourselves whether we want the fruity colored belt or the actual skill set necessary to defend ourselves.

Whether we'd rather stay in our comfort zones, shielding shaky egos with empty compliments <u>or</u> whether we'd prefer to man-the-fuck-up and deal with the prospect of getting face-planted on the pavement if we don't have our shit together.

Couple legendary lines spring to mind here --

Nietzsche's all-time classic -- "Few of us have the courage for what we really know."

Fitzgerald's <u>The Great Gatsby</u> when Nick says -- "I'm thirty. I'm five years too old to lie to myself and call it honor."

And how 'bout a Churchillian cherry on top -- "God hates a coward."

There's pretend and there's what's real.

Know the one place that's especially true? Hollywood. Always been that way. Always will.

Pretend winds up working Hot Dog On A Stick in a funny hat. Pretend talks a lot of shit while eating a ton more. Pretend calls Mommy and Daddy for another cash injection, before crawling home, hands and knees, later on.

What's real? What's real improves your odds, narrows the gap. What's real toughens you up in all the necessary places. What's real puts food in your belly, keeps the dream alive, ensures the Wi-Fi stays on.

What's real gets you where you're going. Gives you a fighting chance.

Personally? I'd rather learn to slay screenwriting's frightful demons than cower under my coffee table hoping they'll just go away. Came hardwired that way from the factory. Never known anything different.

Ultimately, you'll have to decide which kind of writer -- and which kind of *person* -- you want to become for yourselves.

You can keep the Creamsicle belt. Toss me the flamethrower.

What? You didn't think I'd land this one? Shame on you. Hundred or so pages in you should know better. I make a living doing this shit.

FOUR-BY-SIX LOVE

By the time I graduated NYU Film $50K in debt, I'd taken five semester-long screenwriting classes. Not one of them taught students like myself a thing about professional Hollywood screenwriting.

Today, I'm sure things are a lot different. But this was back in the Late '80's, and honestly, most the faculty were faking it -- they were good writers, documentarians and off-Broadway playwrights, but not produced *screenwriters*. Forget about structure, character, plotting, etc... I never got a lecture on proper screenplay format. The coming avalanche of script lit and online stuff people take for granted today was still a decade away, which meant that despite the back-breaking tuition fees, you'd still have to seek out legit knowledge of "Hollywood screenwriting" on your own.

Being an enterprising young man, I hiked the forty blocks up to the WGA East and paid two bucks for their handy 1983 pamphlet "Professional Writer's Teleplay/Screenplay Format". Why sanctimoniously expensive NYU couldn't have purchased these cheapies *en masse* for their film students, I'm still not sure, but everything I needed to know was right there -- proper, professional formatting and other Industry guidelines neatly laid out in black and white.

Shortly after that, I convinced a cool professor to let me Xerox the two "real" scripts he owned -- Paul Schrader's Taxi Driver and Hampton Fancher's Blade Runner. Talk about having the back of your head blown off. Wow. *So this is what real screenwriting was*! This is what legit produced films (movies I'd seen myself in the theater!)

looked like on paper. *Right on.* One-two these wondrous scripts opened my eyes to the endless possibilities of my own cinematic creations.

So yeah, this was great. I'd sussed out *what* a script looked like, and *why* it looked that way -- how those pages were intended as the *de facto* blueprint for the director, producers and actors to make the movie. Cooler still, I'd read a couple genius examples showing what a good writer could do with a great idea. Saying I was pumped would be a massive understatement.

But the most important puzzle piece had yet to drop.

Somehow, by some twist of fate I can't remember, I got turned onto Syd Field's *Screenplay: The Foundations of Screenwriting*. That's right. Same essential text I put on blast in Screenwriting 101. This is the Big Dog that started it all -- not just for Yours Truly, but for generations of aspiring writers before and since.

(Fuck yes, BUY IT, ALREADY! Let me make it easy for you lazy bastards -- http://www.amazon.com/gp/product/B000S1LAYG/)

Getting turned onto *Screenplay* at 22 was a spiritual revelation, my "Neo-jacked-in-and-finally-able-to-decode-the-Matrix" moment. Everything just clicked. All was made clear. Like Peter Finch in Network, I became vivid and flashing, channeling some great unseen life force the Hindus call *prana*.

Put less dramatically -- it was a life-long game changer.

Of spectacular importance was **Chapter 12 -- Building the Story Line**. Not only did Mr. Field definitively outline and explain the Three Act Story Structure Paradigm which governs the screenwriting universe itself (worth twice the price of admission alone), he also dropped a Hydrogen bomb by revealing the single most essential tool for constructing a successful screenplay.

The Notecard Method.

The brilliant simplicity of using of plain jane, off-the-rack, office supply white three-by-five (3x5) index cards to plot out your story.

(Cue God Light and Choir of Holy Angels singing in background.)

Mr. Field didn't invent this device, which has been around since the beginning of Hollywood itself. However, what he did do was launch this concept into the public mainstream for the first time. Many, many, MANY screenwriters across the globe have been thanking his kind soul for that heads-up since 1979 when he first published the book.

(My only humble tweak to Mr. Field's guidelines would be using four-by-six (4x6) notecards instead of the traditional three-by-fives. Four-by's give you *a lot* more real estate to scribble on when you're revising or tweaking beats -- and you will be doing a ton of tweaking and revising.)

The application of the Notecard Method couldn't be simpler or more straight-forward, a fuckin' baboon can do it. You write down one scene per card. First, the location and time of day -- i.e. EXT. BABOON FARM -- LOS ANGELES -- DAY. Next, the broad strokes of what actually happens in the beat -- "Baboons go apeshit when they realize how good *Tough Love Screenwriting* is."

Here are a couple of my cards from <u>Hard-Boiled II</u> which I wrote for John Woo --

H.K. MODIFIED FERRY HEIST
ACTION OPENING!

Classic Woo-INSPIRED ACTION, w/the →
punchline that his EAGER YOUNG PARTNER
bags it.

- Desc. prior b/w them about T.'s not retiring.
This should launch T.'s semblance of SURE EXCUSES to
— TERMER.

LARRY / TEQUILA CHINESE RESTAURANT
SIT-DOWN

Bad start, bad blood, kidnapping!
Q. √ DO WE REVEAL HERE That T. H ain't divorced?
Does T. use this to hunt Larry? THE CELLPHONE RINGS!
OR DO WE SAVE IT FOR POST-T. RESCUE? "Nice Restaurant."
PLUS - FUN TEQUILA DEBT w THE APPETIZER! "Mm, right."

Keep these as broad and short as possible -- "Ferry Heist Action Opening", "Chinese Restaurant Sit-Down", etc. Next, you sketch in any details you've already come up with for the scene. Like most writers, you're probably packing a few key touches and money lines before you even start your script. Perfect. Stockpile all those freebies here in black and white.

You'll also notice that I ask myself <u>questions</u> whenever need be -- "*Q. Do we reveal here that Tequila is divorced?*" This helps remind me of any pending logic

139

or sequencing issues while I'm tentatively juggling my way through these first cards.

Consider this the "discovery phase" where you first roll up your sleeves and do the grunt work of thinking up all the new cards needed to tell a feature-length story. These same 4x6 notecards are the bricks and mortar used to build a solid structural foundation beneath your movie.

One scene per card. That's the ticket. As you start generating cards, lay 'em out in loose chronological order, from script's beginning to end. Days or weeks later, whenever you've gotten a handle on the lion's share of beats you think you'll need, it should look something like this --

That's The Man With The Iron Fists II you're looking at, folks. No joke. And this is the old-school notecard approach capable of turning your flaccid, long-languishing screenplay into a structural marvel with bulletproof logic.

And you thought I was kidding about primates being able to cope.

Obviously, tables are ideal for this. Some people prefer thumbtacking cards to a corkboard. Many times I've just gone stone-cold bachelor with it and laid my beats out on the floor. **Any flat surface will suffice as long as it gives you a bird's-eye, hard-copy view of the story you're constructing.**

Yeah, I know. Now that it's show-me time and you're finally getting down to business, that table top can seem a little, well, *hostile*, right? It looks a mile wide and an ocean deep, and from time to time you seem to catch the cocky fucker eyeballing you. Never fear, boys and girls. Card by card, beat by beat, you'll first establish a beachhead, then begin a steady Sherman's March that swallows up all that foreboding real estate.

Moving forward is essentially a process of freestyling; inking in a fresh card for every new scene you dream up. As you do this, you'll notice these fresh scenes require other new scenes to service them in turn -- building blocks which are structurally tangential to the thrust of your story, but needed to serve the film as a cohesive whole. Here's a bad example of what I mean --

Beat #1 -- the Lead's Girlfriend calls afraid there's someone dangerous lurking outside her apartment.
Beat #2 -- Lead arrives at Girlfriend's place to make sure she's safe and unharmed.

Common sense says you'll probably want/need at least one new scene between those two beats. Say the Lead driving over to his Girlfriend's... or, perhaps more interestingly, Lead getting into his car with Shadowy Figures watching him unseen from down the alley... these Figures then tailing Lead as he drives to Girlfriend's place... and so on.

Watch any movie and pay attention to how many beats are mechanical or logistical in nature, largely used by the writer to move puzzle pieces wherever the larger story needs them. But mechanical shouldn't mean mundane. In fact, bust your ass ensuring they're suspenseful and/or interesting in their own right. Just know that successfully plotting a film requires the less spectacular "Point A to Point B" beats every bit as much as the ultra-sensational Money Scenes studios love to sneak-peek in the trailer.

Guys, these first notecards you lay down are super simple, many of them glorified short-term placeholders. Seriously, they're as straightforward and on-the-nose as "EXT. HIGHWAY -- CAR CRASH" or "INT. BUD'S OFFICE -- BUD GETS FIRED" or "INT. JULIE'S BEDROOM -- WILD SEX SCENE BETWEEN JULIE AND DRUG ADDICT". If you already have more goodies to sprinkle on, cool, sketch 'em out on your card. The big thing is not allowing yourself to get hung up trying to complete or finish the beats at this juncture. Refining and salting in crucial specifics comes at a later stage, when your scenes have been worked into an iron-clad order and are finally ready to be locked. Broad strokes are all you're shooting for. The party's just starting. Nothing more is necessary here.

Overall, pretty simple process, right? The more cards you create and throw down, the more meat you put on your movie's bones and the more your story and script takes shape. This is precisely how all great screenplays are built -- brick by brick by brick, one modest scene after another.

Young writers waste a shitload of time mind-fucking the correct number of cards their screenplays should have. Pay attention, people -- there *is no* correct number ("There is no spoon" anyone?). In the most general sense, I end up with anywhere between 45 and 55 cards when cooking up a feature. Most commonly, I've got approximately twelve cards for Act One, twenty-four for Act Two and a final (you guessed it) twelve for Act Three. If I recall, Syd Field recommends fourteen/twenty-eight/fourteen. But since every writer fills in their cards differently, there aren't any hard numbers to reference. I've heard as few as twelve cards *total* and as many as a hundred.

For example, I may count "CAR CHASE SEQUENCE" as just one beat, but another writer may have, say, three cards which fully flesh it out -- "EXT. TOWN SQUARE -- CARS RACE DOWN STREET" then "EXT. RAILYARD -- CARS SLALOM ONTO TRAIN TRACKS" then "EXT. DOCKS -- CARS CRASH AND SINK INTO BAY". Whatever floats your creative boats while properly building structure is your correct method.

Alright, quick time-out here to underscore a critical point --

When I say four-by-six notecards, I absolutely/ positively mean **four-by-six paper notecards**. That's correct -- those slivers of bleached wood pulp made from murdered trees now sitting neatly shrink-wrapped on CVS, Staples and Office Depot cybershelves.

Accordingly, my advice is not to use Final Draft's "Index Cards", Amazon Storybuilder or any other godforsaken program or interface involving a computer, tablet, phone, app, "smart watch" or Google Glass. You heard right, bitches -- REAL PAPER, with all the attendant evil that entails. Something you can actually (GASP!) hold in your hands.

Listen, I know the brains of tech-savvy slackers like the back of my hand -- each quarter I teach two full classes of you gadget-crazed fuckers. But trust me when I say the Notecard Method remains one of the few instances where digital technology has <u>not</u> improved on an analog-era idea.

Why? First and foremost, because "I'm the Daddy, that's why" -- an even less nurturing version of Sgt. Hartman in <u>Full Metal Jacket</u>. Secondly (and this involves the *rational* part of my brain), because the Notecard Method's hidden, shimmering brilliance resides in providing each writer with **a full-sized physical overview of their script's topography** -- the ability to see their building blocks *en masse*, start to finish, all at once, peering down from on high. This further allows you to reach out, change, adjust and/or rearrange the cards however you need to on the spot. A formerly major scene no longer works? Toss the card out. You discover an extra beat is needed between several others? Easy. Tuck a new card in-between them. You brainstorm a wicked new element to one of your sequences? Ink this brainstorm directly onto the cards so you don't forget it.

Of equal importance is the <u>balance</u>, <u>symmetry</u> and <u>flow</u> of your scenes. Do you have eight shaky cards in Act One, but a belly-busting forty-plus in Act Two? Whoops. That's a problem. Is all the physical action front-loaded (or back-loaded) in your script? Won't work either. You can't get away with wall-to-wall action the first 30 minutes, then nothing but characters stuff the last 90. All those scenes will need to be repositioned for the most effective pacing throughout.

By using the index cards, spotting a plentitude of script-killers such as these becomes possible before writing Word One. Heard the phrase "can't see the forest through the trees?" (a.k.a. "you're too close to your own shit and can't tell which way to go anymore?"). Index cards eliminate that issue by gifting you a macro perspective. They also spare you from trudging sixty pages deep into your new masterpiece only to find yourself mired in an Afghanistan-sized storytelling clusterfuck, nowhere to land, no clear pathway forward.

Am I ringing bells? Do any of these ailments sound eerily familiar?

This one monstrous advantage -- *physicality* -- explains why that flat-chested retina screen you put so much faith in simply won't do the trick. Cutting-and-pasting or "virtually" toggling index cards back and forth will never give you the pro-style perspective being able to physically assess and manhandle the cards by marking 'em up and messing 'em about can.

Per my incessant blathering, the Rosetta Stone on this will always be Syd Field's *Screenplay,* the first text to definitively lay out the notecard dynamics. Bazillions of variations on/pale imitations of his original take have metastasized across the ever-mushrooming galaxy of script lit, so sure, you'll find plenty of other methods under foot and you're perfectly welcome to try 'em all -- it's your credit card or PayPal account. Honestly, if just one of these brings you tangible results and moves the chains forward, then it was certainly worth checking out.

That said, *Screenplay's* approach is the only one I can personally vouch for, and across my thirty professional feature scripts, it's bailed me out and/or carried me to the promised land many a time. The Notecard Method hasn't survived for over a century now because it *doesn't* work. There simply isn't a better diagnostic tool in the craft of screenwriting as far as I'm concerned. Even if it frustrates the most cool-headed of writers sometimes --

145

* * * * *

Should you ever find yourself enrolled in Tough Love Screenwriting L.A., the very first thing you'll do is dive into your notecards.

Plowing ahead without an iron-clad foundation beneath you is pointless. Your screenplay will fail. That's the plain truth, like it or not, and it's better to hear it from me, right now, on these pages, than from a laundry-list of managers, agents, production companies and dead-end consultants begging off or ignoring your shit altogether.

Here's the key thing to remember about each and every beat you work up -- it needs to be there for a <u>reason</u>. **There are no random beats in a successful screenplay**. Period. Not open for negotiation, discussion or rationalization. Don't waste your time scouring cinema history for contradictory examples. Neither Hollywood nor myself -- nor your stillborn screenwriting career -- will give a shit.

146

Each scene has to be surgical in intent and serve a specific purpose. Without this level of premeditation, you'll have neither the strength nor efficiency that all successful structures require. Not only do the beats of real professionals meet this standard, they accomplish it so artfully the viewer rarely even notices it's taking place.

Per my shameless earlier fawning in "What's The World?", David Ayer's *tour de force* Training Day offers us a world-class example of plotting. Not only one of the greatest police actioners in history, the craftsmanship and care at work are top-drawer stuff for *any* genre. This is not just a great cop film, it's a great film period.

From Page One/Line One, there's a jaw-dropping level of screenplay awesomeness taking place here. Exactly what makes Mr. Ayer's script so outstanding? Let me underscore a few of the many terrific elements just to kick things off --

The world is thrilling, fresh and unique. Millions of cop flicks have been made, but again, none have been presented precisely this way before -- riding shotgun inside a corrupt narc's G-Ride as he surfs the violent cityscape of Downtown L.A.

Police-cruising partners are stock even for TV, especially anything set in So Cal. But reimagining the G-Ride into an emotional epicenter for Alonzo and Hoyt's epic battle of wills and worldviews and utilizing it as an observational flashpoint for protagonist and audience alike to process the brass-knuckles, back-alley universe of L.A. narcs was wholly unique and inspired. Nobody had taken it this far -- nor approached it this brilliantly -- before Training Day.

Further, from backroom of a Crenshaw Blvd. wig shop where paraplegic baller Snoop is (literally) forced to cough up his crack, to Latin gangbanger Smiley's claustrophobic Boyle Heights kitchen, to the plush Pacific Dining Car booths where the Three Wise Men hold court, each location is surgically chosen to reinforce the film's sense of uncompromising veracity. I would argue that Ayer's Downtown L.A. plays as big a role in Training Day as San Francisco does in Hitchcock's Vertigo -- becoming an essential character in its own right. Remove the author's specific presentation of either city, the movie we know and love no longer exists. Ballsy statement, I know, and one I'm fully prepared to stand by.

The villain is exceptional. Great villains make for great movies. Denzel Washington won the Academy Award portraying Alonzo, and in the process laid down one of the silver screen's all-time great bad guys. Charismatic and criminally seductive, the Alonzo character takes us on a thrilling roller coaster ride which leaves us enthralled and empowered one minute, off-balance and afraid the next.

One tremendous advantage of villain characters is their being permitted to tell the truth. Following classic Hollywood narrative code, bad guys are allowed to give voice to the real shit because they'll ultimately be killed off/imprisoned/punished/eliminated, etc. Hence, it's considered "safe" in a narrative sense to utilize the villain as mouthpiece for deeper truths, simultaneously validating the film's veracity without upsetting the prevailing societal status quo. Of course, that makes the villain the juiciest part because it doesn't require being "heroic" in the same goody-goody, Stars and Stripes forever way the Lead or Protagonist does. These guys can keep it real and the only cost is paying for it with their cinematic lives.

David Ayer's Alonzo character makes maximum use of this dynamic, if not completely upgrading and reinventing it. Which brings us back around to "movie stars wanting to play movie star parts". Denzel won the Oscar playing 'Zo, and I bet he probably saw that underlying potential the first time he read a draft. How could any great actor not? It's all right there in black and white.

The plotting is wicked sharp. Each piece of Ayer's puzzle drops into place with the utmost precision. Everything previously seeded in or set up pays off perfectly, organically building to the climax and resulting in an entirely satisfying resolution. Key word here -- *organic*. Nothing about Ayer's story strongarms the boundaries of plausibility, insuring Training Day feels both logical and real. This keeps us utterly absorbed within the film's universe at all times, no forced beats or ugly inconsistencies to distract us and puncture the illusion.

Once any audience (or reader) starts questioning a movie's logic, it's game over -- you've lost 'em and they ain't comin' back. You know the exact instant I'm talking about. Sometimes it's as drastic as "jumping the shark", others a whisper-quiet bed-shitting as some film's half-baked logic finally gives way. Watching at home, I can identify this as the moment I unsleep my MacBook to surf vintage guitar porn (you'll have your own porn preferences, I'm sure). The more astute among you will have noticed the majority of these collapses dovetail straight back to the unmet demands and expectations of "Screenwriting 101".

Let's climb under the hood and take a close look at how the Notecard Method informs the immaculate plotting and storytelling of a film like Training Day. And how, whether you've ever noticed it or not, David Ayer is teaching a master class on keeping beats surgically precise, impactful and loaded with critical content.

How do we start? Exact same way you're going to create your own screenplay -- by breaking Act One down one scene/one four-by-six index card at a time.

(Ed Note: If for some ridiculous reason you haven't seen or read Training Day, put this book down RIGHT NOW and go do it. This exercise will mean nothing if you haven't done your homework beforehand. In fact, everyone should try and rescreen it before continuing.)

What follows is what I get from breaking the film down, my own personal take on and interpretation of its structural brilliance -- nothing "official" intended, suggested or implied. Christ, for all I know, Mr. Ayer might eyeball this and suggest I get my head examined... but somehow I think I'll be alright.

Buckle in. Next stop, Big Boy land --

TRAINING DAY -- ACT ONE -- BEAT SHEET

1) INT. HOYT'S PLACE -- MORNING

Establish young police officer HOYT, HOYT'S WIFE and NEWBORN BABY. It's the first day of Hoyt's new assignment in Narcotics. His new boss Detective ALONZO calls to tell Hoyt where to meet.

Okay... when analyzing any film, two specific questions need to be asked of each beat -- **1) What is the ultimate purpose of each scene? 2) What does it accomplish structurally?**

How would we answer this for this first scene of Training Day?

150

A) Scene establishes the Hoyt character's <u>vulnerability</u>, what he loves and needs to protect -- his wife and kid. Immediately humanizes and makes him sympathetic.

B) Shows Alonzo's character interjecting himself into Hoyt's life even <u>before</u> we see him on-screen. In fact, his call starts by chatting up Hoyt's wife, making her giggle, invasively "charming the pants off her" -- adding the sublime subtext of sexual threat/familiarity.

<u>How good is that</u>? Before Alonzo physically appears, his character has already made the power of his presence felt by Hoyt. This is also perfectly consistent with the cunning character we'll come to know throughout the film -- a master of manipulation, someone always three steps ahead, expert at using others' information against them in the shrewdest, most damaging ways possible. So in a very real sense, Alonzo's character is being explicitly established before we first see him.

2) <u>INT. COFFEE SHOP</u> -- <u>MORNING</u>

Hoyt meets Alonzo for the first time -- "Tell me a story, Hoyt." Best Hoyt can come up with is a Valley D.U.I. stop where they found weapons and meth.

Accomplished --

A) Alonzo immediately establishes the balance of power between them -- veteran/new guy, strong/weak, big dog/little dog, top/bottom. This keeps Hoyt's character off-balance from the very start.

B) Hoyt's lackluster drunk-stop tale fails to impress. Why is this seemingly innocent exchange of special note? Because this normal, first day on the job meet-and-greet actually confirms Hoyt's <u>lack of experience</u> for Alonzo.

Think Big Picture. As we'll later learn, Alonzo has plotted out the entirety of this training day well in advance. But to make it all work, he needs a young, green cop he can fully manipulate and control. As the unit's lead Detective, he's gone over Hoyt's file and cherry-picked the kid precisely *because of* his inexperience; because he *hasn't* seen any real action and *won't* have points of reference or larger skills to fall back on once Alonzo leads him into deep water.

That said, no cop's CV tells you everything about the man himself. That's why 'Zo makes a point of vetting Hoyt face-to-face first before launching his training day. When he says "Tell me a story", he's straight-up fishing to see if Hoyt's got another gear, another level which somehow didn't translate into the official Departmental paperwork.

Here's an example -- Instead of the lame drunk-stop, what if Hoyt goes on some adrenalin-fueled rant about how he and his old partner pulled a *de facto* home invasion on some Valley drug kingpin, taking off their badges, putting on ski masks and torturing everybody inside -- including the kingpin's five year-old daughter -- with a blow-torch until the guy gave up his drug stash?

Whoops. Lights out. Game over. Now Alonzo knows he's got a fuckin' cowboy on his hands, a loose canon with his own crazy ideas who can't be manipulated or controlled to the degree necessary. Training day cancelled.

But when Hoyt does fail the test, as expected, Alonzo's plan drops smoothly into place and the "training day" of it all can begin in earnest.

Viewed this way, you can see what the coffee shop scene is _really_ about -- ensuring Hoyt's a legitimately inexperienced young cop, a known quantity who can be handled without any curveballs or surprises.

First time you see this scene, maybe it seems lightweight, a perfunctory throwaway. <u>That's how sublime Mr. Ayer's storytelling is</u>. The larger movie works perfectly fine whether you "get it" or not here, but he's already done his diligence and brilliantly seeded this stuff in for later payoff -- when you and the rest of the audience start doing the real math.

Humbling, isn't it? How fuckin' good this is? For those of you shining the notecards as child's play, something you can do without, you'd best crack that amyl nitrate popper and clear out the cobwebs. This is Bobby Fischer Grandmaster World Chess Champion-level shit you're witnessing here.

Even scarier? This is just the _second scene_ of Mr. Ayer's movie. He hasn't even gotten his swerve on yet.

3) <u>EXT. COFFEE SHOP</u> -- <u>PARKING LOT</u>

Establish Alonzo's "office" -- the G-Ride. Midnight-black '78 Monte Carlo, a spot-on undercover narc machine. 'Zo has Hoyt give him the Chinese Menu left on his windshield.

A) First blush, this seems like filler, a nuts-and-bolts way to move puzzle pieces around. Not so. The G-Ride's appearance not only designates it as real-life or "narc-appropriate" (did I just create a horrifying new phrase?) but also stands as a <u>visual</u> <u>representation</u> of Alonzo's unorthodox methods. The choice of vehicle perfectly externalizes who both the cop, and the man, driving it is -- someone very comfortable coloring outside the lines to get business done. Hard to imagine a more ideal point of entry into the script's heart of darkness than Ayer's narc cruiser.

The cherry on top? The Chinese menu actually plays a larger part in 'Zo's masterplan later on. Can you say "surgical" boys and girls?

4) INT. G-RIDE / EXT. STREETS -- DAY

Alonzo and Hoyt hit the streets. Hoyt checks in via radio, but 'Zo quickly lies about their location, advising Hoyt to never let anybody know where they really are.

This provides Hoyt's -- and the audience's -- first physical entree to the thrilling new world of Alonzo's Downtown L.A. undercover work.

The G-Ride literally becomes Hoyt's universe for the entirety of his training day; a flying saucer, for all intents and purposes, skimming him across the surface of an alien moon with all its bizarre life forms and hostile, unknown possibilities. Within moments, Ayer's Monte Carlo will begin ferrying our young cop deep into the obscene inner workings of a Rampart-style L.A. street policing he never could have imagined.

The instant Hoyt's butt hits the passenger's seat, he becomes the archetypal "stranger in a strange land". Belted inside Alonzo's G-Ride he'll discover the game here is played by a entirely different set of rules with entirely different expectations -- flipping anything and everything Hoyt believes himself familiar with upside-down and inside-out, deepening his disconnection and further keeping him off balance.

Ayer immediately underscores this dynamic with the brief exchange over the <u>police radio</u>. Ever-cunning Alonzo sees the rover as a valuable tool for disinformation and obfuscation -- the exact <u>opposite</u> of what newbie Hoyt expects. And although 'Zo plausibly justifies his approach ("Bad guys are listening."), in fact, he's preemptively cutting Hoyt off from any alternative points of view via contact with the "real world".

All this from six seemingly innocent lines.

5) <u>INT. G-RIDE / EXT. DTLA STREETS</u> -- <u>DAY</u>

Alonzo gives Hoyt the rundown about how the unit works, etc. Hoyt tells him he wants to make detective. 'Zo promises he can help make that happen.

Two big things of note here --

A) Hoyt's <u>primary</u> <u>motivation</u> is made explicitly clear -- he wants to make detective and get his gold shield. This takes us straight back to the "<u>Who's Your Main Character?</u>" a.k.a "<u>Who's your Protagonist?</u>" query in "Screenwriting 101" and answers Syd Field's essential question -- "*What does your main character want to win, gain, get or achieve during the course of your screenplay?*"

Moving forward, Alonzo will use this knowledge to manipulate Hoyt whenever he needs to, a proverbial "carrot on a stick" capable of keeping the young cop in line should he risk losing control.

B) It establishes that Hoyt speaks Spanish. A nice, clean way of slipping that into the mix without drawing any attention to itself.

6) <u>INT. G-RIDE / EXT. DTLA STREETS</u> -- <u>DAY</u>

They continue patrolling. Alonzo busts Hoyt's balls, pushing the family/wife button. Hoyt reacts badly, telling him not to talk about it.

A) Alonzo discovers one of Hoyt's real weak spots -- his family -- giving him yet another card to play against the younger man whenever he wants. 'Zo's offer to "do your old lady up" and give Hoyt a son ties beautifully into the quiet sexual undercurrent of that invasive phone call we witnessed during the Opening.

There's something else worth discussing here. <u>Why even bother showing the wife and baby back in the Opening</u>? From a purely structural point of view, establishing the family is <u>not</u> essential to the script and could be cut quite easily. Having Hoyt kick things off by walking into the coffee shop to meet Alonzo works far better dramatically IMHO, saving you two set-ups, casting/paying a SAG actress, etc.

So why begin the film with two tiny characters we'll never see again?

Because by taking a moment to put a face on Hoyt's wife you successfully <u>humanize her</u> in the audience's eyes. To be honest, it doesn't really matter *what* she does or says in that scene. Having seen her just this once, she becomes "real"; a remembered face for the audience to flash on whenever her character is brought up in the future.

Smart move, right? Left abstract and unseen, Hoyt having a wife is simply a <u>concept</u>; no more powerful or moving than, say, a stranger in some Peet's Coffee informing you they're married. Really, *who gives a shit*?

156

This hypothetical stranger's invisible spouse has no reality for us without a flesh and blood point of reference, hence, any emotion it might evoke is purely conceptual on our parts... if at all.

By putting a face to Hoyt's wife, however, any subsequent threat to this woman becomes a thousand times more suspenseful and impactful for the viewer. Getting maximum mileage from your script's emotional elements whenever and wherever possible is one of superior storytelling's key ingredients.... which is precisely why Mr. Ayer constructed his movie this way.

7) INT. G-RIDE / EXT. NETO'S STREET -- DAY

Alonzo and Hoyt watch as Neto, one of 'Zo's street snitches, deals drugs to hipster university kids in a VW Bug.

A) Gives Hoyt his first taste of how shit <u>really</u> works on the streets. Not only is Neto an off-the-book snitch, but his loyalty is further cemented by 'Zo having sprung his mother from I.N.S.

B) Establishes Alonzo's overriding philosophy that you have to bend some rules and break some laws to accomplish bigger goals in this jungle -- something he'll hammer much harder later on.

Just so we're clear -- this simple truth about cops having to circumvent the strictly legal is something every adult audience member accepts as the real-world price of working narcotics. By co-opting what we know to be true *outside* the theater, Ayer effectively bolsters 'Zo's veracity while deepening Hoyt's uncertainty about what constitutes "right action" at any given time.

157

Lastly, Alonzo's coloring outside the lines continues keeping Hoyt off-balance.

8) EXT. G-RIDE / EXT. STREET CORNER -- DAY

Alonzo hard-charges the college kids in the VW, pulling them over, taking their weed and pipe, then cutting them loose.

Couple really nice things going on here --

A) The action showcases Alonzo's hair-trigger temper for the first time, making explicitly clear his potential for using physical violence in any given situation.

I like to call this a "monster in the box" moment. Just like in our everyday lives, *talking about* being a bad-ass and *being* a bad-ass are two entirely different things. You can vibe a character as being dangerous and lethal as much as you want, but if we never see what they're capable of *with our own eyes* the threat that character presents never feels fully 3-D.

Meaning, if you never let the monster out of the box, the viewer is never certain there's a legit monster inside there to begin with.

Which is why, promptly on p. 18, we're establishing for Hoyt/Audience that 'Zo is definitely one scary dude. Witnessing it firsthand leaves zero doubt he's bad news, a potential time bomb, and Lord knows *what else* this fuckin' guy may be capable of as we move forward.

The cherry on top? Successfully seeding in evidence of Alonzo's temper here will dovetail perfectly into the Ultimate Reveal that 'Zo lost his cool in Vegas and beat a Russian Outfit guy to death with his bare hands. The film's major punchline is that Zo has until midnight to pay a million bucks in gangland restitution for that

158

killing, which is the engine motivating *everything* behind Hoyt's "training day" -- and Alonzo's shrewd plotting of it -- to begin with.

This is how the heavy hitters do it, fellas. The sublime construction of your story on multiple levels <u>simultaneously</u> is the level of work needed to make it stick in the big leagues.

B) Hoyt's reaction to Alonzo's actions say he's not down with this type of policing at all. <u>Visually</u> we're given explicit evidence of our Protagonist's conscience and know instantly this kind of shit will <u>not</u> work for him.

C) Further reinforces that Alonzo is not your standard cop and will go way outside the box whenever he believes it necessary.

D) Lastly, something of quiet importance. Circulating unnoticed beneath all the in-your-face action is Alonzo's confiscation of <u>Neto's weed</u> from the college kids. Impossible to recognize by anyone save 'Zo himself, this will become the <u>first puzzle piece</u> needed to ensnare Hoyt in the narc's training day masterplan.

<u>**Grace Note #1**</u> -- In 2000, what vehicle said "dope-smoking pussy hipster" more than the new VW Bug? Another spot-on choice, one glimpse telling you pretty much everything you need to know about the characters riding inside it.

<u>**Grace Note #2**</u> -- There's a <u>killer line</u> during scene when Alonzo orders the passenger to give him the pot pipe. Reluctantly, the kid replies, "My mom gave me that pipe" -- which absolutely leveled the crowd I saw it with. It was so *dead-on* for California culture it just totally busted them up. Excellent example of how <u>one perfect line</u> can totally legitimize the flavor of a scene.

9) <u>INT. G-RIDE / EXT. STREETS</u> -- <u>DAY</u>

Hoyt's <u>pissed</u> about drug stop and lets Alonzo know it. 'Zo breaks down Neto's weed and I.D.'s it, showing the depth of his street knowledge. The narc tells Hoyt to smoke it. Hoyt says no.

A) This establishes the critical dynamic by which Alonzo manipulates Hoyt -- <u>any time there's a question of propriety 'Zo switches the discussion back to police work</u>. Whenever things get pushed too far and he risks losing the younger cop's allegiance, the veteran shrewdly falls back on all things <u>professional</u>.

During this scene, Hoyt is angry and bridling over what happened back at the VW. He rightfully makes clear that 'Zo's actions were WAY over the line. How does Alonzo respond? By flipping the conversation to a street-pro analysis of the dope he confiscated.

By using this dynamic throughout the script, Alonzo keeps Hoyt questioning <u>himself</u> and his instincts instead of leveling full focus on Zo. Don't forget, backstopping this play is <u>what Hoyt's character wants most of all</u> -- to make Detective. Alonzo's masterful blend of obfuscation and manipulation will keep Hoyt under his thumb for a good long while.

<u>Smarter villains make for smarter movies</u>. Classic case in point right here.

B) Hoyt finally stands up to Alonzo for the first time. Without this showdown, there's no <u>direct confrontation</u> between our Protagonist (Hoyt) and Antagonist (Alonzo) -- and that same roiling conflict and head-butting battle of wills is what's needed to drive the entirety of the film from here forward.

Consider this -- what if Hoyt *doesn't* stand up to the veteran? Say he just goes along with everything 'Zo wants? Joyfully jacks one of the college kids, fondly tokes up Neto's weed like an old Hippie at Woodstock, etc. Hoyt totally on-board for *whatever* without a second thought?

Quite simply, we wouldn't have a movie.

No conflict, no confrontation, no story. In the absence of real stakes -- nothing important to be won or lost, nothing for the viewer to care about or emotionally invest themselves in -- there's no movie worth watching. Accordingly, this scene (and the following) kicks off the conflict which becomes Training Day's primary fuel source from here on.

10) INT. G-RIDE / EXT. INTERSECTION -- DAY

Middle of the street Alonzo slams car to a stop, puts his gun flush to Hoyt's head. Tells the cherry cop if he were a real dealer he'd already be dead. Alonzo lays down an ultimatum -- smoke the weed or get the fuck out of his squad. Hoyt gives in and smokes it.

A) Epic exchange here with 'Zo literally, *physically* forcing Hoyt to make a choice. In or out? With me or against me? The veteran goes straight at his newbie, preying on Hoyt's innate goodness. How does Ayer get this across? Wickedly, with one shrewd line -- "I don't want you in my unit."

Ouch. Making Hoyt feel he's not good enough, that he's incompetent, a failure, is a crippling blow. *What could possibly hurt this specific character more?* Good guy, family man, hard worker, solid morals, Catholic school background (revealed two scenes later) -- and now, for

161

perhaps the first time in his life, he's being accused of *letting someone down.*

Shit gets deeper. Transpose this to Hoyt's life off-the-clock, and it points directly to an inability to provide for his young wife and baby. Yeah, remember them? The very first story elements established in the film? The most vulnerable part of Hoyt's life? Should Hoyt not get the job done, he'll be failing *his own family* in addition to bailing on Alonzo and his unit.

During the opening family scene in the finished film, I believe there's an added line not found in the script -- Hoyt's wife telling him not to "screw this up" i.e. not to blow the opportunity for financial advancement making Detective represents. On a character level, this moment now, proffered weed, middle of the street, directly recalls that line and those concerns for Hoyt.

(Dear Readers -- I profoundly hope you're savoring the breadth of David Ayer's artistry. For screenwriting wonks like myself, this command of storytelling is truly spectacular, something worthy of aspiring to no matter how long you've been a working writer.)

All this comes to a head with an archetypal The Matrix "Red Pill/Blue Pill" moment -- "*You take the blue pill, the story ends, you wake up in your bed and believe whatever you want to believe. You take the red pill, you stay in Wonderland, and I show you how deep the rabbit hole goes.*"

Hoyt obviously takes Alonzo's red pill, and thus begins his spiral down Training Day's darkest of rabbit holes.

B) On Alonzo's end, he needs Hoyt to commit one way or the other for two big reasons --

<u>One</u> -- If Hoyt's going to bail, he might as well do it now so 'Zo doesn't waste any more time. (Remember, the Russians have that ticking clock on him, midnight and a million bucks or it's off with 'Zo's head).

<u>Two</u> -- If Hoyt does commit, Alonzo needs to implement his training day master plan pronto. Step One? <u>Get drugs into the young cop's system</u>.

C) We revisit Alonzo top-coating his nefarious goals with the thinnest veneer of truth, i.e. "Turn shit down on the street and the Chief hands your wife a crisply-folded flag". What adult audience is going to argue that? So yes, it is true -- but it still doesn't have much to do with getting Hoyt to take a puff.

D) Reinforces yet again that Alonzo's the big dog in the mix, able to back Hoyt down whenever necessary -- the exact same strong/weak, top/bottom dynamic set up during their initial coffee shop meeting. It also keeps 'Zo confident he's picked the right kid.

11) <u>INT. G-RIDE/ EXT. DOWNTOWN STREETS</u> -- <u>DAY</u>

Hoyt trips his balls off while Alonzo cruises -- punch line is that Neto's weed was dusted with PCP. 'Zo tells Hoyt not to worry, their Lt. has their backs and gives them a heads up before having to pee test.

A) This puts hard drugs into Hoyt's blood stream -- giving Alonzo something he'll always have over the kid, a huge card to play should it become necessary later on.

If there's one thing I HATE in movies and TV it's when they get the drugs wrong. Nothing takes me out of the dreamscape faster than a writer and/or director shitting their drawers on the dope front. I mean, do some research you square motherfuckers, go to a party once in a while, ask a fuckin' Hipster.

(I remember an uncharacteristically absurd sequence in the normally brilliant Six Feet Under where the mother accidently took Ecstasy... then had wacked out dreams of giant teddy bears and her dead husband. *Man, was I pissed*! To the show's credit, however, the next time Ecstasy was involved Peter Kraus's character played it perfectly. Warm, flushed, drinking water, grabbing people's trap muscles and giving them a tight squeeze.)

So watching Training Day for the first time, I nearly blew another gasket when they showed Hoyt, completely wasted now, looking out his window and then cut to this heavy green-filtered shot of strobing graffiti and eerie pigeons flying over Echo Park.

"You don't trip on weed," I grunted loudly, Santa Monica Cineplex. "That's bullshit."

Then Mr. Ayer played his trump card -- revealing the dusted bud. *"C'mon, dipped in P.C.P? Primos, Sherm, kool, P-dog, angel dust..."*

Dunked all over my smarmy ass, no doubt. Got me hook/line, a deft storytelling facial for the self-appointed Movie Police a.k.a. Me.

What's so sweet is how Mr. Ayer works the reveal for maximum mileage on multiple levels. Upgrading from weed to Sherm takes Hoyt into felony dismissal territory, an immediate career-ender should 'Zo report it. That choice alone upgrades a good scene to masterful. Yet it also serves to put the harrowing depths of Alonzo's venality on display for the first time. If he would dose an unsuspecting young cop that way, what *wouldn't* he do?

Turns out Alonzo boosting the weed from Neto's clients was entirely surgical. Neto is the veteran's long-time snitch, so logic follows he knows the kid sells dusted bud. Alonzo wasn't focused on getting pot into Hoyt's system, that was camouflage for the harder Schedule One stuff. Zo was essentially using marijuana as a delivery system for the underlying PCP.

Besides being superb character work, this points to a pretty wicked level of premeditation, doesn't it? Yet, much like Hoyt, we're so caught up in the immediate action of what's taking place (Christ, we've got a gun to our heads!) we don't pause to do any larger math. The script has given us fair warning... and we haven't begun to fully grasp it yet.

(Much later, after all Hell breaks loose, the script marvelously outs 'Zo's shrewd planning during his classic exchange with Hoyt -- "You've been planning this all day." "I've been planning this all *week*, son.")

B) The deal about their Lt. "having their backs" appears to be a straight-up lie, just another way to mollify Hoyt. As far as I can tell, there's no evidence of this being true anywhere in the film's text. Nobody has Hoyt's back, least of all Alonzo, as we'll soon find out.

By the time this beat ends, Step One of Alonzo's master plan is complete -- hard drugs are in Hoyt's system, leaving him at 'Zo's mercy if he wants to have any shot at becoming a detective one day.

Quick Note -- It's important to recognize *why* every scene is working so wonderfully here. It's because the writer knows his characters so well. Top to bottom, front to back, David Ayer has fashioned sharp motives and come up with deep backstories capable of breathing real life into both men. Never once do you think, "Nah.

165

That character's not real" -- which is critical to the film's success.

12) INT. /EXT. ROGER'S HOUSE -- DAY

Alonzo takes Hoyt to meet ROGER, his road dog. A long-time friend and big-time drug dealer.

The final beat of Act One, which covers an amazing amount of narrative ground before launching us full-force into the beginning of Act Two.

Let me start with the script's description of Roger's house, worthy of special mention --

"A well-tended Craftsman on a steep hill of fixer-uppers in Echo Park."

This is <u>everything</u> a screen description should strive to be. Tight, short and precise while still painting a perfect picture. In twelve short words, Mr. Ayer manages to communicate all this --

1) That we're in a working-class 'hood (Echo Park) located in a somewhat sketchy part of older DTLA.

2) The visual flavor of the place (Craftsman architecture) and that Roger's home is taken care of; an indication the owner takes some pride in living there, which also implies a certain longevity at this residence.

3) Gentrification hasn't taken hold here yet, as evidenced by the houses (fixer-uppers) remaining in disrepair. This makes it a plausible spot for a higher-level drug dealer to do business. Restored and/or renovated Craftsmen mean money -- younger couples with good jobs and new families. These folks do care, will call the cops and have no problem organizing

166

Neighborhood Watch, etc. None of which any intelligent drug dealer wants any part of.

4) Being on a steep hill centered in Echo Park, there's the chance of having a nice view of Downtown laid out before it... which always looks great on camera.

That's how much this *one line* of description reveals. Impressed yet? How 'bout humbled? Twelve words -- the *right* twelve words -- accomplishes all of it.

No, overwriting OCD screenwriters -- we *don't* need to know what color the house is... what type of wildflowers populate the front yard... whether there's a white-picket fence... what year it was built or that Abraham Lincoln stopped by to drop a deuce in 1860. Every detail is a conscious choice by the author to best inform the reader of what's intended for the scene. Maximum impact, minimum words. <u>No purplish writerly excess is permitted to detract from the task at hand</u>, which is precisely what makes it so great.

(Just reviewing this gets me high. Being a first-class film wonk, it's pretty awesome to see this level of craft.)

Now... do *you* have to make every single description you write for the rest of your lives this good? Probably not. You can and will get by with less. Most writers have. But in the words of stoner Wooderson/Matthew McConaughey in <u>Dazed and Confused</u>, "It'd be a lot cooler if you did..."

So try hard. Take time to put real thought into every description. What's more satisfying for a writer than perfection? More rewarding than knowing some stranger in La La Land may pause and perhaps read it *twice*, because it's that fuckin' good -- light years better than all the other shit they're reading.

Okay, back to what this big scene at Roger's house accomplishes --

A) Roger himself is established -- setting up the <u>ultimate target</u> of Alonzo's masterplan and the various machinations surrounding it. Of course, there's no way the audience can guess any of this yet, which is exactly as it should be. The goal here is to subtly seed Roger in, laying the groundwork for what's coming.

B) Alonzo's <u>Las Vegas backstory</u> emerges -- first mention of him having had a confrontation there and the Russian Mob putting out a contract (a "green light") on his ass because of it. Essentially, this is what <u>Training Day</u>'s boils down to -- Alonzo being in debt to the Russians for killing a guy -- and that single event sets the entire plot in motion before film story time even begins. Having Roger bring it up naturally/unobtrusively begins layering this critical dynamic in for a monster payoff later.

C) Hoyt's "Smiles and Cries" monologue serves to humanize the young cop and treat us to an unguarded glimpse of who he is <u>inside</u>. The content confirms he's thoughtful, a good guy whom the audience wants to get behind.

The Alonzo character is so damned STRONG in this First Act (especially as portrayed by Denzel Washington) that he risks blowing Hoyt's character clean off the screen. But remember -- <u>this is Hoyt's movie</u>, he's our hero and protagonist. Accordingly, the writer has to grab the spotlight away from his charismatic villain and point it squarely onto Hoyt, bringing these characters back into some semblance of balance. Without a serious dose of heat and sunlight here, Hoyt risks withering away altogether.

D) Roger recognizing Hoyt as a former All-City strong safety is a super clever device, revealing a shit-ton about what makes the kid tick using organic conversation over obvious, amateurish, ham-fisted exposition.

Strong safety is a tough position in football. Your time is divided between breaking up passes and stuffing run plays -- meaning you have to be cornerback-quick and still hit linebacker hard. Playing strong safety requires speed, power, determination and, most of all, the ability to think on your feet and make decisions under pressure.

Roger informs us that Hoyt played strong safety, straight-up tells us he was good at it ("I follow all the good players"), drawing a direct line between Hoyt and those same key characteristics. Beyond that, being named All-City further elevates evidence of Hoyt's prowess. Lots of guys play safety, but how many make All-City in a talent-rich environment like L.A. which produces its fair share of NCAA Division I athletes? Two or three a year, tops.

So although Hoyt has yet to display any of these defining characteristics on-screen, Roger's dialogue certifies there's a whole other side to the kid, which -- given that he's the lead in a Hollywood movie -- is soon destined to become a factor.

Also consider that Mr. Ayer could easily have chosen a more obvious position, say quarterback. Why didn't he? First off, because it's a total cliché. Secondly, because it doesn't sell the <u>exact</u> <u>qualities</u> he wants Hoyt's character to possess. Hoyt's not some flash front-runner, he's a grinder; a blue-collar kid who knuckles down and gets the job done without fanfare. What about tackle or defensive lineman? They're fast, low profile and even more powerful. That's true. But since Hoyt isn't physically big enough to have played those positions, the implausibility factor risks damaging the film's credibility and obvious street smarts.

Knowing what position some character played back during high school. Seems totally inconsequential, right? Yet, in the hands of an imaginative writer, this one simple detail serves to illuminate a key character from inside-out.

But wait, John. *What if the viewer doesn't know anything about sports?* Say a nunnery-sequestered girlfriend or some cruelty-free vegan non-athlete? No worries, my high maintenance friends. Once they hear the words "football player" it still gives Hoyt the same generous dose of man-cred, just within a broader framework.

E) Alonzo has a choice character reveal here coming via Roger as well. The film version shows us an old photograph, Roger and 'Zo back in the day, and the drug dealer says to the veteran, "You were just like him, you know" -- meaning Alonzo was just like Hoyt when *he* first started out; an idealistic rookie, honest, dedicated to trying to make a difference.

This beat signals the audience that 'Zo was a good guy himself once upon a time, while simultaneously offering the young Hoyt a "Ghost of X-Mas Future" vision of what he may (or may not) become given the choices he makes moving forward.

F) Here's another fun touch. What's one of the first things Alonzo does when they get to Roger's? Puts a glass of <u>whisky</u> in Hoyt's hands, casually tossing hard alcohol into the mix alongside the weed and P.C.P. from earlier. This is an additional card 'Zo can now play against Hoyt whenever he chooses.

G) Lastly, <u>what in God's name is Roger's "snail story" really about</u>? Got me, fellas. I scoured the Net seeking clarity and came up woefully empty handed. Millions of forums have debated it to death and plenty of interesting takes exist. Somewhere, I believe the director Antoine Fuqua claimed it was a complete *non sequitur*; essentially a riddle with no right answer. Personally, I'm not buying it. Given the script's immaculate construction, it's hard to believe David Ayer threw in some meaningless speech for nothing more than shits and giggles. But hey, that's just me and my twenty years experience talking.

Perhaps someday David Ayer will give an interview and finally solve the mystery for the legion of film aficionados out there who'd still like to know, myself included.

This scene brings us to the end of the First Act. A solid Act One should run approximately 25 to 30 pages - - 25 to 30 minutes screen time. <u>Training Day</u>'s Act One ends page 29 in my draft, landing perfectly -- like everything else in the script.

<u>One Last Side Note</u> -- Ordinarily, stringing together <u>four consecutive interior car scenes</u> between the same two characters (followed by another triptych of beats afterwards) would be begging for the developmental kiss of death. *Who wants to watch two static heads riding around gabbing for fifteen minutes*? Nobody, that's who. Especially not professional readers.

However, it's pretty obvious Alonzo's G-Ride is no ordinary car and <u>Training Day</u> no ordinary script. Don't even *think* about trying this in your own scripts. Only after you've fully mastered the rules can you conceptualize successfully breaking them.

171

*****

With that epic breakdown tucked firmly under your belt, I've got just one question for you --

Are <u>your</u> beats this bulletproof? Do <u>your</u> notecards meet this standard? Will they hold up this well under detailed scrutiny by professionals in the business at large? Hawkeyed motherfuckers like myself, just looking for something to rip apart?

(You should be laughing right now, 'cause I certainly am.)

Of course they aren't. Of course they don't.

This is world-class, Academy-award caliber material. The stuff filmmakers' dreams are made out of. A winning Lotto ticket -- only luck didn't have a goddamn thing to do with it.

<u>Hard</u> <u>work</u> brought this to life, folks. Being dedicated. Being smart. Pushing your imagination. Gaining full command of your craft. Doing your homework and working up a no-bullshit/no blind spot blueprint of the story you intend to tell.

This is how the big boys do it, the very best in the business.

Yes, the shit is <u>humbling</u>. It can make you feel small. Even someone like me, who's made a living writing screenplays his entire adult life. If your doors weren't blown off, your knees didn't buckle and your world wasn't permanently rocked by a peek at that monster beat sheet, then something's *seriously* wrong with you. Seek out one of two transplants -- brain or heart -- immediately.

172

Now you know how deep the rabbit hole goes. That level of precision. That level of execution. Each scene surgically servicing your story with a premium of efficiency. Plotting out a movie that actually works is a thousand times more difficult than even the most movie-savvy of weekend warriors ever understand.

Given that, how could anybody hope to produce something of this quality <u>without</u> using notecards or some very similar method?

It's an impossible task, the ultimate fool's errand. Like Manhattan skyscrapers and multi-million dollar mansions, great scripts rise or fall based on the strength of their foundations. Plots like those of your favorite films simply DO NOT come together without concrete architecture. Without that, all you're doing is cranking out pages nobody wants to buy.

Read <u>Screenplay</u>. Get yourself some four-by-six notecards. *Get in the game.* The book's been out for thirty-five years now. If you were waiting for a written invitation, consider this it.

* * * * *

Know what's a blast? Seeing students' minds blown sky-high when they finally "get" the notecards of it all. Watching *their* "Neo-jacking-into-the-Matrix" moments slam home right before your eyes. It's like witnessing somebody's first Ecstasy trip -- only the drug is screenplay structure, and your head doesn't feel like a broken egg shell all the next day.

The rush of empowerment it gives writers is awesome. The realization that, armed with this pretty straightforward knowledge, they <u>can</u> do it, they <u>do</u> have a fighting chance. That all those deferred, semi-sequestered dreams are so much closer to becoming real now than they ever could've believed before.

One Sunday Tough Love class, one of my best students showed up without his notecards. Bright kid, great ideas, über tech savvy -- very much of his generation in the best sense. I politely asked him where they were (translation: "It's your day, Josh. Where the fuck are your notecards?"). My young friend reassured me there was nothing to worry about -- he had this *program* ("Index Cards and Panels") he used instead. It was so much more compact and convenient than dealing with all those messy paper index cards, plus it saved trees!

Imagine my expression. Think late '80's Michael Rooker/<u>Henry: Portrait of a Serial Killer,</u> staring maniacally into that one-sheet bathroom mirror.

Then came the crazy part. *All my other students dog-piled his ass before I said a word.* Rabid fuckers went <u>American Me</u>, treating Josh to a savage little blanket party, if I say so myself.

"No, Josh, it's not the same!"

"What the hell is wrong with you?"

"Suck it up, Josh, you're shitting the bed!" (this from a fifty year-old woman)

"That iPad shit doesn't work, that's the whole point!

I'd have to rank this among my proudest moments as an instructor. It's always nice to have confirmation that your patients are taking their prescribed medicine and that it's actually showing results -- even if one of your best and brightest has to be sacrificially gangbanged by his peers to provide hard evidence.

ANATOMY OF A CLUSTERFUCK

Early 2000's, I was coming off saving a film for a big studio. My stock was surging and I was starting to make my first legitimate splash.

After years of obscure, unpaid laboring, I was really feeling it, finally finding my groove. All that woodshedding had vastly improved my writing. It was becoming better crafted and far more intuitive. Better still, proof of this breakthrough was now coming across on the page, for anyone and everyone to see.

A hungry young agent saw it and took me on, and his agency had enough juice to start getting me into the right rooms (more about this later). They totally had my back and very quickly it became plug and play -- they'd send me out, after that, everything else was on me. As you might imagine, this was a really good time for a young writer.

So... as a last ditch effort (more of a human sacrifice, really), the big studio had hired me to save their struggling film and, against all odds, I'd gotten it greenlit. Not only that, but to everybody's further shock, it became a big hit.

In this town, you strike while the iron's hot. My agents quickly put me in the room with a famous director, one of the real old school legends, in fact. There was a new company in town spending real money, and he'd set up a project there. All they needed now was a writer.

We met on the studio lot, the Director and I immediately hitting it off. This guy was a blast, regaling me with wild tales of '70's and '80's Hollywood, each more x-rated

175

hilarious than the last. Growing up with the classics of that era, I knew and loved them all, and suddenly here I was talking to the guy who'd actually made some of them! We jawed warp-speed for an hour, then spent maybe ten minutes talking broad strokes about his project. It was to be a modern-day Robin Hood -- the big twist was casting a famous MMA fighter as the lead and setting it in violent inner city L.A.

Remember, this is before the whole MMA/UFC thing fully blew up. But within just a few years, Dana White and Co. would radically reinvent the marketing of that world and find themselves sitting on a billion-dollar business.

So in a way -- even though it wasn't premeditated -- the Director's idea of casting an MMA superstar with international appeal in a kick-ass action film was perfectly timed. By the time it was ready to roll out, the U.S. would be beginning its new love affair with the UFC, and we'd be standing there waiting with lightning in a bottle, boffo box office almost certain to ensue.

I drove back home, and later that same afternoon my agent calls. Business affairs from the new company had made an offer -- $100K against $275, or 100/275 in film biz parlance. The Director was crazy about me and knew immediately I was the perfect guy for the job. Word go it became a spontaneous four-way love fest; Company, Famous Director, Agents, Me. My cup runneth over with this highly addictive first burst of adulation.

It was all kinda hard to wrap my head around. A guaranteed ONE HUNDRED THOUSAND DOLLARS for drinking a free bottle of Evian and listening to one of Hollywood's most successful filmmakers tell epic war stories? For just being (GASP!) me???

Abruptly, the lightbulb went on. So THIS is what everybody was chasing. Of course there were heaps of money to be made -- Monopoly money, from where I was standing. But what about having all the heavyweight ego-stroking a film-addled shut-in like myself could desire? Now *that* shit was truly awesome.

Next came a meet-and-greet with the company to discuss our collective vision for the project. My honeymoon continued unabated. We were all on the same page! We all agreed EXACTLY what this film should aspire to! From the top down, everybody onboard was euphoric with developmental glee!

We would set our homage to Robin Hood in the impoverished jungles of East L.A. Forced to flee Brazil because of his heroic actions against homicidal police, our Lead would join his uncle in L.A. to begin building a new life for himself. But after witnessing dehumanizing sweatshop conditions, and running afoul of local gangsters who extorted and violently terrorized the good-hearted (but powerless) immigrants who had befriended our hero, the Lead is compelled to take the law into his own hands, seeing justice done, whatever the cost. I was urged to think of the story as gritty, raw and realistic -- "Robin Hood Xtreme" if you will, with someone like Jay-Z playing Friar Tuck.

Robin Hood is one of the oldest legends in all of Western Civilization, and for good reason. The timeless themes of rich vs. poor, the corrupt haves vs. the honest have-nots, still speak as loudly to audiences today as they did in Medieval times. So our contemporary take involving sweatshops and immigrant labor, oppression and cultural inequality, would fit perfectly alongside the original's centuries-old intent.

After a few frenzied white-boy high-fives ("I love this guy!" cheers one goofy exec), and a second complimentary bottle of Evian, I was sent off to write a treatment so we could haul ass to first draft.

* * * * *

Ensconced back in my bungalow, I set about creating my masterpiece. Like I said, I was totally in my wheelhouse then, doing the very best writing of my young career. I buckled down and poured my heart and soul into the idea. I skipped Radiohead concerts, cancelled dates, ate nothing but bad Chinese and Thai delivery. Twenty-four seven, I labored to make the story not just a kick-ass MMA thrill ride -- the essential dynamic driving the entire project in the first place -- but also a film which actually had *something to say*.

I saw it as a classic have-your-cake-and-eat-it-to opportunity -- killer action and ultra-cool, franchisable genre characters, with a timely message to the contemporary audience nestled behind all the head-butting and hard talk.

Listen, if all you wanted was to see somebody's trachea stomped into tomato soup, or some asshole's nutsack blown off, yeah, you would get that in spades. I mean, this was an ACTION MOVIE after all, mass escapist entertainment. But for the more discerning genre lover (like myself) there would also be a legitimate *subtext* we could hang our hats on. A little something... better.

One month later I submitted my twelve-page, single-spaced treatment. I was anxious, but extremely confident. Never had I felt better about the work and what I was trying to accomplish. I believed it awesome that Hollywood execs were willing to push for a meaningful story, even within the confines of a smaller

178

genre pic like this. Maybe the self-serving, head-time-capsuled-up-ass development stereotypes I'd been brutalized by firsthand in the past would be proven wrong this time around.

A week passed. Then a second. Neither my agent nor myself heard so much as a whisper.

Believe me, if there's anything a writer learns in Hollywood, it's this -- *the silence is deafening.*

Silence is <u>never</u> good. Silence says disinterest, displeasure or -- scariest of all -- *disappointment.* When you put finished pages someone <u>paid for</u> in their impatient little palms and they don't get back to you a.s.a.p. something is terribly, irrevocably wrong. In my experience, there are no exceptions to this rule.

Sure enough, start of week three we finally got word. It wasn't good. Let's just say nobody loved it. The company initially didn't hate it, per se, but, the Director's people did. They hated it with a passion. So that meant the company had started loathing it as well.

Judgment Day took place in the company's flagship conference room. Picture a <u>Hudsucker Proxy</u>-sized oak conference table, all <u>five</u> of my company inquisitors massed at the far end, and me -- best of intentions, isolated, confused -- docked in a half-mast Aeron chair at the other. The Famous Director was now very, very busy, slammed in fact, and sadly could not attend.

Instead, the Head of Development lead the prosecution. He was a real trip, an IMAX D-Guy Cartoon brightly penciled in by Pixar. We're talking an <u>Aliens</u>-level development exec here, with him cast as the egg-laying Queen, not just one of the day player xenomorphs. For the safety and sanity of all involved, let's call him Exec X.

179

"This treatment is too preachy, too grim, too goddamn G-L-O-O-M-Y," his first salvo whistled across my bow. "Where's the *fun* in this world, John? The Lethal Weapon of it all? The hijinks, the wink-wink, the Wow Factor?"

You mean, where's the fun in... illegal immigration? In the callous rich taking advantage of the struggling poor? Is that what he was asking?

"Look, John, trust me -- it's NOT THAT BAD down there. There are plenty of happy stories to tell. Happy stories which give those people plenty of hope."

Whoops. My Spidey Sense suffered an ugly spasm. "Down there". "Those people". When coming from a white guy's mouth, this couldn't be going anywhere good.

"To some, you know, this might sound controversial. But I'm going to go ahead and say it anyway, 'cause frankly I'm not a P.C. person and I could give a shit," Exec X leaned forward, Sunday smile, as if confiding in me. "You know what, John? I have a maid, and she's an illegal. That's right. An illegal. And guess what? She LOVES working for me. Loves it! She's fuckin' overjoyed, couldn't be happier!"

"Me too." The famous director's D-Girl joined in. "My husband and I have an illegal nanny. Always smiling, that woman. Very Zen."

"In fact," Exec X bulldozed forward, "Recently I had a bit of a funny conundrum. My maid's daughter was having her *quinceañera*, and she told me they didn't have enough decorations for it. So guess what I did? This is great -- I let her go around the house and gather up all the old flowers that'd been there a few days and take those to the party! Isn't that terrific? She was soooooo happy."

Another exec in the room I'd met before, a decent guy, coming from the right place. I watched the same horrified shockwave blitzkrieg his face that had already darkened mine. So they weren't *all* Replicants, I thought. Thank Christ.

Oversharing kills. No doubt, I'm every inch as white boy as the next honky motherfucker out there. But there was one huge problem.

I wasn't *that* kind of white.

Both my mother and father had Ph.D.'s from Teachers College at Columbia. Their specialties? Education for Gifted Minority Students. My girlfriend was Hispanic, a social worker born literally -- true shit -- in a dirt-floored shack in Pacoima. So yeah, this wasn't going to be the best of fits.

All this time, Dear Reader, I'd been racking my brain, trying to figure out why they hated my treatment so much. Why everyone was acting like I'd totally butt-fucked the pooch on this one. Now it hit me full-force -- my pages were too, well, Robin Hood. I'd done *exactly* what we'd agreed upon, gotten it pitch perfect... which was worst-case for these folks.

Class struggle? Rich vs. Poor? Wise up, dummy. They wanted our MMA Hero disguised as a grubby street urchin, crashing Beverly Hills parties, stuffing his pockets with hors d'oeuvres and stealing wads of cash from fur coats in the coat room (I mean, is anything funnier than the poor stealing?). And that's precisely the revised take they now pitched me.

181

Everything became a vague blur, Charlie Brown's teacher shot-gunning syllabic nonsense. The only part I remember was Exec X's take on our protagonist -- "It's like Ché Guevara. He was sexy, he was hot, did a couple of cool killings. Perfect, right?"

Talk about mind-fucks. No class struggle, no six-hundred-year-old legend.

Their brainstorm was to take the Robin Hood out of <u>Robin Hood</u>.

Meeting over, we shook hands with the nauseous smiles of strangers who'd eaten the same rotten shellfish. I grabbed my '66 Bug -- the same car I'd driven out to L.A. years earlier -- and puttered straight up Wilshire to my agent Marty's office.

When I walked in, I just *unloaded.* Play by play, line by line, detailing the nuclear winter I'd just lived through. From Marty's expression, I could see he was having trouble grasping it all. He knew my background, knew the man I was, but still. After I'd slaked my desperate need to rant, I punctuated it with this little gem --

"They can keep the money," I said. "I don't want it."

In Marty's entire life, I don't think a single client had ever told him that. And why would they? Idealism and moral outrage are the privilege of a rarified few. In this Biz, at the grunt level, those concepts played worse than kiddie porn. Besides, who the fuck was I? Claude Rains in <u>Casablanca</u>? "I'm shocked, shocked to find that half-baked racism is going on here!" It's not like I'd signed up for the Peace Corps or anything.

Still, I had my principles, and I was willing to put all that Monopoly money where my naive cakehole was.

Marty's advice was to go home, cool my tool and let him do some reconnaissance. Once he'd sussed everything out, he'd get back to me.

Two things bailed me out. First, the exec I knew called Marty and totally vouched for my eyewitness testimony (told you he was a good guy). Second, Exec X himself realized he'd fucked up and called to try and smooth things over. "Listen, Marty," he told my rep, "Nobody over here wants to make an... *irresponsible* movie."

A second meeting was scheduled to try and salvage things, but in many ways it was worse than the first. My time was spent daydreaming about grabbing Exec X and going Sharky's Machine -- pile-driving us through the plate glass and plummeting 200 feet into the crushing calm of warm pavement below.

So that was that -- the deal died. They paid for the treatment, and I -- insisting on principle -- left the other $65,000 sitting on the table. SIXTY FIVE THOUSAND DOLLARS. Just walked away from it. The real world cost of maintaining some integrity.

You may be wondering -- what about the Famous Director, the one guy who surely would've had your back? Predictably, after that first, glorious Hollywood dry-humping, I neither saw nor heard from him again. No phone call. No email. Nothing. To this day, I don't know if *he* actually hated it, or his illegal nanny D-Girl had cut my throat without him getting the real scoop on any of what went down.

And Exec X? Was there any Bad Karma due a producer like that? Would the bold heavens take a stand and angrily smite down what the film industry itself would not?

You're fucking kidding, right? This is the Film Biz.

Years later, I was on autopilot at some friends' place watching a minor awards show. About five hours in, after two dozen self-aggrandizing ass-kissers had hammed it up for the cameras, they finally got around to Movie of the Year.

And who should win but Exec X -- now a full-fledged Producer. Producer X.

This go 'round I *did* crap my pants. Openly and without restraint. But this wasn't even rock bottom. Because his acceptance speech came next --

"I'm soooooo happy you've taken my movie into your hearts, this wonderful little film about racial harmony, the end of prejudice of all kinds, and, of course, hope. Always hope, for those people less fortunate than ourselves."

Producer X had just won a second-tier Indy Movie of the Year award. By playing the race card. In *their* favor. Before he even left the stage, I was stumbling into the backyard, begging a frenzied bong hit. A man can only take so much, and my mind was dangerously close to snapping, the only hope of retaining my sanity a bright, protective sheen of cannabis.

As I slipped into a numbing, stony oblivion, a single thought ran roughshod through my head --

"I wonder if Producer X's illegal maid is back at his house watching this, too?

THE PROCESS

Writing a feature isn't a sprint, it's a fuckin' marathon...
with you cast as a sweat-drenched suburban runner,
gasping for air as fresh diarrhea streams freely down
your legs.

Once you get past the early fun/cool/awesome scenes
you've had swirling around your head forever, there's a
long, *long* stretch of straight-up WRITING still to be
done. Tough, thankless, challenging grunt work that
doesn't exactly start most writers jumping for joy.

If you're lucky, along the way you'll discover a mess of
scenes that become a blast to write. That's the good
news. Bad news is that the plain majority of your beats
will seem to turn on you like drug-addled ex-wives;
digging in and requiring back-breaking labor to finally
finish them off and drive a stake through their hearts
(Marriage issues? Me? Ya think?).

Take scenes such as two characters sitting at a table
across from each other. William Goldman has long
claimed these are the hardest scenes of all to write. Dr.
Goldman, I concur completely. On the surface, they
seem as simple and straight forward as can be, only to
metastasize into a wordless desert without landmarks
the moment you put them under the lamp.

This is but one of the many land mines populating a
writer's day. Minute to minute, slug line to slug line,
there are an infinite number of story choices to be
made, plot threads to explore -- each backed by the
treacherous possibility of self-immolation should you
select unwisely.

When it comes to process, every writer is different, and all I can address here is what I've found works for me. Make use of as much or as little as you want from what follows. Mix and match, experiment, keep the good fits, discard those that don't.

Henry Miller on Writing --

Henry Miller wrote an essential book on writing called (wait for it) *Henry Miller on Writing*. A Kindle edition has finally made its way into the eBook universe and yes, purchase a copy right away (http://www.amazon.com/Henry-Miller-Writing-Directions-Paperbook-ebook/dp/B00LHHFG9A)

Included in Miller's massive treasure trove of invaluable advice are his "Eleven Commandments" for writing. Cooked up while working on the über classic *Tropic of Cancer*, Miller devised this game plan to help keep his writing moving forward with maximum focus and efficiency.

Henry Miller's Eleven Commandments

1. Work on one thing at a time until finished.

2. Start no more new books, add no more new material to "Black Spring.

3. Don't be nervous. Work calmly, joyously, recklessly on whatever is in hand.

4. Work according to Program and not according to mood. Stop at the appointed time!

5. When you can't create you can work.

6. Cement a little every day, rather than add new fertilizers.

7. Keep human! See people, go places, drink if you feel like it.

8. Don't be a draught-horse! Work with pleasure only.

9. Discard the Program when you feel like it—but go back to it next day. Concentrate. Narrow down. Exclude.

10. Forget the books you want to write. Think only of the book you are writing.

11. Write first and always. Painting, music, friends, cinema, all these come afterwards.

What's simply amazing is that Miller's rules still work like a charm over eighty-plus years later. More proof that technology comes and goes, but the core work of writing remains the same.

At first glance, many of these commandments may seem somewhat self-evident -- but when you attempt to put them into practice, day after day, project after project, year after year, that's when you'll begin understanding the brilliant depth of Miller's advice.

These points provide a great launching pad to begin discussion of the process, so let me speak to a couple of them very specifically in terms of my own screenwriting experience to kick things off --

1. Work on one thing at a time until finished.

This is critical. If you divide your energies between projects (several different scripts, etc.) you'll kill any

<u>momentum</u> you're building on the script that's front and center. **Writing is momentum**. Without it, you're as dead as <u>John Carter of Mars II</u>. It's hard enough to face the computer every day as it is, cheating yourself out of a running start at it is downright criminal -- and absurdly counter-productive. You are <u>not</u> getting twice as much done, you getting *half as much*.

3. Don't be nervous. Work calmly, joyously, recklessly on whatever is in hand.

I believe this is an *awesome* attitude to have. Unfortunately, I've never been able to approach screenwriting from this perspective myself. For me, it's mostly war all the time; choosing instead to engage in mortal combat with whatever I'm working on. Believe me, I'm definitely <u>not</u> bragging here, and I certainly don't recommend this approach to others.

But that's only Bad Habit #1. My second all-time shittiest, self-defeating habit is beating myself to a psychological pulp on projects, pile-driving my confidence into the ground and talking myself down during tougher days.

Think Hannibal Lecter in <u>Silence</u> mind-fucking Miggs until he swallows his own tongue. Yeah, unfortunately, that's pretty much how I came stock from the factory. The ol' Jerry West/Fear of Failure psych profile from Day One. You think this book can be brutal? Imagine the searing internal monologue unspooling inside my own noggin whenever I'm on a job. (Then again, don't.)

Lord knows, I'm not the only screenwriter on Planet Earth this neurotic. But in the name of all things Holy, Dear Reader, do whatever it takes not to senselessly beat yourself up like this.

Proven fact -- being a ruthless bastard to yourself doesn't produce better results. I'm here to testify to that. This is not a strength, it's a weakness. It doesn't make you a "stronger" or "more dedicated" writer. There is no moral high ground to be seized here. If anything, it's the exact opposite; hampering your progress instead of motivating you to reach higher highs.

Making yourself more nervous and trashing yourself more than necessary can seriously fuck up your writing, kill your self-confidence and keep you from accessing those deeper, hallowed stages of creativity -- those joyous times when you suddenly find yourself "in the zone" or "totally in the pocket", as if channeling some divine Hindu energy force directly onto the page (What? You haven't felt that yet? WTF?).

Yes -- sometimes you have to dig the spurs in, kick yourself in the twat and get fuckin' fired up again. *Every writer* needs a wake up call now and then. But it's sometimes the sugar, sometimes the whip, and as the old saying goes -- "*Pressure is the enemy of art.*" Few things have I found of greater truth than this.

Many of your strongest ideas will come when you have the clearest mind. Lean on whatever tricks, methods or mind games help you create clean headspace. Breathing exercises. Yoga. Meditation. Going to the gym. Talking a long walk or bike ride. Take it a step further and ask friends and fellow writers what works best for them, get a feel for the different approaches through trial and error. And no, stony readers with "bad backs" and "glaucoma", this is not greenlighting a visit to the local pot clinic every time you "fire up" your script.

Try to bring Henry Miller's calm, joyous, reckless energy to the process as often and as much as you can. If nothing else, remind yourself that no matter *what* you're struggling with, it actually isn't as bad as it might seem in the moment. There's nothing that can't be improved with a fresh head during a later pass, no matter how terrible you believe your starting point.

4. Work according to Program and not according to mood. Stop at the appointed time!

This is a huge note for me personally because it addresses the much-needed discipline and routine writers like myself require to get going. Hell, I don't want to face the white elephant every goddamned day, and I suppose that's true for a vast segment of writers out there. There's a lot riding on getting in that chair every morning, it's a shit-ton of pressure and one helluva lot of <u>work</u>. Who *wouldn't* rather grab some Korean BBQ or go ass-surfing at Venice Beach?

From my first, remedial attempts at screenwriting, I've always needed a "routine" to help force me to get down to business. This involves sitting down to write at approx. the same time, hopefully at the same location (office, coffee shop, kitchen table, etc.), every day I work. Why the same location? Because it helps me establish what Joseph Campbell calls a "sacred space" -- a space specifically set aside for your work and the creative inner journey you plan to undertake there --

> *"This is an absolute necessity for anybody today. You must have a room, or a certain hour or so a day, where you don't know what was in the newspapers that morning... This is a place where you can simply experience and bring forth what you are and what you might be. This is the place of creative incubation. At first you may find that nothing is happening there. But if you have a sacred place, and use it, and take advantage of it, something will happen. ...*

Most of our action is economically or socially determined and does not come out of our life... the claims of the environment upon you are so great, that you hardly know where the hell you are! What is it you intended? You're always doing things that are required of you; this minute, that minute, another minute! Where is your "bliss station"?" Try to find it! Put on the music that you really love... or the book you want to read. Get it done! And have a place in which to do it! There you'll get the "thou" feeling of life."

-- Joseph Campbell, <u>The Power of Myth; Sacrifice and Bliss</u>

Of course, facing the temptation of the Net every second makes maintaining any "bliss stations" pretty hard. Regardless, we have to make a point of shuttering away all the on-going distractions or we won't get legitimate work done.

I've also found that going to this same sacred space on a regular schedule establishes the tone for myself <u>psychologically</u>. My long-time office was literally cinder block walls with no phone, no Internet and one taped-over window so I couldn't see outside. Yeah, it pretty much sucked in there -- which is precisely how I wanted it. Being double-booked with studio jobs, I knew San Quentin-style solitary would provide the level of focus I needed to get my work done.

Basically, only one reason existed to go to that office -- to write. During the short drive over, I'd put on my game face, get my mind right about the day's work ahead and review what I hoped to accomplish in the hours allotted for that particular day's writing. By the time I parked, climbed three flights to my office and hit the desk, I was laser-focused, jacked up and raring to go.

Think of it like putting on a baseball uniform, grabbing your mitt and running the tunnel from the locker room out to the diamond -- there is absolutely <u>no other reason</u> to be at this ballpark other than playing baseball. You wouldn't be surfing the Net or checking out Pinterest while starting in the World Series, would you? Exact same deal... only writers don't get monster MLB paychecks and our process isn't remotely that glamorous.

Perhaps my approach sounds too Spartan for you? Not surprising. Frankly, I'd be worried if everyone had the same take. All that's really important is that you come up with <u>your own version</u> of creating a "sacred space" and stick to it. The specifics of location, ritual, time of day, etc. can all be seasoned to taste. The big thing is that you sincerely commit to creating a work zone and accomplishing your goals within it.

Which brings us to the second part of Henry's Commandment #4 -- <u>stopping</u>.

Knowing when to stop is hugely important. A la Clint Eastwood in <u>The Enforcer</u> -- "A man's got to know his limitations." This has never been more true than when writing. Having a stopping point keeps you honest. It keeps you focused on how much time there is left to work, which helps you adjust your pace/tempo accordingly. If you're moving too slowly, the clock will make that clear to you. By saying something as simple as, "I'm going to stop at 5:00" you help maximize your own precious effort beginning at the start of each new day.

More importantly, STOPPING keeps you from plowing past the point of legitimate productivity. Sure, you can work for ten hours instead of five -- and sometimes you simply *have to* -- but you're fuckin' kidding yourself if you think those extra five hours are going to be as productive as the first five.

For starters, all you accomplish by going long and exhausting yourself one day is siphoning away some of the fresh creative energy you're going to need the very *next* day.

You're a boxer. Start of the fight, you press hard, thinking you've got a chance to knock your opponent out. But you don't knock 'em out. You're not fighting the type of fighter that gets knocked out. So all you've done by pushing too hard in the first round is ensure you'll be punched out, busted up and flat on your back by the fifth or sixth.

Writing a script goes all twelve rounds, every single time. Screenwriting is a brick-by-brick prospect -- if you don't pace yourself, *you'll* be the one on the canvas, confidence cooked, energy spent, unable to continue. You'll have endangered your own <u>momentum</u> -- the most vital energetic component of the process.

Push for the K.O. on Tuesday, you're too burnt to write well on Wednesday. *How in the Hell can that be a winning strategy?*

Digging this hole deeper still, I've found that I <u>lose my objectivity</u> about what's good or not good after I've pushed past my prime working hours. There's a very definite vanishing point where you get burned-out, wasted, fried, outright silly and punch-drunk sometimes. And as you sludge onward, you kinda start feeling like maybe what you're doing is actually working. And you know, what? Once in a unicorn's ass, it might be. But ninety-plus percent of the time you're the Looney Toons guy marooned on a desert island with Bugs Bunny -- so starved and heat-stroked that every

193

time you look over at that damned rabbit you're seeing a savory drumstick standing in his place.

In my experience, these pages often reveal themselves as fool's gold. Often whatever work came out of my forced march will have to be re-evaluated for quality control, much of it reworked or even discarded altogether. Cranking out ten shitty pages not only hasn't helped, it's actually *cost me* twice as much effort -- the hours pushing through the first time, then the hours spent to patch them up later on.

There are always exceptions, of course, professional circumstances when you have no choice but to keep writing whether you're feeling 100% creatively or not. Sometimes you simply have to suck it up, soldier on and fix things on the fly best you can. Alas, this is a big dynamic of both the film business and the paid screenwriter's journey. In any case, coping with such high-class problems is something every writer should look forward to someday.

End of the day, page count means nothing. Every good writer understands it's all about the quality of however many pages you produce, not quantity. William Goldman estimated that walking away with three good pages meant he'd done a great day's work. This is a guy with Oscars (plural), who's written some of the world's all-time best movies. If he's not measuring himself by page count, why should you?

5. When you can't create you can work.

Some days, you just aren't feeling it. You struggle to get it up and there's simply no good wood to be had. It happens, even to female writers. But there's still plenty of essential work to do beyond just inking in new pages.

Great place to start? Reviewing your beat sheet --
brainstorming over the scenes you've notecarded but
not yet written.

Put the whole circus under the microscope in search of
something to improve or dramatically heighten. What
you've got may already be good -- but what the hell,
test-drive making it better just for kicks. One big
advantage to having a rock solid beat sheet beneath you
is that it makes experimenting with outside the box
ideas risk-free. If you push too far and start getting
wacky, simply circle back to H.Q. Every once in while,
just by getting loose and playing with things this way,
you'll find yourself stumbling onto the truly inspired.

It's not uncommon to find story or character points
feeling too rushed, or to discover things you *assumed*
were built-in actually MIA from your beats altogether.
Sometimes the lightbulb pops on and suddenly you see
how rearranging certain scenes can triple their impact.
This is the ideal time to get a handle on all this, perfect
the best version of your project, so free up your mind
and have a blast sussing out the many options.

On the flipside, there's also looking to <u>cut</u> whatever's
extraneous to the story and certain to be dumped later
on anyway -- no matter how much you may have fallen
in love with it.

Also try thinking your characters through on other
levels, giving them deeper subtexts, working up
idiosyncratic touches that make them more vivid and
intriguing. You always want characters to feel 3-D, and
giving them interesting, identifiable ticks and habits,
etc. can really help draw a reader in.

Think Clooney's Zippo in <u>Out of Sight</u> -- he only does
lighter tricks when nervous. Jon Voight as Joe Buck in

<u>Midnight Cowboy</u> -- wearing that sad, boyish cowboy outfit in the unforgiving heart of Times Square, perfectly underscoring his naïveté and displacement. Kurt Russell in <u>The Thing</u> as McCready -- getting beaten at computer chess then pouring Scotch into the hard drive, ruining it; making clear he's a man who refuses to lose no matter what. And one of my all-time favorites, William Hurt in <u>Body Heat</u> -- jogging the full length of that beach, then stopping to light a cigarette -- a loveable loser, best of intentions, but who can never quite follow through and do what's best for him.

(That's right, Smartphone Spawn, if you haven't seen these classics, rent or DL now. It'll help your writing way more than <u>Spring Breakers</u> or some godforsaken Katy Perry "documentary".)

Last, but not least, there's also reading and proofing the pages you written so far, which we'll talk about in more detail shortly.

6. <u>Cement a little every day, rather than add new fertilizers</u>.

Back to brick-by-brick mode here. Do the small, steady work that a project requires, as tedious as it may be, rather than go all flashy and try to reinvent the wheel while inking in a properly plotted draft. The thirst for excitement can cause a writer to do terrible, terrible things. Slow and steady always wins this race, as agonizingly incremental as it may seem at times.

7. <u>Keep human! See people, go places, drink if you feel like it</u>.

This has been one of my biggest problems throughout my career -- physically and spiritually lone-wolfing it, going underground, hiding out, "hitting the mattresses", immersing myself so deeply in the self-imposed pressure of getting shit done that I become an epic douchebag to those around me, especially (but not limited to) my girlfriend and anybody else still within my immediate blast radius.

Taking a break, unplugging, leaving the house, having some fun, etc. does help, big time. I dare say it's even essential if you don't want to go completely bat-shit and wind up with no friends on the flip side of finishing your draft. So once your allotted work hours are done -- don't feel guilty about checking out and doing something fun. (Operative concept being -- "once your allotted work hours are done".) Believe me, your draft will still be sitting there waiting to do battle with you tomorrow, regardless. By blowing off some after-hours steam, you may actually be *energizing* yourself for that next go 'round.

8. <u>Don't be a draught-horse! Work with pleasure only</u>.

Yours Truly has been a draught-horse all his life, so I'm clearly the wrong guy to lecture about this one. I rarely work with pleasure, even when I know I'm generating good pages. I also tend to go straight for a script's throat. Once I've notecarded the project out, it takes me approximately eight weeks to write a first draft. This is the short end of the standard contractual length a writer gets to submit their work to their employers -- eight to twelve weeks.

But I'm also going after it *every day* -- four to six hours a day, six days a week. Many of you haven't broken through yet and have real jobs, making that impossible to do. So the real trick is <u>making time</u> to write on a regular basis, and try and enjoy it at the same time. **And let me stress this -- you don't "find" time, fellas, you**

make it. Sit around waiting to find the time, you and your precious screenplay are going to be some unfinished, gray haired motherfuckers.

The young Lawrence Kasdan, writer of <u>The Empire Strikes Back</u>, <u>The Big Chill</u> and <u>Body Heat</u>, offers us a fantastic real-life example of doing what it takes to get it done despite having adult responsibilities to deal with. The famous story I've always heard was that Mr. Kasdan worked a serious day job in Advertising. God knows, that type of work alone will suck the creative energy out of anybody. I worked a paralegal job on Wall Street fresh out of school, and my total number of pages written during that gig were <u>zero</u>. Yet despite this, Mr. Kasdan promised himself to write a couple hours each night no matter what. Following dinner, after the kids had been dealt with and before he needed to sleep to be fresh for the next day, Mr. Kasdan <u>made time</u> to work on his scripts. Was this ideal? No. Did he make it work? Fuckin' A right he did. Three decades, <u>seventeen</u> produced writing credits and a ton of hit films later, it's pretty obvious that his sacrifice was well worth it.

How much of this is urban legend? Don't know, don't care. The message remains the same. If you can't commit to screenwriting -- often at a level of financial and energetic discomfort completely alien to the average American taxpayer -- how the hell can you expect to reap any of its rewards? The ol' "you get out of it what you put into it" dynamic.

Did Larry Kasdan refuse to be a draught-horse and "work with pleasure only"? I don't have the slightest idea. Maybe you can ask him yourself when you meet peer-to-peer as a successful screenwriter in your own right someday?

10. Forget the books you want to write. Think only of the book you are writing.

Substitute the word "scripts" here for "books" and it's still a perfect fit. When you get neck deep into a screenplay, say forty, fifty pages in, even with a script you've been *dying* to write for an eternity, you kinda hit the wall for the first time. You realize you're in deep water now, no doubt about it, with no life vests in sight.

Even worse? Being forty/fifty/sixty pages is the worst possible place to be -- *you're essentially halfway to nowhere*. You've already done a ton of work to get as far as you have, yet half a script doesn't count for a fuckin' thing. Further, you've got another sixty, seventy pages to go before it will count, which by now feels like its going to take at least five times as long as those first sixty did.

This is where your mind can drift, and you start thinking of all the other super cool movie ideas you have that would be WAY more fun to write. You may even spend valuable time noodling on those ideas rather than sticking to the program to finish the grueling fucker you're slaving away on now...

...And that's exactly what Henry Miller is telling you not to do.

These other super cool movie ideas are a mirage, my friends, and you will totally rat fuck yourself by seeking their shelter out of your current sense of despair. Believe me, they will not be any "easier to write" -- all marathons are the same length. In fact, many may have a host of monstrous logic holes you haven't scratched the surface of yet, completely preoccupied as you are with the cool scenes you're going to slam dunk, what the one-sheet might look like, who you'll get to play the lead and all the folks you definitely need to thank during your Cannes, Golden Globes or MTV Movie Awards speech.

<u>Get back to work on what's in hand</u>. That's really the best advice I can give you.

Or as Tom Berenger so cheerfully says as Sgt. Barnes in <u>Platoon</u> -- "Take... the... pain."

11. <u>Write first and always. Painting, music, friends, cinema, all these come afterwards</u>.

Another note to procrastination -- Do your four/five hours before you allow yourself to do anything "fun"... even surf the Net or deal with your email. If you go fun first, it's absurdly easy for your will to wane, and all that great momentum swinging your way to begin slipping through your fingers. Plus -- working *after* fun will never be as good or productive as seriously committing and doing the thankless grunt work of writing first.

* * * * *

Here are some additional "tricks of the trade" I've been guinea-pigging for two decades now. Again, compare and contrast, season to taste, use whatever works for you and forget whatever doesn't.

<u>Punching In</u>

If I've had a single stroke of legitimate genius in my twenty-plus years of screenwriting it was this --

Start keeping a time card.

Check out the big brain on me, right? Keepin' it way old-school -- straight out of the 18th Century.

I created a Word Doc called (wait for it) "Time Card", and whenever I sit down to begin writing I type in the Date and my Start Time. Whenever I break for lunch (or any other extended and/or unexpected absence), I put down however long that took. Lastly, after a hard day's work, usually distraught and balled up in the fetal position, I enter my Finishing Time.

Tallying it up is simple math. Total hours spent - break time = *actual hours worked* on any given day. As a sweet bonus to myself, I also leave a comment about the *quality* of my work in the margin. Something to the tune of "*Great Day*", "*You're the Boss!*" or, conversely (and much more common), "*That sucked ass*", "*You totally shit the bed*" or "*Quit pretending and get a real job*".

Essentially, my time cards look like this (based on a real project!) --

John Jarrell -- *Project Name* -- Time Card

9/1/14 - 10:50am to 2:30pm
3:30pm to 5:30pm
8:30pm to 9:00pm

(5 -- Welcome Back to the Rodeo)

9/2/14 - 12:40pm to 3:10pm
3:40pm to 6:30pm

(5.5 -- Who am I? WTF?)

9/3/14 - 11:45am to 2:30pm
3:30pm to 5:30pm

(4.5 -- Mama told me there'd be shitty days like these)

9/4/14 - 2:00pm to 6:00pm

(4 -- Late Start/Real Life)

9/5/14 - 5:00pm to 9:00pm (4)

9/6/14 - 12:00pm to 6:00pm

(5.5 -- First Good Day...)

9/7/14 - 1:00pm to 5:30pm

(4.5 -- Another Good One)

9/8/14 - 12:00pm to 2:30pm
3:30pm to 6:30pm

(5 -- Pick up friend at LAX)

9/9/14 - Day Off

(0 -- Pitch at Warners)

9/10/14 - 1:00pm to 3:00pm
4:00pm to 5:00pm

(3 -- Whatever)

9/11/14 - 1:00pm to 4:25pm
9:00pm to 11:00pm

(5 -- Should have done more)

9/12/14 - 12:00pm to 2:00pm
3:00pm to 6:30pm

(5 -- Friends stop by, but still killed it!)

9/12/14 - Day Off

        (0 -- Sunday/Brunch/Fun)

9/13/14 - 3:00pm to 6:00pm
        8:30pm to 11:15pm

        (5 -- Meeting/Late Start)

9/14/14 - 12:30pm to 2:30pm
        Lunchtime Proofing

        (3 -- Real-life intrudes)

9/15/14 - 12:00pm to 2:00pm
        Print out thru p.31

        (2 -- Clusterfuck of calls kill
        progress)

9/16/14 - 12:26pm to 4:21pm

        (5 -- Indefinably grueling.
        Got in a few late...)

Okay, so why have I found this such an amazing innovation in my writing life?

Because the time card never lies.

<u>Committing to keeping a time card forces me to be one-hundred percent honest with myself</u>. About my writing. About how real my effort is. About how real *I* am.

When you're responsible for entering your own hours -- or lack there of -- there's nobody else to blame or bitch to if you don't like what you see. Visually, zeroes and low totals reinforce the stark truth that getting this script done is squarely on you, and that presently you're not making that happen.

Whenever I notice a run of recent days where I'm sucking wind, being a pussy and only putting in two or three lightweight hours per, I get downright ruthless with myself. After twenty years, I've elevated self-flagellation to performance art; nobody alive can make me feel shittier about my failures as a human being than, well, me. I'll let the guilt and despair and disappointment simmer for a while, then come down *hard*; cutting loose an avalanche of the purest self-loathing to bury my inner-lazy bastard.

Self-love has clearly never been my strong suit. I'm an obsessive-compulsive tight-ass and beating myself to a pulp is just how I like to roll -- in fact, I'd be lost without using it as my primary motivator. Undeniably, I'm one of those Jerry West/Fear of Failure guys; all whip, no sugar, no fun allowed. But I certainly do NOT recommend this approach to other writers. I can't stress this enough. The emotional and energetic costs are astronomically high, and if I could do it all over again, knowing what I know now, I would definitely seek out a far more balanced approach.

However *you* ultimately chose to deal with your own lack of effort and imagination is strictly your business -- just be sure to find methods that actually do motivate you when your spirit and resolve dips to its weakest. A writer's recurring "crisis of faith" is an entirely normal and expected part of the writing process.

Time cards can either reassure you, giving you a nice boost when you're totally kicking ass, or they can crucify you, offering fair warning that shit needs to be dialed up, pronto, if you want to succeed. Throughout my time in Hollywood, I've found there's simply no substitute for having the exact amount of energy you're expending down in cold black and white. Whenever I assess a written-in-stone accounting of what I'm *not* contributing, it paves the way for those "Come to Jesus" pep talks all of us need once in a while to get refocused and back on track.

Right now, perhaps the time card of it all doesn't seem like that big a deal, and I fully understand that it may not work for everybody. That said, *give it a shot and try it yourself next project.* There's always the possibility that, like with Yours Truly here, this one tool can help maximize your productivity big time.

<u>Writing Days and Editing Days</u>

Sometimes you simply need to break stuff up, get a breath of fresh air, take a time-out from the grind of pure creation. One way to do this -- and still keep making progress -- is to have an **Editing Day** after every major section of pages.

The idea is that on Editing Day you don't do <u>any</u> writing or create any new pages. Instead, you print out and read over whatever you've created so far; proofing, marking scenes up and looking for potential edits/changes/improvements you might want to make. This is obviously a valuable part of the process while still working on your script because it gives you an overall sense of how things are tracking and flowing, tonal or character adjustments you discover you need to make, etc.

Basically, editing days keep you marching forward while giving you a break from the actual bricklaying and hard fucking work of writing.

205

I take editing days at the logical junctures -- first ten pages (hook), the first thirty (First Act), then intermittently throughout -- probably the Midpoint around p. 55 or 60, definitely end of Second Act, and then I'll read the Third Act as a stand-alone thirty pages as well. This seems to be the right amount for me -- too much editing can fuck up good pages, too little can leave you without an accurate understanding of what's working and what's not.

While we're on the subject of editing, here's an epic no-no for <u>anyone</u> <u>and</u> <u>everyone</u> writing a screenplay, veteran and newbie alike. Perhaps the most important piece of advice offered in this entire book --

<u>Never</u> edit the fresh pages you've written the <u>same</u> <u>day</u> you write them.

Repeat -- <u>Never,</u> <u>ever</u> do this. Give these newborns at least two days *minimum* before going over them again -- in fact, a full week is a thousand times better.

Here's why -- **when you edit the same day you write, you end up cutting/hating on/killing off a ton of material that was actually pretty good upon later, rested, clear-eyed reflection**. You're too close, my friends, you can't see forest through the proverbial trees, and your exhaustion and frustration with what you've inked in -- which NEVER appears to be good enough vs. what you'd originally intended -- will psych you out and black-cloud what's left of your mind.

How do I know? From vast, sprawling, tragicomic experience. Done this silly shit to myself a million times. Using that final, deflating hour of a brutal day's work to hack up pages that are actually pretty decent, repeatedly tweak and fuss over lines of dialogue until they're nothing but mush, and damn-near every other bone-headed thing a writer can do last minute to destroy their own project. It's tantamount to blowing off your own foot with a .357 because your sock's bugging you.

Don't do it. Put the gun down. Forty-eight hour waiting period *at least*. Trust me, you'll thank me for saving a lot of innocent, workable pages from the slaughterhouse.

What's that old playground saying? "He who turns and runs away lives to fight another day?" Yeah, that.

Trouble With Certain Scenes or Sequences

Additionally, you may work on a scene for several hours and still feel like it sucks ass. Hell, maybe it <u>does</u> suck ass. But after a certain amount of time/expenditure of energy the way to crack it is simply to <u>put it down</u>. That's right, put the gun down and walk the fuck away.

I had one incredibly complicated sequence during an assignment Regency had hired me for back in the day. The major problem was there was a shit-ton of information to get out to sell the concept, and it was all coming out as expository dialogue -- which is the last thing you want. Movies are <u>visual</u> -- don't tell me, show me -- and when you have one or maybe two characters just standing there blabbing on and on and on about whatever the fuck, it just KILLS a script, it sits like fucking lead on the page. Even while writing it, you can already see the reader's eyes glazing over when he sees those long, thick, black rows of dialogue.

This was crushing me. How the fuck am I going to make this scene work? I literally came back at that scene <u>seven</u> consecutive days. So remember, that's seven days I'm not generating any other <u>new pages</u> either.

I've brought my own forward momentum to a dead halt -- all to try and conquer this one fucking sequence. To strongarm it into oblivion.

Of course, I'm the one who got bulldozed. The scene got the better of me, not the other way around.

Finally, I decided to put it away and concentrate on a few subsequent scenes I knew would be somewhat "easier" relatively -- nothing's ever truly easy, of course -- allowing me to get my groove back. It worked and I did.

Then a week later I took another look at the sequence and what needed to be done leapt straight out at me. All it had taken was a fresh perspective. **Hey, it may take revisiting something several times over several weeks or even months**. But that really doesn't matter, does it? Continue onward with the project and come back to it whenever it feels right. That way you can hold onto your groove and not come to a dead-stop.

Editing In General

One of the hardest things is letting go of what you've written -- spent so much time and agony writing constructing piece by piece, word by word -- to begin revising it and making it better. You see it locked in, written in stone, so to speak. To be really good, you have to see what you've written as a good jumping off point... because most every scene can be improved applying a different perspective or point of view.

Like many screenwriters, I'll write a rough or first draft "long" -- meaning I'm overwriting description, adding extra thoughts and flourishes, etc. during my first pass, knowing full well I'll need to weed-whack the shit out of 'em next time around. The thinking is to stay focused

208

on getting down any cool lines or ideas you're generating while in the pocket on a scene. Channel the potential of all that tasty stuff onto the page, collect the very best of it, then you'll have a ton of options when you return to shorten and reshape it. Go big, then pull back. Having too many good ideas to sort through is a high-class problem, and far preferable to not having enough, or worse, having discarded some real winners you didn't recognize at first blush.

Next pass, days or sometimes weeks later, I'll begin refining this material and paring it down. Say I've written a pretty cool character description but it's four complete sentences -- way too long. To get her down to proper one or two-sentence fighting weight, I start mashing-up all my contenders, toying them back and forth, cut and paste, in search of the perfect combination. Sometimes I even end up combining half of one line with half of another; whatever it takes to construct the most powerful description. <u>Ideally, whatever you land on carries maximum impact, saying the most about who the character is the shortest possible length of time</u>. Essentially, this is the goal of any scene, character or description -- brevity and precision. You tend to know when you've hit paydirt because it just sounds and feels *right*. This is where a writer's instincts kick in, bringing us back to Tony Gilroy's killer Chester Conklin description -- "Ivy League Oliver North. Buttoned down. Square jaw." Doesn't get much better than that.

What I'm saying here is to "kill your darlings" -- just don't kill them too quickly. Give them a chance to breathe first, then return and max out their potential with fresh eyes and ruthless, judicious editing.

Voice Over Sucks

I thoroughly discourage my students from using voice-over (a.k.a. V.O.) in their projects. There are a couple excellent reasons for this.

General rule of thumb, V.O. in modern features is a dead giveaway there's bad storytelling ahead. The age-old film-writing commandment **"Show me don't tell me"** goes straight to the heart of this. <u>Voice over is largely a cheat, a crutch, a painful admission of defeat by writers and/or filmmakers that they don't have the skill necessary to tell their stories without holding the audiences' hand and talking them through everything play-by-play</u>. By spelling everything out in the most ham-fisted way possible -- literally <u>telling you</u> what they want you to think or know or feel -- the movie's authors become mouth-breathing strangers in the multiplex, anxious chatterboxes who won't shut the fuck up, living in rightful fear of their images failing to sell the story as hoped.

Legit *Film Noir* of the '40's and '50's offers one of the few historical exceptions. This genre elevated V.O. to stylistic high-art, giving audiences a sneak peek into the reeling psyches of taciturn post-WWII tough guys loath to say much about their feelings *at all*. *Noir*-era voice over allowed viewers to bear witness to the existential struggles and complex psyches of these troubled characters *from the inside*. It helped audiences navigate these largely unsympathetic protagonists' waking nightmares alongside them, hell, as one of them, bringing empathy and a sharper understanding to the myriad of moral dilemmas confronting these chiaroscuro loners.

Just as importantly, <u>this device was used to enhance and deepen the film's text</u> -- not simply explain away plot gaffes, excuse thin character development or make ridiculous and implausible events sound somewhat less ridiculous and implausible. V.O. didn't serve *Film Noir* as a crutch, it became a fascinating key component, a sublime accoutrement, if you will, of the story itself. Wikipedia calls this era "The Golden Age of First Person Narration". I couldn't have defined it any better myself.

Obviously, there are some brilliant modern exceptions to V.O. as disingenuous cheat -- <u>Taxi Driver</u>'s Travis Bickle, <u>The Usual Suspects</u>' Verbal Kint, Jack Manfred's aspiring novelist in <u>The Croupier</u>, among select others spring to mind; all residing within the one one-thousandth of the top one percent ever to utilize the device.

Unfortunately -- and I'm being extremely polite here -- the lion's share of today's cinematic voice overs sag woefully shy of such lofty storytelling. During the contemporary/post-iPod era V.O. is primarily used as narrative caulking to disguise, patch and explain away substandard material which most likely shouldn't have been put into production given its present state.

Being a younger/aspiring writer the odds are pretty good you haven't quite reached the <u>Taxi Driver</u>/<u>The Usual Suspects</u> level yet. With twenty-plus years and a bunch of big league scalps under my belt, *I'm* still not at that level and have zero issues coming correct and owning it. Writing true God-tier V.O. is hard fuckin' work and not every writer will master the skill despite the best of intentions.

More deeply, reliance on V.O. can seriously stunt a writer's storytelling growth. <u>Forcing yourself</u> to come up with interesting ways of telling your tale visually and through fresh action is ultimately what will make you good at it. Think logically -- is there *any* skill out there you can truly master without practice? When a Mr. Olympia contestant wants to build muscle mass, what does he do? (No, I mean *after* the anabolics, blood doping and creatine shakes.) Very good, my fair-haired friends -- big-assed homeboy hits the gym. So how does your skinny ass expect to build the monstrous screenwriting biceps, quads and delts needed to compete if you won't do the heavy lifting your discipline requires?

Don't think V.O. fools anyone. It doesn't. Quality execs filter the shit out to see if your story holds water without it. And God Forbid your scripted V.O. isn't spectacularly compelling, because if it drags or reads awkwardly, it could risk hogging the spotlight, becoming the very focus of things, and working *against* you by killing what otherwise might have been a pretty kick-ass script.

Once again, repeat after me -- "Show me, don't tell me." If there's a better general guide to keeping your script's storytelling on point and in check, I haven't come across it. Remember -- you're not writing a podcast, radio skit or Off Broadway show. Motion picture is the most spectacular visual medium that's ever existed, the screenplays accompanying them the most precise visual writing ever practiced. Your script needs to reflect those dynamics at all times.

Heard the old chestnut "a picture's worth a thousand words"? If somehow you missed that one, let me bring you up to speed --

Once more, from Wikipedia -- "*A picture is worth a thousand words*" *refers to the notion that a complex idea can be conveyed with just a single still image. It also*

212

aptly characterizes one of the main goals of visualization, namely making it possible to absorb large amounts of data quickly."

That's precisely what movies themselves are all about. Thinking in pictures. Using the full weight of the <u>visual</u> to create an impact far exceeding what the spoken word alone can accomplish.

This is what all good screenwriters shoot for. Do I even have to say it's what you should be aspiring to in your own pages as well?

* * * * *

Conversely (or should I say perversely?) there's a disturbing new fad of studios, production companies and even (most tragically) filmmakers themselves slathering a bad Betty Crocker frosting of V.O. onto *everything* -- whether a movie needs it or not. A good deal of it reeks of hasty retrofitting in post-production (during editing) or being force-fed into later drafts -- and with every new release this sorry trend seems to be growing.

All this reeks of developmental paranoia, the bald fear that if one popcorn-belching fishhead out in Movieland isn't spoon-fed every last story point then *that* fishhead might discuss their epic lack of comprehension online with *another* fishhead who's similarly flummoxed, and a grass-roots tsunami of dim-witted displeasure might arise to collapse a film's box office receipts.

Pretty condescending take, don't you think? Completely lacking trust in the average moviegoer's intelligence... which directly translates to calling you and me and everyone else paying $14 a ticket "stupid" (a.k.a. "a fishhead"). Consider this. During the Golden Age of intelligent American cinema in the 1970's, you didn't have theaters being shuttered because <u>The Godfather</u>'s storytelling was too sublime or <u>Dog Day Afternoon</u>'s personal relationships too challenging for John Q. Moviegoer to decipher, did you? These films strove for excellence, and the studios and distributors did just fine, thank you, winning many an Oscar in the process.

By today's hand-wringing standards, <u>Chinatown</u>'s legendary "*She's my sister... (SLAP!) She's my daughter... (SLAP!) She's my sister <u>and</u> my daughter*" scene would be anxiously rewritten to spell everything out -- "My father had non-consensual vaginal intercourse with me and I gave birth to an illegitimate child because of it!"

Jake Gittes' would promptly repeat the *exact same* information in NEW VOICE OVER to ensure EVERYBODY got it, no matter what -- "*Mrs. Mullray said her father had inappropriately diddled her youthful shunt, and that the little strumpet being hidden in the house was the product of his foul, incestuous lust...*"

Simple physics -- <u>when you dumb *anything* down far enough to ensure the LCD "gets it" without the slightest struggle you irrevocably damage the quality of your product</u> (see "Education in America" file). Yes -- from time to time paying adults will wait for the dumbest kid in class, but given any choice at all we damned well won't seek the experience out.

When measured statistically on the Stanford-Binet, people in 1975 were just as dumb -- or as smart -- as they are now. So why are so many shot callers in today's Hollywood so insistent their product be rendered so stupefyingly obvious?

Let me personalize the damage this can do to a somewhat healthy human brain. Bored out of my skull

214

the other night and determined not to text around for cut-rate hallucinogens, I V.O.D'd a cruddy low-budget comedy, perfectly aware it was going to suck donkey balls and wildly disappoint (for the masochistic-minded readers out there, it rhymes with <u>Better Life Through Chemistry</u>. RottenTomatoes -- 17%).

Yet even then, expectations already lowered to the floorboards, the movie doubled-down its own idiocy by slapping the limpest, lamest, most pointless voice-over in the history of limp, lame, pointless voice overs onto its agonizing ninety-one minute running time. A legit Hollywood legend -- and Oscar-winner no less -- was somehow Shanghaied into doing the honors, and I'm sure they loathed laying down the track every bit as much as the six or seven paying viewers worldwide hated listening to it.

What made it worse than the everyday shitty V.O.? For starters, it was even *more* shallow, unfunny and uninspired than average -- commonplace but still unforgivable cinematic sins circa 2014. Next there was my shocking realization that its inclusion was <u>completely</u> <u>unnecessary</u>. You heard me right. <u>Not a single word helped -- or even helped excuse -- the so-called story</u>. That Hollywood legend could've been reading adorable pet posts from Aww Reddit for all the difference it made. The V.O. didn't better define the characters (using the term loosely), didn't give additional insight into the paint-by-numbers plot, didn't point out a single thematic subtext worthy of serious contemplation, and certainly didn't attempt to bewitch and/or beguile the viewer with poetry-for-poetry's sake.

None of what was scripted in V.O. bettered the movie. Quite literally, you could've pulled the entire

V.O. track, start to finish, and <u>no</u> <u>discernable</u> <u>difference</u> would be apparent to the viewer. None. Nada. Zilch.

Once I grasped this, I was swept with panic. *Why had they done this? Was it some brave new mind-fuck being pioneered on behalf of marketing bots everywhere? Padding a shitty project with hastily-scripted V.O. to give the <u>impression</u> so much more was going on than actually was? Cinematically stuffing saline falsies into an Angelyne-sized boulder-holder in some foul attempt to make this runny-nosed anorexic seem deliciously full-figured? Or was it simply those responsible for this mind-dulling turd deciding <u>Better Living</u> needed an after-the-fact V.O. because, well, all the other uninspired, unsuccessful comedies out there had one too?*

All of these answers are pretty frightening, and I fell to my knees, praying like hell this wasn't some new trend and that I'd never again have to witness such a vulgar, low-brow theatrical bra-stuffing. Right then it hit me -- scoring some bathtub blotter or MDMA-sautéed 'shrooms was far healthier for my brain than this movie and I invoked the full weight of social media to try and rectify that mistake pronto.

Having narrowly survived the VOD's attempted lobotomy, here's my sincere suggestion to aspiring writers of all stripes --

<u>Do not use voice over in your scripts</u>.

With certain projects, narration or V.O. may be necessary, even expected, depending on your starting point or source material. Good films are sometimes bookended or bracketed with V.O. beginning and end to set the table. I get it. Each project is different. But beyond those limited exceptions, you need to focus your efforts on writing your script <u>the</u> <u>right</u> <u>way</u>, without safety nets, Lady's Helpers, crutches, excuses or cop-outs.

I steadfastly believe that if your story is good enough, it won't <u>need</u> voice over or any of the creative baggage that comes with it. Or put another way, there's no great story that can't be told <u>without</u> voice over. On this point, I remain intractable.

To many astute writers, using or not using V.O. may seem yet another example of Hollywood's hateful "Do As I Say, Not As I Do" policy -- i.e. <u>you</u> shouldn't use it in spec scripts, but then <u>they'll</u> go ahead and slap it on anyway. No doubt, these slippery caveats can drive a writer nuts. But hey, if somebody wants to pay real money to have you or so other writer mummify your script with lousy voice over, well, God bless 'em. That gets filed under "High-Class Problems". Meantime, man-the-fuck-up and build your screenwriting muscles by using the very best storytelling skills you have.

Titles

Many of you have probably noticed that coming up with the perfect title -- the word or series of words that sounds *just right* -- can drag out into an endless quagmire of ever-worsening options.

Traditionally, I've had a good title in mind before inking a project in. I wish I could claim this was conscious on my part, but no forensic evidence exists to support such a claim, so I suppose it's simply a matter of how my mind works, a.k.a. blind luck.

On the rare occasions I didn't have a title going in, coming up with anything I was satisfied with was excruciating. *Nothing* seemed to fit or feel right. Writers being somewhat perfectionist by nature (read:

neurotic and obsessive as hell), lingering questions over a title can become a nasty thorn in any scribe's side.

The importance of choosing wisely should be obvious. Titles don't simply headline your script, they also help successfully market the movie as well. Solid, impactful titles set the stage for coming coolness, jumpstart a myriad possibilities in the imaginations of many others who'll get involved along the way. When you whisky-dick yourself with a soft title, you're missing out on a huge opportunity to kick things off with a bang.

If you've created an unquestioned masterpiece, sure, I expect you could entitle it Glory Hole, Poo or 'Taint and still find a good home for it. Truly great scripts are always rare and at a premium. But short of banking on a long shot, why *not* grab 'em by the balls with something catchy? Some resonant title which sets the hook, gets 'em wet and starts 'em fumbling for the ol' iPad to take that first peek?

"Come on in, reader," a world-class title whispers. "The water's fine."

Thusly, each writer's quest for title gold begins. Ideally, you'll find a name for your project which intrigues, enchants, frightens and/or delights even the most calloused reader. Beyond that, it'd be awesome if your dream title was also *completely organic* to the material you've created. Cut from the same thrilling cloth cloaking the very beating heart of it.

Little Miss Sunshine is a great example. Goodfellas is money. Vertigo spot-on. And how about Se7en? Fuckin' intense, right? They all nail the essence of the film, while still providing some mystery, humor or intrigue about it.

Sometimes your protagonist is idiosyncratic, quirky and uncommonly compelling enough to name the entire film after them. Juno. Precious. Michael Clayton. Shrek. However, this obviously isn't best-case for the vast majority of movies. Sgt. First Class William James over The Hurt Locker? Eddie Adams or even Dirk Diggler over Boogie Nights? No thanks, not so much.

Steven Segal's Dreadnought was renamed Under Siege to avoid unnecessary head-scratching by potential ticket buyers. Apparently, the original conjured up horrifying images of the chubby Aikido star launching kicks in an 18th century barrister's wig. So they dumped it and the movie went on to become a hit.

J.F. Lawton's big Late '80's spec sale was aptly named 3000 -- the film was hella dark, with $3000 being the fee for spending a full night with the prostitute protagonist. When the studio shrewdly flipped the story on its head, re-envisioning it as a broad, bantamweight "Hooker with a Heart of Gold" tale -- and cast Julia Roberts -- it became a behemoth global blockbuster. Release title? Pretty Woman.

The use of American Graffiti in the '70's escalated into a battle royal between filmmakers and execs. The studio felt that it would be confusing for audiences ("What is this? Some Italian movie?") and suggested something more, well, on the nose -- Another Slow Night In Modesto. Thank Baby Jesus the filmmakers won out on that one.

Basic Instinct works nicely. Is it speaking to sex, survival or murder -- all of which play big parts in the film, and all of which involve primal human behavior?

Flashbacks of a Fool is a fantastic little movie -- heart-stirring and insightful with solid performances and a

219

perfectly chosen soundtrack which deepens its bittersweet scope and sense of nostalgia. (Not a bad description, right? Maybe they should've hired *me* to market the sucker.)

Regretfully, its also one of the worst titles for a drama ever. Sounds "beach book" up the butt, doesn't it? Like some faux Danielle Steel knock-off old ladies sneak their menopausal jollies from.

Obviously the light bulb went on for somebody after the fact, because for later Blu-ray and home-rental advertising they blew up the word FLASHBACK to dwarf "of a fool" and added a glossy Daniel Craig, the newly-minted James Bond, wearing Ray-Bans in a "running after the terrorist" pose. Take it on faith that Mr. Craig performs precious little 007 action during this bittersweet coming of age tale.

Much of today's marketing has become a clinic in reductive thinking, obsessive suits working overtime to distill titles down to the essence of their most dumb. This sad trend creates painfully obvious titles telling you EXACTLY what the movie is -- Horrible Bosses, Snakes on a Plane, We Bought A Zoo. It's a surgical strike of sorts, keeping customers from having to use to their imaginations or indulge any curiosity when selecting a movie. High-concept comedies get somewhat of a break I suppose, given the broad pandering of the product by nature. But recently this trend has devolved further to Sex Tape, Let's Be Cops and Airplane Vs. Volcano... and despite the apparent nadir of Sharknado, somehow I have a sinking feeling we haven't hit rock bottom yet.

Gone are the days of One Flew Over The Cuckoo's Nest -- today it would be called Nut House, Mental Home or Electroshock. Apocalypse Now would also be front-seated on the short bus, becoming <u>Vietnam War</u> or <u>Willard vs. The Crazy Colonel</u>. And <u>The Sixth Sense</u>? A brain-numbing <u>The Boy Who Sees Dead People</u>, giving away the whole shebang.

Look, it is what it is. Today's reliance on "branding" has affected every industry, not just the movie business. My personal take is not to go Dumbo until brute-forced into it. If your Manager or Agent *absolutely insists* you change it, I'd hear them out. They know the trends and the marketplace, what's "sexy" and what's selling. Ultimately, should good fortune smile and someone buy your project, whomever paid for it -- a.k.a. the People That Now Own It -- are going to do whatever they want anyway, with or without your blessing... whether you know about it beforehand or not.

...But I wouldn't worry your scruffy little Hipster beards over imaginary title feuds with fictitious studio heads just yet. That stuff only takes place in the Super Bowl and you haven't even been drafted yet.

Titles are very important. Go for the gold. Give potential buyers something they can really sink their fangs into. Charming. Foreboding. Fun. Dangerous. Whatever you pick, just make sure it's *imaginative* and packs a punch. Your "writer's intuition" will tell you when you've nailed it. It'll just click.

There's that wonderful line in Cameron Crowe's <u>Almost Famous</u> when Billy Crudup/Russell says to the young William, "Just make us look cool."

Precisely what I'm telling you. Just make your title sound cool.

Upgrade To Specifics

New writers' descriptions invariably suffer from a crippling lack of specifics. Locations are often blasé and one-note ("INT. BAR" or "INT. SUPERMARKET"), personal descriptions vague and uninspired ("He drives a yellow car and wears dark sunglasses" or "She's an exotic beauty that men want to possess").

First problem with this approach is making the writer look lazy as hell -- not the critical first impressions any of us should be striving to make. Lame "choices" such as these just sort of sit there, don't they, like moist, listless turds. Level of difficulty? Zero. Any dyslexic first grader could have done as much. By keying them in you're offering public confession to your lack of imagination and creative involvement -- a *de facto* "I could give a shit" and/or "I don't want to work too hard at this".

Dude, where's the passion? What happened to the Rock 'N Roll?

If the writer isn't passionate about these choices, how the hell can they expect a reader to get fired up about them?

Potential readers are like any good Friday night crowd seeing an up-and-coming band. They can only feed off whatever energy the performer (you) gives them. If your shit's out of tune, your guitar playing low-energy and lifeless, motherfuckers ain't gonna dance.

The tragic thing about going soft is that you're forfeiting an opportunity to enrich your screenplay so comprehensively. Because one massive benefit of using well-chosen specifics is that it *personalizes the writing* for anyone reading it, making it feel textural and a thousand times more *real* in their eyes.

Screenwriting is essentially a process of turning nonsense into make-believe. Nothing accomplishes that better than scripting your people, places and things (*Schoolhouse Rock* in da house!) in Technicolor, giving readers a vivid, visual point of reference they can quickly internalize and make their own. Minor as they may seem, detailed specifics provide the figurative "dirt under the fingernails" capable of bringing any writer's narrative to life.

Instead of the mundane "INT. BAR", push yourself into more textural terrain. Something along the lines of say, "INT. FIREFLY LOUNGE" -- a Barfly-era L.A. nightspot where top of every hour they light the bar on fire. Or "INT. THE ARSENAL" -- a Westside speakeasy decorated wall-to-wall with ancient weapons; battle axes, muskets, samurai swords, WWII pistols, etc.

See how these examples offer ten times the descriptive firepower? They engage you, pique your interest, get you *involved* in what's happening from the location alone.

Isn't that the trick of any great writer? To get the reader's imagination doing a lion's share of the heavy lifting, enlist them as willing accomplices to better sell your dreamscape? Anytime you recognize legit truth in a description, it elevates the material, makes it that much more personal. And personal connection is what good storytelling is about.

All of us love to get lost in a good story. We're delighted to take that trip whenever possible -- which accounts for the tens of millions of books, movies, TV shows and graphic novels available across the globe. Folks will suspend disbelief about as far as intellectually possible if you'll simply give them something they like, something worthy of committing to.

Professional reads of a screenplay are no different. Entertain the nice people while spinning your yarn, make them glad they took the time, and whether they buy, consider or pass, they'll love you for it.

Going back to our example, bare minimum something like "INT. SUPERMARKET" is swapped-out with a common chain like "INT. RALPH'S" or 'INT. WHOLE FOODS MARKET", etc. But kids, you can still go *so much* bigger. The sky's the limit, everything from "INT. CLOWN LIQUORS" to "INT. JUNIOR'S MEAT-A-PLENTY" just waiting for your invention. Remember the name of the '50's malt shop in Pulp Fiction? Jackrabbit Slims. Perfection, right? Try seasoning your choices to taste along these same lines. No matter what the situation or what you're describing, it should always seek to service the story at maximum capacity.

Another big league upgrade? Character specifics. When done expertly, how your characters are presented within your screenplay's world gives readers revelatory glimpses of who these folks are on the inside. Personality stuff that plays awkward at best if forced to reveal it through expository dialogue.

"He drives a yellow car and wears dark sunglasses." Again, think specifics. What *kind* of car? A bumble-bee yellow Testarossa or a Reagan-era Mazda 280Z with the driver's door smooshed in? See how much difference that one detail gives us at just a glance? Specifics. What *kind* of sunglasses -- $2000 Chrome Hearts or BluBlockers bought off QVC? Big gap between those two customer bases, don't you think?

224

"She's an exotic beauty that men want to possess." Exotic *how*? Are we hinting at ethnicity? Is this jaw-dropping hottie French, Persian, Inupiat or Vietnamese? Or is it more a question of style? Her yellow 1950's Bouton D'Or dress or that Cartier necklace brashly sprinkled with pink diamonds? (Or are you politely trying to say she has big breasts? If so, try "stacked", "buxom" or "built like a brick shithouse" instead. No worries, on the house. Happy to help.)

While we're on the topic, let's all agree to quit using the word "beautiful" in any script ever again. It's a wasted word with zero impact. *Of course* the dramatic female lead is beautiful -- it's the *movies* for chris'sake. Ugly people don't get cast in those roles.

One of the finest character descriptions I've ever seen is found in Tony Gilroy's <u>The Bourne Identity</u>. It's of Chris Cooper's C.I.A. character Chester Conklin -- *"Ivy League Oliver North. Buttoned down. Square jaw."* How's *that* for specific? Eight words tell us *everything* we need to know -- the first four alone putting it in the hall of fame. I aspire to sell characters with that same surgical level of coloration in my own writing, and yeah, shit is <u>hard</u>; but great writers do it all the time. They invest the necessary effort working and reworking a passage until it's as refined and impactful as possible.

(By the way, Gilroy's description of C.I.A. underling Zorn is also top notch, and it's only *three* words -- "Brilliant bloodless lapdog.")

Don't forget -- characters' <u>names</u> are also capable of saying a lot in themselves; becoming evocative and surprisingly informative, whether in tone or feel or by literal interpretation.

Michael Douglas' "Gordon Gekko" in <u>Wall Street</u> -- as slippery, cold-blooded and cunning as his namesake lizard. Christopher Walken's "Hickey" in <u>Last Man Standing</u> -- a psychotic killer with menacing facial scars. Robin Williams' "Seymour Parrish" in <u>One Hour Photo</u> -- creepy and odd and forever out of sorts. James Earl Jones' "Thulsa Doom" in <u>Conan The Barbarian</u> -- the ultimate source of towering evil which dominates the film. And what about little "Damien Thorn" in <u>The Omen</u>? Sweet-sounding nick for the Kindergarten-sized son of Satan himself, right?

Cooking this stuff up is actually fun for me, one part of the process I sincerely enjoy. There's an infinite palette of shadings for any writer to explore in this arena, and it's a killer device for further racking your characters into focus.

<u>Specificity plays a key part in any great screenplay</u>. So please, fellas, consider all these elements with great care. There's meat and there's a Morton's ribeye. There's music and there's <u>Exile On Main Street</u>. There are books and then there's <u>Fear In Loathing In Las Vegas</u>.

For legit writers, surgical grace notes such as these can enhance the stranger's read a hundredfold. This is truly one of those cases where "God is in the details.

<u>Anything Stock</u>

What's a "stock beat"? Any scene that's already been done to death a million times. Straight-off-the-rack hackneyed movie standbys for predictable characters and predictable actions in predictable locations and situations.

The Hero halting the bomb from going off with *exactly* one second left on the timer (never three seconds, never five, always one). The heavens suddenly erupting with rain as lovers begin to kiss. A cat jumping out to scare teens searching a creepy house (How come it's never a dog? Or better yet, an angry toddler in a wet diaper? That'd be cool.). Bad Guy holding gun to Love Interest's head as Hero tries to talk him down (because so many homicidal maniacs just, like, give up, right?). The Villain about to kill the Lead when somebody from off-screen kills Villain instead. High-Ranking Government Officials ignoring the Lead's pleas to do something even though you'd have to be brain damaged not to see he's right.

...and that's just the tip of the iceberg. You could fill the Library of Congress with stock beats alone, the list is literally *endless*. Additionally, the phrase "stock" can (and will) be applied to almost any dog-eared device within a screenplay --

Stock characters -- The Drunken Irish cop. The Mexican/South American Drug Lord. The overweight African-American Police Lieutenant who screams at his two rebellious (but results-driven) Detectives whenever they enter his office. The beady-eyed Muslim Terrorist, full black beard, wire-rimmed spectacles (in it for political/religious beliefs). The Eastern Bloc Terrorist -- Chechnyan Rebel, Rugged Ukrainian or Former KGB, always wearing black leather (in it for the cash). The Millennial Hoodie Computer Whiz, ten seconds and a broken Sidekick he/she can stop a nuclear device or pinpoint the Public Enemy #1's home address.

Stock locations -- The creepy house in the woods where dark shit has happened before and/or the creepy house in the woods quietly inhabited by bizarre-looking psychotic maniacs (you know, wandering eyes, distended foreheads, gangrenous, festering bald patches).

My all-time favorite? The "Abandoned Flame Factory" -- that wonderful brick warehouse on the outskirts of

227

town where Freddy, Jason and legions of their lesser, derivative brethren take victims for the final showdown. Although long vacant and derelict, fresh fires burn inexplicably throughout -- boiler rooms, trash cans, basically wherever the D.P. (Director of Photography) thinks they'll look the coolest.

Stock Dialogue -- Freckled Young Boy to Heroic Father -- "*Daddy, are the bad men going to hurt us?*" Cop/Detective to Bad Guy/Bank Robber -- "*Put the gun down and just walk away!*" Platoon Sgt. to Cherry Private with violent, sucking chest wound -- "*Don't die on me, damn you!*". Any Angry Male Lead to any Evil Male Antagonist -- "*If you touch one hair on her head I'm going to kill you!*" And let's not forget the most insipid stink bomb ever -- "*Bingo!*" Usually said aloud by the character to themselves when discovering anything the writer wants to draw *extra-special* attention to -- locating the heavy's hideout, a secret computer file, etc.

(Somewhere I read that "*We've gotta get outta here!*" is the most used line of dialogue in cinema history. After I learned that, I started noticing that it's in *everything* ever produced... and pretty much everything I've ever written.)

Please, my friends, avoid this clusterfuck of zombified clichés like the plague. Fuckin' cobwebs are growing over my fingers just typing this. Take my word for it -- nothing rolls eyes back into a reader's skull quicker than being sandbagged by one of these stanky chestnuts. Talk about buzz-kills. It's like stepping in warm dogshit right before Senior Prom. Worse, their discovery can extinguish any precious cool points or writer cred you were accumulating up until that point.

One reason so many of us unconsciously auto-pilot this stuff is that our screenwriting forefathers kind of aced it the first time around, and it's been further knocked-off and drummed into our heads a million times since.

Whenever you find yourself facing stock situations, basic storytelling mechanics painting you into somewhat inevitable narrative corners, my suggested standard operating procedure is to start by flipping the stock solution on its head. One-eighty the sucker and see if you can squeeze something fresh out of it. Take that spreadsheet of well-worn clichés we've been enduring all our moviegoing lives and move decisively to renovate them.

Ask yourself this -- Do you really want to be the freshman scribe with "*Danger is my middle name*" or "*I'm too old for this shit*" blemishing your pages like chickenpox? Don't just phone it in with the rationalization that "*everybody else does it*". That's chickenshit and won't help your cause one bit. Whatever time you spend writing the stock out of your scripts will be well worth it.

Other Notes And Quotes

Writing is MOMENTUM. I've found this to be an essential truth. Whenever you find yourself in The Zone, down in the pocket and totally feeling your shit, you've got to protect that precious energy at all costs. General meeting? Yoga class? Coffee date via OKCupid? Fuck you. Cancel them.

Writers know the type of flow we're talking about is impossible to plan for. You can't predict it, you can't bottle it, and once it starts flowing you certainly can't put it on "pause". Strike while the iron is hot. Days like these don't come around too often, so you'd better channel that divine voltage for all it's worth in the here and now.

229

Squander it, waste a good writing session in favor of something trivial, you'll end up regretful and hating yourself for it... like you always do.

"If it should occur to you to cut, do so". This comes from Somerset Maugham via Paddy Chayefsky and 99% of the time it's absolutely the right move.

Have that nagging hunch you really don't need something, despite the fact you LOVE the writing or witty turn of phrase or whatever else is giving you wood? Cut it. You've gotta get ruthlessly real with yourself. Shit just has to be done if you want your pages to have any longer-term chances of survival.

Believe me, I don't dig cutting decent material any more than you do. I'm no different than any other stubborn screenwriter. "Kill your darlings"? Over my dead body, Faulkner, you dick.

But knowing this simply has to get done no matter how I feel about it, I got constructive and came up with a healthy consolation prize for myself; a way to remove good stuff without eternally damning it to the dark oblivion of Final Draft's "delete" key.

My miraculous solution? **I keep a trims page -- a separate FD or Word document where I stockpile all this surplus cut-and-paste evidence of my genius**. Now whenever it occurs to me to cut, I do so... promptly pasting that stuff into my trims page. Couple cool things about this. First, you don't feel like you've "wasted" good stuff after working so damned hard on it. This reduces the agony factor a thousand-fold whenever you're forced to trim. Second, if you ever want to backtrack, reversing your earlier Supreme Court decision to give that material an appeals hearing, you're covered. You simply pluck it off the trims pile and bugger it around some more. No harm, no foul.

(In fact, I'm keeping a trims page for this book, too. Whenever my logic completely hops the reservation or one of my rants gets psychotically long, I cut-and-paste that shit right into my Word doc.)

I'll be totally honest -- the total number of times I've resuscitated material from my Trims Pages and made it stick back in the same script is very, very small. Okay, almost nonexistent. Like I said, 99% of the time your nagging instincts are right. It had to go.

However, I have taken these same trims and nicely repurposed them in <u>other scripts</u> a number of times. Say you've worked up a pretty cool description, it's just a little too long, doesn't quite fit or perhaps you had a bake-off with another take on it and that version won out. With just a few revisions, these also-rans from trim page purgatory often turn out to be <u>perfect</u> for another character, location, scene or sequence in a different project somewhere down the line.

My feeling is that if you crafted this stuff so well you didn't want to cut it in the first place, it's entirely logical there might be lasting value in another context later on.

"<u>Movies are real life with the boring parts cuts out</u>." Decades later, Hitchcock's quote continues to impress, as both observation and instruction.

Here's a basic example of what this means. Say one of your characters arrives at their apartment building, unlocks the front door, climbs two flights of stairs, unlocks their apartment door, walks inside, puts their backpack down, opens a can of cat food and feeds their cat.

That's pretty much real life, right? Many of us live our own version of this every day.

But say this were a <u>movie</u>, something professional you paid to see. How would the filmmakers re-present this same action?

Basically, they'd have one shot of the guy walking up to the building... cut to a second shot of him topping the stairs and unlocking his apartment door... cut on the action to a third shot of him spooning out cat food while a purring kitty rubs up against him.

That's real life with the boring parts cut out.

<u>We simply don't need to see him do all this extraneous stuff</u>. Unlock the building door, climb each of the sixty steps leading up to his floor, watch him walk inside, set his backpack down, sort through his junk mail, take a quick piss, step into the kitchen, call for his cat, choose a can of cat food from the cupboard, get the can opener out, begin prying it open, and so on...

In fact, there's a good argument that you only need <u>two shots</u> total -- the guy walking into the building, followed by a direct cut to him spooning out cat food. Doesn't get any tighter or more economical, <u>and it still sells exactly the same thing</u>.

When screening older films (say anything from the Eighties back), many of you have probably noticed a ton of them show *everything* -- every single goddamn step up the staircase, every single goddamn step across a parking lot, etc. <u>It's absolutely agonizing to watch this today, isn't it</u>?

Recently screening an old black-and-white, I started feeling queasy when a scene opened with this sprawling master shot of a woman standing atop sand dunes. These dunes wall-to-walled the letterboxed 16x9 and she was positioned in the *extreme* distance.

"No. NOOOOO!" I gagged on my salty caramel waffle cone. "They are not going to make us watch her walk all the way across those fuckin' dunes, are they?"

Oh yes, John, they are. Black-and-White Woman began a Bataan Death March towards camera right on cue. It took her a fully thirty seconds to get there. Thirty static seconds is an *eternity* on-screen (try it -- one thousand one... one thousand two...), the audience held hostage with nothing else to look at and nowhere else to go.

I resolved to use this time constructively, checking three Gmail accounts, winning an eBay auction and P2P-ing all six seasons of The Larry Sanders Show before her face was finally racked into focus. Of course, by that time I'd been sucked into a cyber-coma and didn't care anymore.

Modern cinematic storytelling has evolved into lightning-quick cuts and tightly framed visuals, shortcuts which compress and collapse screen time with a maximum of brevity while still managing to impart the essential content.

This is also how we live our lives now -- in shorthand. All our mind-bending new tech reflects the same dynamic and reinforces these same expectations. Net-consciousness dominates, dots connect at light speed. People process twice the info three times as quickly. Readers and audiences not only "get it" faster, they bring shorter attention spans, amplifying their impatience. Bore folks for an instant, the channel's been changed, a fresh Chrome window's been opened and the app closed out.

233

Which is why your screenplay needs to be stylistically in sync with these same times and expectations as well. <u>Accordingly, you'll need to go through any script you're working on and pay particular attention to rooting out Mr. Hitchcock's "boring parts"</u>.

First things first, fellas. Don't spaz out, trip major ballsack and cut your own nose off to spite your face. Chillax and let your pal Big Papi here tour guide you through how you want to do this.

First step -- <u>finish a draft</u>. Any draft. Rough draft, first draft, words-on-paper draft, *whatever*. No excuses, you need a legit pass under your belt with all the blanks filled in to get the full benefit of the exercise.

Do it the other way around -- "Hitchcocking" the boring parts first -- you may accidently cut into bone and carve up good material. Taken out of context, especially during its initial creation, pages are hard to judge. You want as much backbone as possible in place before diving into this.

Now the fun part. Begin ruthlessly scouring your pages for boring passages, unneeded action and description where nothing really happens, then excise them with the surgical ferocity you would a malignant tumor. This is vital business, the down-low secret to making your script "tight" and a "fast read" and all that other good stuff which makes sweet music to developmental ears.

Here's the litmus test I apply to my own pages. I try and visualize the actual shots I've scripted, essentially staging them in my head. Picture them like you're actually watching the movie (you'll probably want to do this privately as I've caught myself making hella weird "movie face"). If I foresee any slack during this "mental cut", I eliminate it.

234

What continually amazes me is how little is actually *needed* on the page to sell things colorfully if the artistry is there. First pass you often spend three sentences describing something that final pass you realize only needs one.

I've also discovered the more time that passes between first writing a scene and then coming back to rewrite it, the more obvious this dynamic becomes. Things I wouldn't have dreamed of exiling to my Trims Page become easy cuts with the fresh perspective of two or three weeks away from them.

DON'T BE A HERO

Perhaps the most tragically misguided, crack-is-whack script I've ever been sent (quite an accomplishment given the unrelenting competition) featured an Anal Lube Magnate antagonist smuggling drugs inside industrial-strength barrels of his "Gooey Duck" lubricant.

This was being developed by a major studio. I shit you not.

And like every other tortured project referenced in *Tough Love*, I have a Cloud-stashed, password-protected PDF you'll never see to prove it.

Shamelessly looting Walter Hill's archetypal '80's masterpiece, it fancied itself a "Gay 48 Hrs." -- with predictably catastrophic results. The Nolte character was "reimagined" as a dour, humorless, jar-headed homosexual-hater (wait, wasn't he that in the original?). His Eddie Murphy-esque partner was presented as pound-for-pound the most offensive black "gay" caricature imaginable. A loud, obvious, ass-wagging tornado of finger-snapping and "You go girl!" and every other stereotypic favorite from darker, less-evolved yesteryears gone by.

The "twist" (such as it was) was having Gay Cop give Fag-Hater Cop a hot homosexual stud makeover, which enables him to go undercover in West Village N.Y.C. and solve the case -- ultimately busting the Anal Lube Magnate (perhaps "busting" wasn't the ideal word choice).

I challenge you, Dear Reader, to name a single cliché not represented within the script's pages. Lock-jawed Bull-Dykes? Check. Transsexual hair stylists? Check. Laser teeth whitening and *Freshman* magazine? Check. "Butt Pirate" license plate. Check. Even the obligatory (groan) Mariah Carey and Celine Dion songs being belted out in place of Eddie Murphy's legendary "Roxanne" bit. Double check.

In all honesty, I'm not sure if the project was working overtime to empower the Gay Community or embarrass it. Even assuming it was written with the very best of intentions, everything that ended up on the page was an epic backfire, Exhibit A for the most offensive take possible.

Why was it sent to me?

Because it was also an open studio writing assignment.

Studio gigs are the *crème de la crème* of the screenwriting world. Nabbing one feels like a call-up from Triple-A to the Majors, from Scranton/Wilkes-Barre to God's Holy New York Yankees. These jobs put you on the biggest stage, under the brightest lights, working shoulder-to-shoulder alongside legit Industry players with enough juice to actually *get shit done* in this town, to make things real. Sometimes you even get the bonus of *Variety* or *The Hollywood Reporter* announcing your hiring -- big-time boosting your stock with the civilians back home.

Major studios are the original Dream Factories, one-stop shopping with all the necessary tools and toys already in place. Nobody can jump-cut a writer from page to screen faster, and *any* project a studio owns -- good, bad or ugly -- can be greenlit and fast-tracked for production with a simple nod of the right someone's head.

Studio gigs also pay full-freight. That means they can pay whatever your full quote is when you're hired on a project. At that time, my quote was a modest $300K a draft.

So I did what any ambitious young screenwriter would do -- I went about coming up with a fresh take. Complete overhaul, take the house down to three studs and start over. I shit-canned the "Gay 48 Hrs." of it all and went hardcore Mike Hodges/<u>Get Carter</u>. The drama was folded into a darker, more street-savvy context; friends from the old neighborhood finding themselves on an abrupt collision course years after choosing separate paths.

The Nolte character would become an old school hard-charger who made his bones during the N.Y.P.D.'s run-and-gun days -- a man unafraid of bulldozing over a few laws if it means getting his man or closing a case. Playing him straighter and out-of-sync with the times would provide some much-needed texture, for sure, but I also wanted him to read as a results guy, a cop interested in the best ideas no matter where -- or whom -- they came from.

Next up was creating the classiest possible version of the Murphy gay cop; stylish, intelligent, wicked funny, but all said and done, a fantastic policeman. Despite the endless shit he takes from fellow officers, Murphy chooses to take the moral high ground and remain "radiant in the filth of the world" as James Joyce once said. Other characters mistaking that for weakness, however, could prove an unfortunate miscalculation.

Most importantly, any mention of anal lubricant, butt pirates or the like would be forever banished to Screenwriting Siberia.

* * * * *

Two days later, I began dancing the same dance all screenwriters do when making a run at a job.

First, I met with Dana, the project's producer. He was a sharp guy, and we got along like the proverbial house on fire. Everything I pitched him he loved, and having read my samples (previous scripts your agency sends out as examples of your writing) and digging where I was coming from, Dana decided I was a good choice for the project.

Two weeks later, Dana and I met with the studio exec on the project, Daniel. This kid was a real up-and-comer and a ton of fun. He knew movies, *good* movies, inside-out and had a bizarre sense of humor rivaling my own. We pitched Daniel and he also believed our take was a nice fit for where the studio wanted to take the project.

Everything's coming up champagne and cheesecake at this point. Dana and Daniel and I are all on the same page, they *love* me, I *love* them, everybody *loves* everybody, and all that remains is a *pro forma* close-out session pitching the Head of the Studio.

No writer can better position themselves for an open assignment. Producer and lead exec both have your back, and behind the scenes -- with your agency providing heavy air support -- they're pushing hard for the Studio Head to pull the trigger on hiring you. This, my friends, is the fabled catbird seat. The place ambitious young scribes are eternally striving to be.

One week and a thirty minute pitch later, I would become the proud new owner of a lucrative Hollywood writing assignment.

* * * * *

Showtime was soon upon me. The three of us arrived, a united front, grinning as we accepted our free bottles of Evian and marching into the Studio Head's office.

This particular studio chief was notoriously humorless and a tad, shall we say, cold. Shaking hands was like having an ice-boxed Sprite trust into your mitt, and despite having reached the pinnacle of success and power as one of Hollywood's Elite Chosen Few, *El Supremo* wore this permanent expression which seemed to say, "*Meh.*" They could've been wholesaling carpet remnants or managing a Budget Rent-A-Car for all the enthusiasm evidenced in that room.

Didn't matter, though. Was not a factor. Never had I been more ready or deeper in the pocket, and once small talk was dispensed with I leapt out of the gate, Secretariat grabbing the inside rail and never looking back. This third pitch was easily best of the bunch. My presentation was flawless, Dana and Daniel laughing and smiling theatrically at all the appropriate junctures as if it was their first time hearing such an *amazing* pitch, too.

Landing gear lowered. Tires barked. The Eagle Had Landed. Everyone exhaled. The office seemed refreshed by the unmistakable aroma of success.

As expected, *El Supremo* gave me some lightweight notes, nothing problematic, and Dana/Daniel began discussing whatever details producers and execs discuss knowing it was a complete lock. Clear as if it

240

were last Friday, I remember sitting there in the afterglow thinking to myself, "*I can finish this meeting without saying another word and the gig's mine.*" That's how much of a slam dunk it was. No further comment on my part was necessary. My only remaining task was to smile, shakes hands, get up and walk out

Then, at the *last possible instant* before the meeting adjourned -- Dana extracting her Blackberry, studio exec Daniel halfway out of his chair -- the Studio Chief mentioned one other little character thing they'd like to see tweaked.

A quick "no problem", one affirmative nod, game over, $300K paycheck assured.

Instead, God Only Knows why, I took the writer bait and decided to be a hero.

"Well, actually..." I started off. "The dynamic *wouldn't* work that way because..."

Believe me, I was <u>not</u> trying to be a smarmy douchebag. I was actually attempting to be *helpful*. Informational. Share some of the knowledge I'd accumulated working the project out. Certainly they'd want a strong, comprehensive take from the writer, right?

Microscopic energy shift. My radar alone picked up this foreboding blip, Dana and Daniel completely oblivious. It was as imperceptible as a tiny bone breaking, but nonetheless something had been shattered. The only people aware of it were Yours Truly and the Studio Chief.

"Yes, well, I'd still like you to take a look at it."

Right then I knew. *I'd blown it. I'd lost the job.* Bottom of the Ninth, nobody on, last batter, two quick strikes, perfect game no-hitter being prepped for the record books, I'd gotten lazy and hung a curveball... and WHAM! now I was watching in slack-jawed horror as the ball went sailing straight over the fence.

* * * * *

The *moment* we left the office, I interrogated both Dana and Daniel --

"Did you guys feel anything... *weird* at the end of the meeting? You know, like I'd upset her during that last exchange?"

Absolutely not, they assured me. I hadn't been disrespectful or out of line in the slightest. Chillax, brother. It went like clockwork. Done deal, Miller time.

But in my gut I knew better.

Sure enough, six hours later my agent Marty called. I *had* fucked up. Big time. *El Supremo* went for the kill switch, concerned I might be "out of control", some "cowboy" who won't listen and refuses to take notes. No Studio Head wants to feel like they're being "challenged", however inadvertently -- least of all by some cow-licked middle-class writer in Birkenstocks. I'd been given the death penalty for what Amnesty International would deem an officious misdemeanor. My "done deal"? Crushed as casually as a McDonald's ketchup packet pitched under a moving school bus.

Dana and Daniel, my three-way love fest partners? That jolly producer/exec tandem who'd been hailing me as the next Preston Sturges just hours before? Suddenly, they *did* seem to remember me being a little, well... *unwieldy* in that meeting. Aggressively pushing the envelope. Refusing to take "yes" for an answer. The way they ducked my calls after that about-face, you'd think I'd pulled a Louis XIV and gone dookie behind the Versailles curtains.

Blatantly unfair? An egotistical overreaction? Concepts like these are inadmissible and entirely academic. Rightly or wrongly, I'd overstepped, and that's something any writer has to own. Jesus, I'd told *myself* to close my cakehole and shut the fuck up. *How much more direct can communication get?*

Real-world cost of five-second error in judgment?

Three-Hundred Thousand United States Dollars.

Mangled look on Venice screenwriter's face?

Priceless.

Takeaway? "Helping" kills. Don't be a hero. Par is plenty good enough to win big tournaments on difficult courses. Overconfidence -- however slight, however unintentional -- can blow a writer's balls off in half a beat of a hummingbird's heart.

Didn't matter that I'd get a much better job at a much better studio with a much, much better script paying a lot more money not two weeks later. That I'd be substantially upgrading from anal lube to big league Action Star and that slogging through a "Gay 48 Hrs." page-one would have been root canal anyway.

Silver linings are for assholes. Quote me on that. Three-hundy is three-hundy, no matter how you slice it.

What'd you pay for *Tough Love*? Maybe ten bucks? Same life lesson cost me over a quarter million. Seems you might be getting the better end of the deal.

READ AND SEE THESE FILMS

In my L.A. Classes, I'm constantly shocked by some of the seminal films students haven't seen and sometimes haven't even heard of. I'll reference, say, David Lynch's <u>Blue Velvet</u> only to find blank young faces, completely unaware of Frank Booth's amyl nitrate-enhanced charms. Forget about <u>Chinatown</u> (winner Best Original Screenplay), fifty-plus-percent roll snake eyes on <u>L.A. Confidential</u> (winner Best Original Screenplay) and the numbers are exponentially worse for <u>Tender Mercies</u> and <u>Breaking Away</u> (both winners Best Original Screenplay). This stunning list of omissions seems to grow longer with every new session, and often leaves me head-in-hands, muttering to myself like the bitter old hater I've always feared becoming (i.e. "Hey you kids! Get off my lawn!").

Here's the deal -- Continually educating yourself by viewing <u>the very best scripted films in history</u> is every bit as important as knowing what's crowding today's multiplexes. In fact, from a screenwriter's point of view, I can make a superb argument that it's about a thousand times *more* important.

Why? Because there's a level of craftsmanship and storytelling involved in past eras that simply isn't being required of content these days. The vast majority of new studio films are neither intended nor expected to have the same life-altering impact perhaps they once did. Previous generations were rewarded differently by their moviegoing. Real people would make *life choices* after particularly soulful cinematic experiences they felt spoke directly to them -- decide on which careers to pursue or exotic places to live, expose themselves to bold ideas about whom they might *become* someday.

244

One of America's greatest treasures, the incomparable Martin Scorcese, provides undeniable proof of how powerful this dynamic was for an earlier generation of movie lovers.

Even today's "A-List" -- the "go-to guys" -- seems less and less capable of landing their stories and being able to "close". Both *The Sopranos* and *True Detective*, brilliant and beloved as they both are, pulled epic collapses at the finish line -- and they're still light years ahead of 90% of nonsensical theatrical releases. Most cynical IMHO are projects like *Lost* or <u>Star Trek</u> (2009), which don't seem to give a shit whether they land or not -- they make open declarations of faking it, ignoring the most rudimentary logic or plausibility in smug confidence the public will pay out for half-assed storytelling anyway.

In both cases they did, justifying this approach to many. But realistically -- was <u>Star Trek</u> that good or the *brand* that big? The same case can be made about <u>The Phantom Menace</u> -- perhaps the most reviled (and most profitable) stinker in sci-fi history. Here on *Tough Love's* pages, honesty is job one. In the spirit of that, let's be entirely honest with one another -- you could project a fuckin' Pop-Tart on screen for two hours and it'd be a hit with the <u>Star Trek</u> or <u>Star Wars</u> brand backstopping it. How much credit should the writers and filmmakers really get for that? Especially when there's no argument the story blows?

But hey, free country, to each their own. Maybe you savored <u>Star Trek</u>'s plot holes and pained coincidences, believe Jar Jar Binks is pure genius. Convincing you otherwise is a fool's errand I'll decline to undertake at this stage in my life.

<u>Educating yourself with the unrivaled best is what's critical</u>, that's the takeaway here. **Learn from the highlights, not the lowlights**. Your goal is to become a legit five-tool threat, the Derek Jeter of Final Draft -- not some slacker hoping to sneak by invoking the dirty little secret that convenience trumps quality and nobody really cares. Evolving writers will benefit greatly from not drinking the Kool-Aid and getting caught up in the hype. If you're naive (or uneducated) enough to believe some graduate of the <u>Star Trek</u>/*Lost* school (flashy concept/fast-and-loose plot/epic failure to land) could carry the ink-stained Underwoods of legendary heavyweights like Paddy Chayefsky (<u>Marty</u>, <u>The Hospital</u>, <u>Network</u>) or a young, N.Y.C. taxi-driving Oliver Stone (<u>Midnight Express</u>, <u>Scarface</u>, <u>Salvador</u>, <u>Platoon</u>), then I'd urge you to lay off the OG Kush Wax and read a real fuckin' screenplay sometime.

There's an old saying -- "In the land of the blind, the one-eyed man is king." Yeah? What about the guy with *both* eyes? What kind of advantage will he or she have whenever things boil down to the pages at hand?

I get it, my malnourished Millennials -- if you're under thirty some of the vintage titles seem prehistoric and glacially paced. Older films do use medium shots pretty generously (reason -- so you can figure out where the fuck you are during the action) and they steadfastly refuse to shake the camera like it's got a king-sized vibrator jammed up its joy tunnel. Guilty as charged. They also used (GASP!) *real fire* for the explosions instead of CG, and no, the pyro crew on <u>Apocalypse Now</u> didn't give a shit about "keeping it green". You'll just have to deal with the joyful injustice of that.

Revisiting several favorites from back in the day, I couldn't help but notice the lead actors also looking like <u>normal</u> <u>people</u> -- they hadn't sand-blasted their teeth

246

Liquid Paper white, didn't have <u>Brazil</u>-level plastic surgery stretching foreheads drum tight, hadn't subjected themselves to multiple alkaline lemon cleanses and the Lap Band. So yeah, I can see where you'd be lost and slightly disoriented when viewing one of these cobwebbed chestnuts and its forgotten race of surgically unenhanced human beings.

(See, exactly what I'm talking about -- *Brazil*. Another seminal film you probably haven't seen yet.)

There's no denying it can be hard to find many titles these days. Older catalogues often get short shrift on streaming services in favor of <u>Transformers 19</u>, and unless you have the cashish for collector-priced DVDs on fleaBay you may be shit out of luck. However, in a fascinating digital-era twist of fate, film fanatics worldwide have somewhat taken matters into their own hands by sharing out-of-print classics via BitTorrent sites. The quality isn't always great, VHS or low-quality TV rips are common, but thanks to these dedicated cappers, sharing the cinematic lessons of many lost gems is still possible.

Insane as it seems, rights holders appear perfectly content to let these titles continue vanishing into the abyss -- despite the emergence of lower-cost streaming technologies, legal downloads, etc. There's a blanket assumption they can't be profitable or no longer have any "commercial appeal". Meanwhile, they're voluntarily *giving away* a king's ransom in potential online income to P2P. One hundred percent of nothing is nothing, fellas. The math doesn't get more basic. When reasonably priced, I believe most people would honestly prefer buying the real deal from the official studio. It guarantees quality and it's something they can feel good about -- making it a win-win for everyone.

*****

Make no mistake -- consciously or unconsciously, anytime a screenwriter watches a movie, they're adding to their database of what works and doesn't work.

Sometimes you'll find yourself learning far more from bad movies than good ones. Happens all the time, counterintuitive as it sounds, if for no other reason than crappy films show you what NEVER to do. Beyond that, there's the fun of trying to cook up potential cracks, fixes and better ways to approach the same scenes and situations on your own.

When it comes to working up your own projects, my suggestion is to <u>always try and learn from the very best examples found in any given genre</u>. These are the handful of legendary lighthouses staggered across a largely blasé cinematic coastline, existing in perpetuity to help guide aspirants in a variety of insightful ways.

Here's a practical example of how this tracks. You decide you want to write a cop movie. The three cop films generally accepted as the modern cornerstones of the genre are <u>Dirty Harry</u>, <u>The French Connection</u> and <u>Bullitt</u>. Educate yourself by screening the ones you feel might best inform your script (personally, I'd watch them all). Late '80's <u>Lethal Weapon</u> defined the modern day Buddy Cop flick. Throw that on your list, too, if you haven't already seen it. Yeah, these grey-haired classics may be older than your Dad, but age is not the focus here -- structure and superior storytelling are.

Brushing up on the bona fides gives writers a much-needed B-12 shot in the behind. It familiarizes you with the wealth of amazing material these entries pioneered, which *still* works or Industry insiders wouldn't be trying to purloin their storytelling goodness to this day.

248

For younger/newer writers, reviewing these films provides a massive Clockwork Orange-style eye opener -- you'll be blown away by how much of their original content has been borrowed (Hollywood translation: stolen) and regurgitated by inferior wannabes many decades later.

In a single year taking generals and going up for jobs, I heard both Steve McQueen/Bullitt and Budd Schulberg's A Face In The Crowd referenced probably twenty-five times. These titles were floating around the developmental ether at that moment, companies interested in fresh ideas about how to "take them sideways" (remake them differently enough so the original rights won't be needed). So as a screenwriter always on the look-out for potential work, if you hadn't seen either film you were already out of the conversation. No job for you.

Next step -- salt in other great pictures which similarly address key elements of your project. Internal Affairs showcases the psychological cat-and-mouse between good cop and bad. L.A. Confidential explores ideas about law enforcement and morality in earlier eras and deftly illustrates how to use period for maximum effect. Rampart offers a taut character study of a Daryl Gates-era cop quickly becoming obsolete given the new L.A.P.D. expectations of political correctness.

Do your homework, kids. Seek out and get turned onto the good shit, whatever the appropriate genre. With the Net at your fingertips, it couldn't be easier to ferret out what professionals need to have seen.

Following that, I'd binge-view the best of what contemporary television has to offer. Both premium and free cable networks have been breaking hella new ground in recent years -- trouncing the meager storytelling innovation found in features. When it comes to cop projects, I'd bee-line straight for *The Shield, Luther, True Detective* and *The Wire* among others (Did I mention you should watch *The Shield*?). Every bit as essential as knowing your history is possessing an understanding of the current narrative landscape as well. What are the new takes out there? How have they shifted or upgraded audience expectations? Which traditional elements will still "play" and which won't in light of newer projects changing the game or raising the bar?

When *True Detective* aired in early 2014, it blew *everybody's* doors off. The whole town was buzzing about it. This was an important show, fresh, dynamic and stunningly unique. Overnight, writers were forced to rework pitches and reconceive storylines to accommodate a host of savvy new narrative possibilities. Once that amazing Pilot aired, making the rounds with your grandpappy's same 'ol series idea was a laughable exercise in futility. *True Detective* simply had to be factored into the mix from that point forward. Plain evidence of this halos the structuring of Showtime's new series *The Affair,* among others.

This also pointed out the fascinating new cross-pollination between TV and film which previously hadn't existed. Television has traditionally taken its creative cues from the silver screen. Now it's largely becoming the opposite. Features have to pay attention to little brother cable or risk seeming passé before they can reach release.

Whether we're talking National Film Registry classics or next Sunday's new Showtime series, in the room nothing's more impressive than showcasing your knowledge of the narrative roots of the project you're discussing. Packing a big-league database also helps protect against any surprise blindsidings should some director or producer reference a critical genre standard you're commonly expected to know. Rest assured, whiff on one of these and you'll want to kill yourself by the quickest means possible. As Yours Truly can testify, sitting there lock-jawed as that plum gig goes spiraling down the toilet is an ugly feeling you will never forget.

Last Fall, while working on this book, I went up for a writing assignment where the original writer, unconsciously or not, had written a lightweight shoot-'em-up borrowing heavily from <u>Shane</u> -- perhaps the greatest and most iconic Western in Hollywood history. Knowing and loving the film as I do, the moment the studio sent the script down I knew *exactly* was it was, and more importantly, exactly how to fix it.

Sure enough, the veteran producer's eyes lit up the moment I threw <u>Shane</u> into my pitch. This is a gentleman with real credits who's done some big movies, and the instant I referred to the classic bloodlines and unrealized mythic potential of his project, I knew we were in sync. I had him hooked. Having that cinematic point of reference on my mental SIM card provided the perfect jumping off point for my take, and essentially I was hired before I left the room.

After you've updated your own hard-drive with the appropriate cornerstones, you'll want to consult any <u>current</u> <u>releases</u> applicable to your idea, however tangentially, for better or worse. For example, if a bowel-churningly bad thriller has come out recently and cratered, familiarity with it can help you construct a bulletproof case why <u>your</u> <u>project</u> isn't the slightest bit similar. Nobody -- and I repeat NOBODY -- is going to invest in a dead-ringer for something already D.O.A., whether it came out fifteen minutes or fifteen years ago. Successfully delineating the vast differences in world, characters, theme and action can extinguish any developmental "guilt by association" and keep your movie alive and in the hunt.

Opposite end of the spectrum, should a fantastic thriller come out and start breaking box office records, you want to halo your project with its success; pointing out positive parallels and pushing that film's big payday to prove there's plenty more box office waiting there to be mined.

Either instance, genre classic or contemporary also-ran, you'll want to break down their core elements insomuch as they apply to whatever story you're creating. Among the biggest of these tend to be underlying structural conceits.

Exactly as we did with Training Day in "Four-By-Six Love", you can break down any film for further study. Simply type up your own beat sheet while watching the movie start-to-finish. This is the shorthand version of the notecards, chronologically listing each scene, its location, the characters involved and the key action or import of what takes place. Remember, these don't have to be wildly intricate. Alien, for example, might look something like this --

Act One --

1) Establish Nostromo travelling in deep space.

2) Establish Interior of Nostromo, ghostly, mechanical, empty. In-coming message awakens ship's main computer, Mother.

3) Crew begins awakening from cryosleep pods. Each character initially sketched out through different appearances.

4) Mess Hall -- Crew eats a big first meal together, more fully establishing each character. Ship mechanics Kotto and H.D. Stanton haggle over contract demands.

...and so on. Breaking films down this way is Industry-standard, providing a road map to better analyze and understand the successful structure of a particular movie that may apply to your own. Twenty years later, I still break down films regularly for writing assignments, spec scripts, pilots, whatever. It keeps you sharp and provides an on-going education (or re-education) as your career progresses. As far as learning tools go, beating out film structure is invaluable, and like so much of screenwriting, what's wonderful is that *anybody* can do it, pretty much anywhere, at any time, completely free of charge. All you need is your brain, a keyboard or pen and paper.

Want to discover how Oscar-Winner Ted Tally immaculately crafted his intercuts between Jodie Foster stumbling onto Buffalo Bill's place and Scott Glenn and his F.B.I. guys kicking in the front door of the wrong house? Break it down. Mr. Tally's approach is one of the most artful examples you'll find of this technique. Who better to learn from than the best?

Want to find out how archetypal villain Scorpio's scenes were layered into <u>Dirty Harry</u>? At what intervals his victims are revealed to ratchet up pressure on both Clint the cop and the City of San Francisco itself? Break it down. It'll provide an evergreen example of how intelligently laddering cat-and-mouse elements can drive a script relentlessly towards climax. This pioneering dynamic is still being lifted by film and TV to this day -- the trailer for <u>A Walk Among The Tombstones</u> lifting scenes and shots wholesale.

Want to echo Chris McQuarrie's surgical care in seeding in <u>The Usual Suspects</u>' Keyser Soze. Understand how Chris brilliantly obfuscated his way to an Academy Award by keeping the bad guy in plain sight for a solid one hundred minutes? (*All together now!*) <u>Break</u> it <u>down</u>.

* * * * *

Throughout *Tough Love's* various rants and raves, if I've positively referenced a film then you probably want to have seen it. Additionally, any of the essential titles I've cherry-picked below involve some spectacular contribution in either the writing, direction or performance that you should have on your radar. Figuring out what's important about them and why they're key to your budding growth is homework I feel confident leaving in your hands. I could've easily come up with another fifty or so, but I don't want to fry anybody's brain. This should get you started --

<u>Almost Famous</u>

<u>The Matrix</u>

<u>Who's Afraid of Virginia Woolf</u>

<u>Network</u>

<u>Alien</u>/<u>Aliens</u>

<u>Prisoners</u>

<u>The Bourne Identity</u>

<u>L.A. Confidential</u>

<u>The Bad News Bears</u> (1976 Original)

Se7en

When Harry Met Sally

Your Friends and Neighbors

American Beauty

Lethal Weapon

Fargo

Training Day

Ghost

Unforgiven

For screenwriters hungry for an even deeper education, reading the actual scripts is about as good as it gets. When studying the writing of a legit master, past or present, this is equivalent to a young architect being allowed the privilege of perusing Frank Lloyd Wright's blueprints. The mechanics of how a great writer's dialogue looks and tracks on the page, their stylistic choices for presenting the actual words, slug lines and editorial passages -- all of these offer invaluable insight to even the most experienced scribe. This is not a substitute for breaking a film down as described above, rather it's an upgraded and more detailed extension of that same process.

Obviously this exercise involves getting your hands on the actual screenplays themselves in the first place. Getting a hold of produced scripts can be somewhat hit-or-miss, but you'll find thousands already floating around in cyberspace and on film-wonk forum boards. Quick heads-up -- **physical scans** are always preferable to retyped/re-entered "digital copies" which often suffer from abridged descriptive passages, typos and other unforgivable errors. There are a myriad of websites (such as hollywoodscriptfinder.com among others) that have legit scanned production drafts available and many noteworthies are now being published in proper format, like the Newmarket Shooting Script Series, for example. **Whatever the case, real drafts are what you're looking for.** Accept no substitute.

Here's a quick list of a few screenplays I love -- As well as a brief word about why I recommend you read them as originally scripted by their authors. You may want to prioritize these titles when starting your search.

Larry Kasdan's <u>Body Heat</u> -- Good God, what a great read! Every single detail of the story is so artfully laid out and sublimely seeded in, and the scorching heat of it, the lust and aching desire, just sizzles off the page. The very definition of a page turner which still packs a mammoth punch. They certainly don't write 'em like this anymore.

Hampton Fancher's early draft of <u>Blade Runner</u> -- For pure enjoyment of the writing itself, I personally prefer this undated 141 pg. draft to David Peoples' later rewrites. I find it more textural and evocative, with some interesting differences that I think are pretty cool. It may feel a little prose-like and "purple" (i.e. overwritten) by today's minimalist standards, but it remains a magical script in my opinion.

Oliver Stone's <u>Scarface</u> -- People today seem to have forgotten what a world-class screenwriter Stone is, easily one of the best who's ever lived. What's so mind-blowing about this particular draft is that damn-near *every line* of Pacino's dialogue is right there on the page as Stone intended it. As badass and balls-to-the-wall a

screenplay as you'll ever read -- right up there with his
<u>Salvador</u>, <u>Midnight Express</u> and late '70's draft of <u>Conan</u>.

Paddy Chayefsky's <u>Network</u> -- No surprises here. This
is pretty much the Holy Grail for screenwriting as far as
I'm concerned. Mr. Chayefsky's command of subject,
character and dialogue is unparalleled and highly,
highly unlikely ever to be equaled. You find yourself
reading these long, thick passages of dialogue --
something no writer alive could get away with today --
and suddenly it hits you that <u>every word</u> is necessary,
every last word *counts.* (How many of us can say that
about our own scripts?) This towering masterpiece is
entirely surgical, not an ounce of narrative fat on it, and
it's also coming at you at lightning speed. Unreal. Even
the best of screenwriters stand humbled by this
astonishing accomplishment.

Andy Kevin Walker's <u>Seven</u> -- The greatest serial
killer movie ever written (yes, I have it one tiny click
ahead of the also-amazing <u>The Silence of The Lambs</u>)
and yet another project that'll never be eclipsed. When
it first hit town, I remember a friend at Warners wildly
praising it and messengering it down to me. Late that
night, I started reading and it absolutely scared the piss
out of me. I was living alone in a Venice Beach studio
the size of a postage stamp, yet when I got to the
sequence with desiccated victim "Victor" and the
Polaroids, I literally got up to make sure no boogie men
were hiding in my five-by-three closet. Not kidding.
Andy really is the master of brilliant twist on top of
brilliant twist, and one of the very best writers out there
period.

Joel and Ethan Coen's <u>Miller's Crossing</u> -- A criminally
under-seen and under-appreciated masterpiece of both
screenwriting and period filmmaking. On the page,
you're simply AMAZED at how clean the presentation is.

No long swaths of technical description or editorializing to bog things down, just precisely what's needed to tell the story to perfection. And then there's the dialogue. *Goddamn, it's spectacular.* Much like <u>Network</u>, razor-sharp lines being delivered warp speed, a crackerjack patois of Prohibition-era patter every bit as cutting and insightful as it is colorful. This is one of those rare screenplays where you could cross out everything editorial and the dialogue would still stand on its own. A brilliant accomplishment every aspiring screenwriter should be familiar with and one of my desert island scripts without doubt.

You may have noticed my personal tastes stray to the outer fringes of the slam-dunk commercial mainstream. So I asked my good friend producer Craig Perry (<u>American Pie</u>, <u>Final Destination</u>) what scripts he would recommend to aspiring writers as well. Craig advised reading and having a solid knowledge of the following scripts if you're serious at all about working in modern-day Hollywood --

<u>Groundhog Day</u>

<u>Raiders of the Lost Ark</u>

<u>The Apartment</u>

<u>Pulp Fiction</u> (for dialogue)

<u>Jaws</u>

<u>Chinatown</u>

<u>The Terminator</u>

<u>Back To The Future</u>

... and *any* Coen Brother's script for clarity of language.

258

SLEEPING WITH THE ENEMY?

One perpetual thorn in any screenwriter's side is the looming question of <u>representation</u> -- how to get a professional agent or manager to represent their work.

In *Tough Love's* early pages, you shared in my own seat-of-the-pants, right-place/right-time, you-lucky-motherfucker origins story, so you can probably guess this chapter doesn't offer any groundbreaking loopholes or revelations. During even the best of times, finding decent representation has always been frustrating as hell. Today's Business is caught up chasing some lasting new model yet to fully take shape. A flash-frozen uncertainty about which type of content or method of distribution will ultimately win out has taken hold, meaning fewer viable paying gigs and fewer agents and managers taking on new clients -- exponentially growing that wicked level of difficulty from the word go.

As if that weren't sadistic enough, the roles agents and managers play have changed significantly over the past six or seven years. Many managers now do much of the primary day-to-day servicing, with agents at bigger agencies focused more on packaging and larger deals -- things above the ten-percent client's pay grade. Before the crash, none of my screenwriter friends had managers, myself included. Why sacrifice an extra ten percent when our agents were taking great care of us? Now we <u>all</u> have them. It's become somewhat essential if you hope to stay in the hunt.

Once you've psychologically prepped yourself for all this, the next question concerns which avenues an aspiring young pimp like yourself with zero connects should investigate. My producer friend Marcy was kind enough to share her thoughts once again.

The consistent answer she hears year-in and year-out is contests. Cold calling will get you nowhere. "Pitch fests" mostly appear to be a scam, if not an outright joke. They're poorly run and teeming with shady producers and low-level kooks. She honestly doesn't feel many people there ostensibly to hear pitches actually take them seriously. Her veteran impression is that execs go primarily to see friends and network peers, never really expecting to find any worthwhile product.

Pitch fests are also expensive. An agent recently pointed out to Marcy that they're somewhat of a hustle in that they charge aspiring writers for this shot to "pitch execs", but Monday through Friday those same execs might hear twenty pitches for free as part of their regular jobs.

Granted, those workweek pitches are set up through agents, but that underscores the idea that anyone worth their salt will dig up a rep on their own -- i.e. the cream will rise -- and they'll get a chance to pitch legitimately without paying for some crappy fluorescent-lit ballroom experience in the bowels of the Valley. Ironically, people working pitch fests end up being the exact same execs new writers are sent to by their new agents -- only this time they're paying a lot more attention and the experience is 100% different.

Craig Perry echoed both Marcy's and my feelings and experience in regards to "the cream rising" -- "*In the end, good writing almost always bears out. If you're actually GOOD, you will get found.*" Again, that's coming from a real-deal producer whose films have crossed the $100 Million Dollar line, a guy who has absolutely no motivation to blow smoke up undiscovered writers' asses.

Does this mean you should just chillax, kick back and expect some CAA agent to parachute through your window dying to sign you? Please -- whatever universe rolls like that, teleport me there. Key to this "you will get found" dynamic is consistently putting yourself in the right *space*, with the right material at the right time. Tupac-style keeping yourself on-point and game-tight so when daylight at long last appears, you're ready to pile drive on through to the promised land.

Or as the old saying goes -- "Pray for good harvest, but keep hoeing."

Because Marcy's a real straight-shooter, I asked her point blank -- "Is this ultimately what we're telling aspiring writers? That if they're good, some random/lucky/unexpected happenstance hook-up will appear to help them along?"

Her answer? "Yes, that's exactly what we're saying. Write a lot, read a lot. Enter contests that seem aligned with your style and taste and that have judges who can help your career. See where past winners have progressed to get a sense of this. Paying for someone to hear your ideas is a waste of money when, at the right dinner party or networking function, you can pitch someone of real merit for free.

Bottom line? Word of mouth is your strongest weapon in this business."

Marcy's final suggestions were similar to my own in "The Good Read" -- network assistants to start funneling your work into the system, join writers' groups and classes likely filled with ambitious people also serious

261

about advancing their careers. Cherry-pick the classmates you can tell are real comers, stay in touch with them and begin building up your peer group that way.

These are what they are -- broad points of entry, backed by uncompromising truth. Wish I had something more instant grat to send your way, but I don't. I expect many readers have already started traversing these roads with limited success. What can be said but "Rome wasn't built in a day" and "the journey of a thousand miles begins with but a single step" (been waiting to mashup two hackneyed Twentieth Century truisms like that for a good hundred pages now).

When forced to confront the daunting agent/manager question, taking a "first things first" approach is by far the most constructive thing you can do as far as I'm concerned. Here's what I mean --

First Thing -- Is your script there yet?

Hate to cold-cock you with it that way, but *Tough Love* is nothing if not an Astroglide-free zone, and this may be the final word on why you're not getting any traction out there.

There's an old joke -- "If one person tells you you're drunk, laugh it off. If three people tell you, lie down." This speaks perfectly to screenplays as well. If multiple parties keep telling you certain specific elements aren't working, it doesn't mean they're wrong or "they don't get it" -- it means that as the author, *you're* failing to communicate effectively. **The burden of proof is always on the writer, not the reader.** Your job as a craftsman is to ensure they get it, by any means necessary.

Consider falling back and taking another swing at it. Take a couple weeks off, clear your head. Then gather up your solid feedback, give it a second look and see if there's some legit value there you may have blown off too casually before. <u>Fix whatever needs to be fixed and re-engineer things anew, regardless of how long it takes or how much extra work is required</u>. Do Not Pass Go until you're firing on all cylinders and your business is taken care of.

Let me hit this point hard -- **<u>Looking for an agent or manager with a screenplay that doesn't work is a complete waste of everyone's time</u>**. Yours. Theirs. Whomever made the introduction, etc. Reps know the good shit when they see it. *They have to.* Precious little of it around to begin with, and being able to separate the speculative wheat from the chaff is quite literally what pays these peoples' bills.

You get one read in this town. Why waste a legit open door because you're anxious, impatient, exhausted by waiting and tired of striving to improve things yet again? Only you can decide if you're taking your best possible shot. The odds of success will radically increase by only putting work out there which lives up to 100% of the potential you see in it.

Second First Thing -- <u>Do you have anything brand new to give them</u>?

Agents and managers need <u>fresh</u> <u>material</u> to have any incentive to take you on. They can only do *their* thing after you've done *your* thing. What exactly do you expect they can do if you're not armed with something they can sell?

Operative word here -- <u>F-R-E-S-H</u>. As in "brand spanking new". Hot off the press. Not the same dog-eared script that won you the "2004 Daughters of the American Revolution Screenplay Competition". Not the same 'ol recycled spec <u>Buffy The Vampire</u> episode you've been pedaling since Alyson Hannigan (God Bless her hot little soul) was twenty-three.

Brothers and sisters, there is a *reason* nothing ever happened with that old script. Feel me? Great scripts don't languish five-plus years without interest. Not if they've seen even the outermost fringes of the legitimate film biz. Think of this like an old-school B-horror movie, with you playing the protagonist who discovers her BFF's Freddy or Jason-butchered body. I'm the peripheral supporting character (high-school quarterback, class nerd, etc.) holding you back from the corpse who pleads, "*She's gone, Trixi. Let it go. Just let it go!*"

<u>Let</u> <u>it</u> <u>go</u>. That spec you're coddling is a losing lottery ticket from a jackpot held five years ago. It's matted with metaphorical cobwebs and reeks of expired milk.

<u>New material is the name of the game</u>. Projects unseen and unexposed to the business at large. If you've already "burned" your script (exposed it to most of the legit buyers out there) that ain't gonna help either. Potential reps expect a factory-fresh Lexus, not some Clinton-era Ford Probe with balding tires. They don't want sloppy seconds with some toothless ol' streetwalker (a.k.a. your script) the whole town's already spluged on and defiled. Where's the potential profit in that?

Know what I still regret, despite having written something in the neighborhood of thirty features? *Not having generated more original material*. This is critical throughout your career, but when seeking some kind soul to take your orphaned ass in off the street, it's essential.

While on the topic of managing expectations, let me disabuse some newbie knuckleheads of one particularly absurd pipe-dream I keep hearing bandied about --

You cannot expect to get a TV staffing job as a complete unknown. The odds are better of you winning a Nobel Peace Prize. These gigs are highly prized, the pinnacle of the Business. They not only pay exceptionally well, they put what you write -- i.e. what you have to say -- directly on *television*. Are you seriously coked-up enough to believe that with zero pro experience you have anywhere near the skill set that requires? That you can even handle it yet? Fuck'sake, pard, there are *Emmy-winning writers* out there who can't get staffed. Do you honestly believe a sample episode of Two and Half Men or participation in some studio "diversity program" is going to move you to the front of that long-assed line?

Perhaps nobody's had the heart to tell you this yet? Well, please, allow me. You are not qualified for this job yet. In the same way you're probably not qualified to be a nuclear engineer or an air traffic controller. Writing is an occupation, like any other. It requires very specific skills and experience. The FAA doesn't hire just any asshole off the street, and neither does Sony Television.

The best way to get a foothold in TV is to create your own series idea and pitch it. Networks are always on the hunt for first-rate new shows, and they'll buy from less experienced writers with the built-in fail-safe of adding a Show Runner (a broadcast-experienced producer and/or writer) who can deliver no matter what should your pilot get produced. When it comes to getting work, selling an original pilot is about a thousand times more likely than you getting staffed.

Which wraps us right back around to first things first. **Come prepared with solid, brand new, unexposed material to show potential managers or agents or don't expect to be picked up**. Empty-handed writers are about as attractive -- and as useful -- as the Ebola virus.

* * * * *

My buddy Certain-Persons and I decided to write a new spec together. It was one of those "why the hell not/let's have some fun" deals. We had a decent idea, C-P had a few months off before starting a new production company, and I needed something to kickstart my sagging career and propel me back on the big board.

One day while writing, I mentioned my agent hadn't called me in months. I joked that I'd probably get a X-Mas card before she actually called again. This was September, hence the joke.

C-P had a brainstorm, as he's prone to do, and suggested we call my agent on the spot, right then and there, with him listening in on the other line to get a fair sense of what was up.

That call played out like they all did. I'd go over open writing assignment grids in advance (hand-offs from friends working big agency desks) and circle whichever projects I'd be right for (or at least have a shot at). Straightaway I'd go over these jobs and suggest she put me up for them. Having already done all the legwork, I figured it would make things as easy as possible for her.

With the precision of an atomic clock, my agent would reject these ideas, squashing each of them with the stock list of agent excuses -- *"The town's slow right now,"* *"Your samples aren't right for it,"* *"They're only looking at produced writers,"* etc.

(FYI -- There are *at least* a thousand of these half-hearted half-truths struggling writers and actors are both intimately familiar with. I'm kind of surprised nobody's compiled them into a comprehensive list on some website yet.)

And that, as they say, would be that. End of discussion. Case closed. Appeal denied. Let's (not) do lunch. Certain-Persons rejoined me as I was hanging up.

"You don't call your agent to find out why you're *not* going out," came his wise counsel. "You call to find out *when* you're going out."

To be fair, I wasn't exactly burning up the town at that point, slam-dunking spec after spec. But still, wasn't there something she could do? Anything? Even the most modest effort she could make on my behalf?

"I guess I need a new agent, huh?"

"You don't need *an* agent," C-P scolded me, uncapping his second early morning liter of Mountain Dew. "You need the <u>right</u> agent."

Sure enough, a week before the holiday I discovered my agent's X-Mas card slouching inside my mailbox. I brought it with me to Certain-Person's place, and we basically laughed our balls off. My pal stuck it to his 'fridge using a <u>Jurassic Park</u> swag magnet and we went back to bickering about the next scene in our script.

* * * * *

It shouldn't come as any surprise that the "right" agent or manager can make all the difference to your career.

Ask anyone thriving -- or even just surviving -- in the film industry, they'll confirm that for you. There's not a creative alive that's gotten wherever they are without having dedicated, dynamic people behind them pushing with all their might. Not Matt Damon. Not Selena Gomez. Not Carrot Top.

The perfect way to attract this caliber of representation, despite being some F.O.B. Joe Schmo who doesn't know his dick from a Beverly Blvd. pothole?

Write top-notch scripts that will force people to pay attention.

Winners attract winners. When you've got the real stuff, others with the real stuff find you. "The Devil recognizes his own." Beyond that, there simply ain't that much screenplay gold being written to begin with.

Certain-Persons and I finished our spec. While he started his new company, I went back to work on my own script that'd been languishing nearly a year. I'd been suffering a huge case of approach-avoidance, but the two of us working together had been so much fun it got me fired up to jump back in the trenches and finally tackle it.

My buddy gave it a read and (to my great relief) confirmed it was good. Not the most overtly commercial thing ever, but it would certainly do the trick. During our months writing, C-P had promised to help a honky out and do me a solid finding a new agent. Now I had the fresh material necessary to make that leap possible.

* * * * *

From the instant the world's very first talent agent
signed their very first writer client, agent bashing has
been *de rigueur*. Buried inside some anonymous UCLA
archive, I have little doubt silver nitrate negatives exist
of some four-eyed dork with coffee breath and a six-
hundred-page screenplay carping about his rep from
behind the wheel of a Model T.

*Whom else can we blame when shit doesn't go the way we
want? We can't blame ourselves now, can we?*

Paranoia is an inescapable part of what underlies any
writer/rep relationship. Most everything between you
is based on the intangible and ephemeral; queasy grey-
zone stuff you can't actually put a hand to. Potential.
Patience. Blind faith. Loyalty. Good timing. Bad and
good luck both.

On the writer's end, you must trust your rep's going to
do everything in their power to get producers and execs
to pay attention and *read you*; to overcome any
prejudices and/or outright indifference to your work
and your being unknown, then alternately bust down or
sweet-talk doors open, gaining you entry into the very
rooms that can change a screenwriter's destiny.

On the rep's end, they need to trust you're sitting on a
reservoir of raw skill and talent (very different things)
which will continue evolving. Flash-in-the-pan "one
script wonders" have limited value -- one-and-done
doesn't feed the bulldog much these days. They want to
know you're resilient enough to surf the coming highs
and lows with positivity, bright enough to embrace each
experience and learn from it. Much of this business is
sink-or-swim OJT (on-the-job training), a galaxy of
crucial subtleties left for the individual to puzzle out

269

then try and master on their own. Grasping this in real-time, without wet-nursing, is an implicit expectation of quality representation.

Maneuvering new talent into the kill zone is a crazy amount of work -- largely invisible labor you won't fully appreciate. Once your peeps put you there, first and goal, ball in hand, they expect confidence in you doing your best, without coping an attitude, throwing a shit-fit, straight up choking and/or shitting the bed -- all legitimate concerns when dealing with the neurotic, sadomasochistic psyches of baby screenwriters.

It's best to avoid nurturing needless illusions when starting out -- there's nothing romantic about the union between writer and rep. It's an arranged marriage based on practicality and the ceaseless creep for cash. The writer's dowry includes commercial ideas and stories which have profit potential. The manager or agent's dowry contains keys to the golden doors behind which real money is made. You have something they want, while they have something you <u>need</u>. They're the top and you're the bottom. They're the "D", you're the "s". This is the beating heart of the Faustian bargain you collectively strike when doing business together.

This certainly doesn't mean to act like some grim and serious tight-ass all the time, or that you won't come to deeply enjoy some of these folks. Contrary to popular portrayal and endless cinematic lampooning, reps are human beings, too. Many agents are bright, delightfully charismatic people, with whom you'll share some of the best times of your professional lives. When you finally hit a gusher and that oil geysers out, it's a rush of euphoria and relief and empowerment second to none. Suddenly, you feel like *somebody*, like you have class, like you're a contender. What once was the Gobi has become a honeysuckle oasis with Bedouin hotties popping peeled grapes in your mouth. Calls get taken, cell digits are given out. Fab lunches are scheduled, party invites emailed, Lakers tickets and a cornucopia of other sweet industry perks start cascading into your lap like it's the most natural thing in the world.

All of this is a <u>blast</u>, and I cannot recommend it highly enough. Goddamn right, becoming successful feels good. For once, you finally get to see how the other half lives, get to hang with the cool kids at school. That Butt Town bully forever kicking sand in your face? Now he's passing you a shatter-stuffed G-Pipe, shouting "Party On, Motherfucker!"

My only words of caution? Don't forget during these best of times what you knew all too well during the worst -- that this is still *business*. All of it. Those flattering texts and warm shoulder grabs aren't fake, they're just, well... temporary; an expected and well-established part of the dance. Come on, when a stewardess smiles, it doesn't *really* mean she wants to fuck you, dummy. Once the heat subsides, and your stock undertakes a disorienting plunge from peak to valley -- as it will in *any* Hollywood career -- few agents I've known will be asking you to godfather their kids or join Hawaiian vacations. You can certainly choose to take it that way, but ain't a damn thing *personal* about it.

Know who nailed this? Cameron Crowe in <u>Almost Famous</u>, when Philip Seymour Hoffman/Lester Bangs warns -- "You cannot make friends with the rock stars."

Or as an ICM agent shared with me somewhat prophetically -- "That's why they call it 'Show Business' and not 'Show Friends'."

* * * * *

Certain-Persons sent my new spec to three different agents he had relationships with. The only set-up he gave them was that I'd been in the Business, sold a few things, gotten a few gigs and was looking for new representation. If they dug my writing, great. He'd be happy to make an introduction. If not, no worries. All it cost anybody was a quick read and a phone call.

Agent One was a well-known "spec monster" -- selling big money scripts was what gave him massive wood. But everything *after* the sale -- career building, focusing the writer on the right material, putting them together with the right producers, etc. -- didn't turn his crank so much. The guy was a frontrunner, a home run derby specialist who jollied himself jacking lob balls out of the park and making a big splash. The time-intensive aspects of agenting, like actually digging in and learning the entire gamut of skills required of any good agent, didn't interest him in the slightest.

We met at his world-famous agency offices. One of the senior partners rode shotgun, and I was surprised to recognize him. We were both Northbeach regulars, an upscale Venice watering hole with a twenty-foot-long illuminated fish tank. Couple times I'd seen this same guy shithoused and stupefied trying to puzzle out the freshwater eels.

Long and the short of it, Agent One wasn't convinced he could sell my new script. A <u>The Wild Bunch</u>-flavored thriller set in the world of home invasions, it had nagging elements of the Industry-reviled "character piece" -- despite a generous helping of action and some climax-goosing, four-alarm theme park explosions, there was no denying that, sooner or later, somebody cast in the film would actually have to *act*. This annoyance kept my pages from becoming a first-pitch homer. Putting this spec over would require legwork,

272

the ceaseless championing of a young writer, following up wherever there was the slightest hint of daylight...

Nah. Too much work. Agent One's face betrayed his mental exhaustion even considering it. Forty minute mark, he reiterated his interest, said they needed to think it over and told me they'd give me a call. Corralling my free Evian, I shook their hands. The Senior Partner said he'd catch me at Happy Hour.

Next day they called to pass.

Agent Two was a fun guy working at an agency considered demonic and egomaniacal even by Hollywood standards (narrows it down to twenty or so, right?). After C-P made the handoff, Agent Two touched base by phone, which was a incredibly nice gesture. Getting *anybody* to call you back when faceless and unknown seems to require a miracle, nothing short of Moses parting the Red Sea or finding an NRG focus group who still believes Nic Cage has real hair. We talked briefly, I thanked him and said to hit me back whenever he'd a chance to look the script over.

Couple weeks flew by before our follow-up. Agent Two told me he'd enjoyed the script, and from his brief notes I could tell he'd actually *read it* -- even more miraculous than that first call-back. In all honesty, though, Agent Two had another client sharing somewhat of the same creative wheelhouse, and servicing one writer coloring outside the traditional lines was already a handful as it was.

This shit happens. Agents don't need many duplicate clients on their rosters, meaning writers working within the same specific genres or overlapping in the type of material they write. Agent Two was totally cool and gave it to me straight, like an adult -- which, end of the

day, is all any writer can hope for. Very warmly, I
thanked him for taking the time.

Passes didn't get much better than this. Hearing "no"
didn't bother me in the least. Why? Because rather
than viewing it as rejection, I chose to see it for what it
really was -- a *confirmation*. Whether or not I'd gotten
signed, my script was proving strong enough to gain
serious consideration from big league Industry agents.
May not seem like much to the casual reader, but for
any anxious/hopeful young writer this is a massive
victory. *Now you <u>know</u> you're not just tilting at
windmills.* That everything's not just inside your own
head. Professional strangers don't waste time
bullshitting struggling wannabes. Just getting
confirmation I was on the right path and not completely
delusional about my prospects gave me a huge shot in
the arm.

Last up was Agent Three.

He was a little different than the rest.

His name was Marty, from the Motion Picture Lit Dept.
at an upstart new agency. Marty called me bright and
early one Monday morning having gotten to my <u>Wild
Bunch</u>/Home Invasion spec on the weekend read. To
my complete sleepy-eyed bewilderment, he seemed
pretty pumped about it.

Straight out the gate, Marty told me I was a fantastic
writer -- qualifying "writer" as in someone who can
actually <u>write</u> instead of just getting lucky with a
concept or being connected. He acknowledged the
script wasn't an outright million dollar sale, but still
thought with the right positioning it had a shot at
happening. This guy was all about business, zero
bullshit, zero hustle. More importantly, Marty said, and

I quote, "I can get you working, no problem. It'll take a little time, but it'll happen."

Evidently, this complete stranger had glimpsed what few others seemed to pick up on -- that I had solid skills which could be put to good use making money for everyone involved.

The things Marty was saying were fuckin' poetry to this struggling young writer's ears. He didn't communicate using "agent speak" -- he was pragmatic and friendly, nothing but good vibes, a *real human being*. He was the only rep I'd spoken with who talked Big Picture instead of little picture, writing instead of specs. Marty saw a long-term investment, a career to build and nurture, instead of the hit-and-split mentality of many big agency poster boys like Agent One.

This guy wanted to meet, pronto -- promptly cancelling his breakfast the next day to make it work. Wow, it hit me, this *must* be serious.

Whenever an agent calls you after seven p.m, it means they're rolling their call sheet and just tying up loose ends. You're not a priority, but they want you to feel properly serviced. Should you ever enjoy the good fortune of an agent calling before eleven a.m., it means they're way fired up and ready to move Heaven and Earth over something.

(F.Y.I. -- having a hallowed "breakfast meeting" is one of the highest levels of interaction in the Hollywood Mealtime Meeting Hierarchy. In order of importance: breakfast or dinner -- sometimes interchangeable in terms of importance -- then lunch, then drinks).

Marty gave me the agency's address. I assured him I'd be there.

275

"Holy shit," I thought hanging up. "An agent that gets where I'm coming from and wants to run <u>with</u> me. Someone who can open all those magical doors and help me become a real professional."

Certain-Persons followed-up soon after and Marty said, "I've only talked to him over the phone, but it sounds like this guy could really light up a room."

"You don't know the half of it," C-P shot back. "You won't be able to shut him up."

Marty's agency was still settling in, their new office space under construction. Coming off the elevator, I helped an Irish kid crabwalk a copier into the only conference room. Then Marty and I sat down for about an hour. What I heard in that room was twice as thrilling as what he'd said on the phone. One major topic of discussion was building me into a "call-in client" -- someone whom producers and studios specifically call to book for a job, instead of having to pitch and hustle for gigs with every other low-level schmuck on the make.

Marty also stressed that getting worked into the mix would take time. Maybe a year, maybe longer. We'd send my script out, see what kind of interest it drew, start taking generals and organically create relationships from that. My new spec would be a great way to purchase entre into this larger development world, whether it sold or not. Neither he nor the agency were in any big hurry. Doing it right was the important thing.

Finally, I just asked straight-up -- "Should I quit shopping around for an agent?"

"I'd like you to stop, yeah."

Marty shook my hand and the deal was done. I was finally off to see the Wizard.

* * * * *

That first year, I took a million meetings behind a cool spec that ultimately didn't sell. We came hella close, everyone from Sly Stallone to Sam Shepard to Christopher Walken showing interest, but for whatever reasons we couldn't punch her into the end zone.

Far more importantly, I was introduced to a motley crew of mid-to-lower level producers, execs and assistants who went on to do amazing things -- run studios, win Golden Globes, start big companies, get filthy rich -- many of whom I've maintained close relationships with to this day. Didn't get a single job out of that first big push, did not make a single dollar, but that process set the table for the next five years to come.

Exactly as he'd promised, Marty eventually got me working -- using that same unsold spec as the sample which helped me bag a bunch of studio jobs.

As usual, my buddy Certain-Persons had been dead on the money.

I didn't need an agent, I needed the <u>right</u> agent.

Key to getting them was being right place/right time with a brand-new, wholly original script already in hand. Without that, I might still be bitching about early X-Mas cards from uninspired agents.

* * * * *

Once you at long last score an agent or manager, many of you will be exchanging one dictator for another. A nagging new paranoia will soon burrow into your brain

277

with the ferocity of that fucked-up sandworm in <u>The Wrath Of Khan</u> -- constant worry and wonder about whether or not your new rep is "working for you". That's Industry parlance for whether they're actually cutting through all the attendant agent/manager ADHD and making time to focus specifically on *your career alone*; with all the energy and intelligence needed to help it take flight.

Truth of the matter? You'll never know for sure. Nobody ever does. This is where that trust part of the equation comes in. But here are a couple key points for neurotic, success-starved scribes which might help keep them from embarrassing themselves, freaking out and/or publicly shitting their drawers.

Fact -- <u>Your agent/manager only gets paid when you do</u>.

That's right, Rambo, your rep doesn't make any money by setting you up to fail. Excepting rare, bizarre circumstances, they are not your enemy. To the contrary, they're perhaps the only person alive in this shitty business who cares enough to go to bat on your behalf. Good reps don't waste time signing or even "pocketing" (representing without signed paperwork) clients unless they see real potential for success. This ain't the March of Dimes or the Make-A-Wish Foundation. No motivation exists for taking on dead weight that can't produce results.

The unspoken truth of it is that every client is given a <u>limited window</u> within which to succeed. A *de facto* trial period where a rep invests a hundred percent to make it work. Some agents have generous windows, others keep 'em narrow as a doggy door. What it all comes down to are personalities and their gut-level belief in you. Humphrey Bogart's agent stuck by him for *years* while he struggled to find his wheelhouse, convinced to the depths of his soul Bogart would make it big. Turned out he was right. Together they went on to achieve the legendary.

Then again, gas was nineteen cents a gallon and people still believed in a blonde haired/blue-eyed Jesus back then. I highly doubt that same heart-warming level of loyalty has been seen in Hollywood since *Gunsmoke* was Number One in the Nielsen's.

Whatever size your rep's window (rimshot), only one surefire way exists to get (and keep) them servicing your career with maximum optimism, effort and efficiency.

Start delivering.

(You're the writer, Holmes. What did you expect? That somehow this *wouldn't* come back to you?)

First spec doesn't sell? Write a second one. Start planning a third. Couldn't sell your series during pitch season? Cook up another, better one -- many networks buy year-round now. <u>New material is always worthwhile</u>, whether you dunk it straightaway or have to play out the hand for a while.

Per my earlier testimony, delivering doesn't have to equate with immediate dollars and cents. Putting yourself in the hunt, making positive impressions, coming close on projects and becoming a factor to be reckoned with can all yield excellent long term dividends.

Strip away all the bullshit, agents, managers and attorneys want to know that you're <u>trying</u>. That you're busting ass, going after it, treating the process of career-building with the dogged dedication it requires. *Why should they knock themselves out if you're not willing to commit at the same level?* They won't. Action is character, talk is cheap. <u>Show</u> <u>them</u> you mean it. Top-tier reps don't wanna hear fairy tales about how dynamite your next (currently imaginary) script is going to be, they want that sucker in hand. How else can they make you into the star client you so loudly and persistently claim you want to be?

Please pay attention, because I'm only gonna say this once --

Nobody can sell what you don't write.

So if you're falling short on your end -- not providing good new material, failing to make the most of opportunities, etc. -- that shit is on <u>you</u> and you alone. Everything writing-related begins and ends with your efforts. Climbing up your agent's butt won't change that one bit.

Best way to keep *anyone* motivated in *any* business? Get results. Quit wasting time worrying about your agent and concentrate on the part <u>you</u> play in things instead. It'll make both your jobs so much easier.

Fact -- <u>Your rep has other clients</u>.

Shocking as hell, I know, but you're definitely not the only person your agent or manager represents.

Let me ask you something -- who's your rep's Number One breadwinner? The screenwriting rainmaker with the monster quote bringing in the epic bucks? Because if it ain't you, then you can't reasonably expect to be top dog when it comes to being serviced. The squeaky wheel gets the grease in this Biz, and when this particular wheel gets to squeakin', mountains of money come sprocketing out.

Want to be first in mind, top of your rep's list?

Start generating income with what you write.

The real players know that's what it all boils down to. You can't control what clients your agent or manager may or may not be doing more for. **All you can control is making _yourself_ the most attractive client possible from a business standpoint.**

It wouldn't be unusual for a good rep to have thirty clients. That gives them thirty chances to hit the jackpot, thirty bingo cards to play. Writers? We get one. Professional agents don't live or die by us as individuals. That would be suicide. Can you imagine _your_ livelihood, your very survival, hanging on anything as scatterbrained, self-obsessed and completely unreliable as a _single screenwriter?_

Fuck that. _I'm a writer_ and I'd rather shoot myself than face a prospect that harrowing.

But we do live and die by them. These people singularly serve as our lifelines to the Business at large.

Get what I'm trying to tell you here?

You need to learn your place.

Man, that was fun to write! Gets your hackles up just _reading_ it, right? Like I'm some hair-lipped cracker plantation owner snapping a bullwhip across your back, barking at you to go slop the pigs or make me a straw hat or some shit.

Of course, what I actually mean is that having a clear-eyed understanding of what place you occupy in your rep's pecking order and where you stand in the film biz food chain -- and becoming entirely comfortable with that -- can become a critical tool for success.
Admittedly, it's a concept that came to me late, but once adopted I've found it invaluable in keeping me centered and somewhat sane while traversing Butt Town's schizophrenic sinkholes.

Listen, when I get sent a script, I'm already assuming *at least* six or seven other writers have seen it before me. Probably more. Does that wound my ego? Hurt my feelings (reader: *what* feelings?)? No, it does not. Not in the slightest.

Who the fuck do I think I am, anyway? Who knows better than me what I've done or not done? Accomplished or not accomplished? Have I sold a million-dollar spec? Power-scribed a global blockbuster grossing in excess of a billion bucks? Created a franchise worthy of action figures, lunch boxes, condoms, iPhone covers and all manners of merchandising crack that gives bean counters across the L.A. Basin stage-four priapism (*noun*: a painful and persistent medical condition where the penis refuses to return to its flaccid state)?

No. Not yet anyway. My memory ain't great these days, but I'm sure I would've remembered something that fuckin' awesome.

The people who have proudly stuck any number of those feathers in their caps? They're way ahead of me when it comes to any Approved Writers List. Only logical, isn't it? Why *wouldn't* it be this way? There's a sort of "screenwriting seniority" involved, I suppose you could say. They're currently more "successful" in a movie biz context, their names "mean more" than my own right now.

What's to get peeved about? That's what the scoreboard reads... today. Nothing says you won't get bigger, do more, knock a couple massive sales out of the park further down the road. Just means you can't expect to be first call with the vast majority of plum open writing assignments out there. That's a rare advantage earned, not given.

When looked at this way, without ego, wherever you currently stand, I think you'll find it both a source of strength and a <u>relief</u>. Quit torturing yourself with a myriad of paranoid variables. Other writers' successes, "better" agents, more powerful agencies -- all this shit is simply white noise. A distraction keeping you from the vital business at hand.

Concentrate your efforts on the only thing any writer *ever* controls -- what you choose to write, and how often you choose to write it.

* * * * *

Here's some friendly advice about leaning on <u>personal hookups</u> during your quest for representation.

Historically, handoffs from established peeps already making their way in the Business tend to yield the best results. Totally obvious, right? The shortest distance between two points is a straight line... with a trusted human face on either end. What's critical to remember for bit-chomping new scribes burning holes in the carpet is that asking anyone from close friend to men's room attendant to pass your script along is <u>never</u> the no-brainer you think it is.

283

Passing along an unsolicited project is a public assumption of responsibility. Your connection is allying themselves with you not only as a person, but with the underlying quality of your material as well; which equates with putting *their own reputation* on the line whenever lending a hand. Let me assure you this is no small thing. Per the laws of any good mob movie, vouch for someone, now it's on you.

This is just one of the many reason star assistants, up-and-coming execs, agent program trainees, etc. are loath to call in markers unless its absolutely critical. Favors are a precious commodity in this town; the less you ask for 'em, the more compelling (and hard to refuse) eventual requests become. Your hookups are busy kicking ass and eating a ton of bullshit to build *their own careers*. Why would they associate themselves and their names with lackluster material? Or some goofball known citywide as a capital "D" douchebag? Spamming Industry pals with dubious scripts leads to closed doors and unanswered emails. To backstage questions about your hookup's ability with new material -- a seed no serious future player can afford planting.

Much as it might hurt, sometimes connects steadfastly begging off may be all the answer a writer needs. It can only mean two things. They seriously don't want to read it <u>or</u> they already *have* read it, didn't dig the horrors glimpsed within, and don't have the heart to tell you so.

Don't become so preoccupied with emotionally bullying and badgering your peeps to get what you want that you can't hear what the fuck they're trying to tell you. Genuine sensitivity and self-awareness in this dept. is highly recommended if you plan on keeping your Industry friends friendly.

* * * * *

Not all marriages last forever -- not even the most passionate. Hollywood's arranged couplings of convenience are no different.

Sometimes a client/rep split becomes inevitable. Nothing's in the flow. Things quit clicking. Calls dry up. No-look passes start sailing out of bounds. Once winning early and often, gigs now become further and farther between, like Chevron stations on a parched stretch of Death Valley asphalt.

Six months or six years later, *it's just time.* To go your separate ways, freshen things up, see what the future holds. One (or both) of you have lost that loving feeling... and there's no tenderness like before in your fingertips.

I'll assume any writer inhabiting this space is calm and rational, acting from a place of great equanimity after having tried direct communication (i.e. voicing their concerns <u>out loud</u>, not through a pussy email or text), taking a sincere whack at fresh material, sitting down to restrategize together and/or attempting anything else capable of breathing life back into a faltering relationship. Alas, sometimes things simply are what they are, and you can't fit the genie back into the bottle. Even the best agents and clients don't always succeed together, the same way all great thoroughbreds and their jockeys don't win the Kentucky Derby. Timing, luck, chemistry... you can't necessarily hang these on anybody, writer or rep. Sometimes that's just how the cookie crumbles.

With divorce imminent, let me suggest you cut the cord with as much dignity and appreciation possible. My personal preference is saying your professional goodbyes face-to-face. Make it a celebration of what was accomplished, not a bitter post-mortem of what fell shy. Perhaps this person was a huge help to your career at one point. Perhaps you made some good money, shared some fantastic highs before it petered out. Or maybe all they did was keep you in the game, help you live to fight another day -- no small feat itself. Either way, like Yours Truly, you may want to convey your sincere thanks in the most respectful way possible.

Odds are breaking the news ain't gonna blindside 'em. They're professionals. Neither managers nor agents live in an emotional vacuum. To the contrary, most reps are highly attuned to client energy. Whether you know it or not, they can pick up the disgruntled writer vibes leaping off you like you're a human tuning fork.

I already know what you're thinking. Depending on the circumstances, especially if it's the *agent* who feels jilted, they may not be too jazzed about this whole face-to-face deal. Or maybe it's just not that big a thing to them, whatever existed (or didn't exist) between you failing to justify the inconvenience versus a quick kiss-off call. However your rep decides to handle it, what's of lasting importance here is *you* making the gesture in the first place.

Facing this same situation once, a few Industry peeps of mine nearly psyched me out -- advising me to end it via email, telegraph, carrier pigeon... basically *anything* capable of bypassing the powder-keg potential of going face-to-face.

Being a stubborn sumbitch, I went with my gut, called "bullshit" and sat down with my agent anyway.

Guess what? We had a fantastic conversation, revisiting the many twists and turns we'd encountered, sharing things we wished we'd handled better, each fully owning our parts without the slightest hard feelings. I know, sounds like some sappy Seventies encounter group, right? But getting to express my thanks this way when parting was a very good thing, fully justifying my decision.

Two schools of thought exist about the process of leaving. Number One is that it's easier to get an agent when you already have one; similar to job hunting in the straight world. I don't believe there are any Rand Corp. studies on Hollywood agents laying around, but there's a proven logic there. Perhaps it makes you a more appealing client to some and helps set you up with a ready-made place to land.

But there's also potential blowback. Outing your search publicly exposes you. Hollywood is the smallest fuckin' town in the world. The walls have ears -- and so do the menus, tablecloths and toilet stalls. Your rep discovers you're "cheating" on them this way, there won't be any making nice. Expect excommunication and a permanent stain as your rewards for trying to backdoor them.

Number Two was the choice I made. Taking the high-road. The "do the right thing" approach -- an uncomfortably close first cousin to the "nice guys finish last" approach. Worse case scenario, you end up like Pesci in Goodfellas; walking in and hearing heavy plastic rustle underfoot a nanosecond before the muzzle flash. Best case, you get to bask in the honesty and evidence some quantifiable integrity to the outside world.

Discounting all the touchy-feely Good Karma stuff, burning bridges is always a messy business, and you rarely emerge unscathed. Venting spleen and giving 'em both barrels may *feel* orgasmic at the time, but no writer can predict when it might wrap back around to haunt them -- especially since so many agents/managers move into development or producing at some later juncture in their careers.

Bottom line, why *not* end your partnership on a positive note? The benefits are many, negatives none. Trust me, you'll end up making plenty of enemies in this town inadvertently, for no apparent reason, not even trying hard. Why not keep that body count from spiraling any higher if possible?

My hard-earned experience is that the Hollywood D-bags you despise most end up hanging around the longest; post-apocalyptic cockroaches who survive every flop, shake-up and setback to emerge four times as douchey and diabolical as before. Worse than not being able to rid yourself of these hard-shelled fuckers, they always seem to pop back up at the least opportune times; when the very last thing you need is an unexpected cockblock coming out of the blue.

My take could not be cleaner -- avoid any and all emotional entanglement with these loathsome creatures whenever possible. Should the potential for squabbles arise, the middle-class writer (having the least power) inevitably eats the bullet. Make a habit of reaching for the easy, insincere "thanks" over the more satisfying "fuck you" whenever there's a choice. It'll make your climb a helluva lot less taxing.

WHAT ZIZ ALL ZEEZ MONKEY HAIRZ?

My agency called. This time it was Seymour, not Marty.

The Lit Dept.'s dominant strategy was to divide studios and major production companies into "territories" and assign individual agents to cover the action at each of them. Say there was a job at Sony. Whoever covered Sony would be the rep to contact you directly. They played real team basketball back then, which moved things along much faster.

Seymour covered Studio X. Like pro ballers, guitar players and game show hosts, lit agents tend their business with a wide variety of styles. Seymour was the exact opposite of my main guy Marty. He was a living, breathing outtake from Barton Fink; the same schmoozy Hollywood agent populating The New Yorker cartoons since 1912. Regardless, he was a solid guy, and after a decade surviving on rice cakes and 49-cent tostadas, any call from *anybody* about a paying gig was like fuckin' X-Mas morn. Nipsey Russell and Charo could've called about a Love Boat reboot (Google if under 35) and I would've burst into tears of joy.

Seymour ran it down for me. Studio X was looking to hire a new writer on a big summer blockbuster. Based on a recent film I'd written, the VP Tony wanted me to come in and conjure up something "urban, contemporary and totally kick-ass!" to help get the script back on track.

The film's premise was pretty straight-forward -- a wheelchair-bound homicidal maniac computer hacking genius (think evil Stephen Hawking) decides to take over the Internet and destroy America with it. All the other little essentials beyond that (stuff like the plot, the characters, their motivations, etc.) were still vague as hell and wide open for interpretation.

What sweetened the deal was the involvement of a world-renown European director named Giorgio, a filmmaker I'd long admired. The studio was adding him to the mix as a producer in vague hopes he'd eventually relent and agree to direct the film himself.

The precise instant Seymour called, I was shot-gunning Peet's in hash-marked boxers, cracking the shrink wrap on the new Radiohead CD and praying like hell it had A LOT more guitar than their previous effort.

"Hell, yes, let's get it on." I gave him the greenlight. "Send me the script and I'll read it a.s.a.p."

"Well, actually," Seymour hesitated, pumping those invisible Film Biz brakes. "The VP wants to meet with you *first*, just to walk you through things. He said the previous drafts totally suck donkey balls and he's afraid they might poison the well with you creatively."

"Totally suck donkey balls" ain't exactly the starting point any writer's hoping for. My Spidey Sense commenced a vague, unsettled tingling.

But outside my 400 sq ft. Venice bungalow it was 78° and breezy and all was well. Rent was coming due, my '66 Bug needed a new syncro *and* a Northern Cali hookup was FedEx-ing me a plump Z of (street name) "Warm Helmet of Clay". As any struggling young writer from any era can tell you, none of this shit came cheap.

(Note to confused Millennials: this was back in Prehistoric times, before the advent of "legal" cannabis clubs. Back when you actually had to have some game, be cool and do some legwork to get baked instead of just ordering home delivery with an iPad app.)

But beyond all that silly shit, I'd prayed to be in precisely this position most of my adult life -- *making a living writing movies.* Fuckin' A, I mean, what's not to like? With the Movie Gods finally smiling (or were they smirking?), I'd taken a few baby steps towards The *New* American Dream -- screenplays having usurped the crusty ol' Great American Novel of years prior. Basically, with one sale you could make more than Faulkner, Henry James and Jack Kerouac in their combined lifetimes.

Or as my best friend so succinctly framed it -- "Doc, you're right where you want to be."

Cerebral cortex haloed by all this uncommon (and awkward) positivity, I pulled the trigger, taking a confident step forward into the unknown.

"No worries, Seymour," I pledged. "Go ahead and set it up."

* * * * *

Driving onto a legit studio lot has always given me massive film wonk wood. The toxic twin towers of L.A. and the Movie Biz have left precious little history standing, so any chance to relive <u>Nightmare Alley</u> on the New York Street, picture F. Scott Fitzgerald staggering shit-housed from the faux Swiss Chalet Old Writers Building, or role-play the <u>Starsky & Hutch</u> pilot... well, it's a rare and wonderful gift for anybody who's ever truly loved the movies.

We met for a Cobb salad in the Studio commissary. Tony was alright as far as VP's go. If you dug a little, dropped a few crucial safe words, you could uncover a stand-up guy Robocopped inside the cookie-cutter corporate blue suit. Tony legitimately *loved* classic film, and he tried hard to juggle what worked best creatively with what could be sold upstairs in real-world terms.

But we are talking about the studios here, and the majority of times even the most sincere Exec's efforts get cockblocked into oblivion.

Poor bastard. What torture this must've been. Playing monkey in the middle was the cross many a studio VP had to bear, regularly forced to navigate that age-old tug-of-war between commerce and art for their movie-loving souls. The harrowing, relentless pressure to bandwagon extremely profitable dogshit vs. their yearning to champion far better scripts whose complete lack of box office appeal could cost them both parking space and paycheck.

As Nietzsche so famously scowled, "*Even the bravest of us rarely has the courage for what he really knows.*" I wondered if Tony knew this quote... and if he'd ever considered it while voting thumbs-up for Freddy Got Fingered or Speed 2: Cruise Control.

The junior exec on the project? No issues there. Having no soul to begin with, movie-loving or otherwise, he had none of his boss's high-minded concerns.

Brooklyn was an unabashed bootlicker, a cradle-to-the-grave studio lackey who'd adopted the ever-popular "failing upwards" approach to Hollywood after four silver spoon years at Yale. Brooklyn was neither prescriptive nor profound, understanding a hundred times more about the seating chart at Barney Greengrass than <u>The Godfather</u>.

For working screenwriters, execs like these are potentially lethal non-entities; unseen Claymores strung in Hollywood's jungle vines. They never add anything creatively, give the broadest story notes possible and will sell you out in a heartbeat -- even when they completely agree with you. Goofballs like this passionately *loved* something until someone senior to them hated it, then they passionately *hated* it, too. For sycophantic brown-nosers like Brooklyn, "being their own men" never entered into the equation.

So there we sat, this unholy trinity -- screenwriter, D-Boy and V.P. -- grinning over commissary salads like constipated chimpanzees. V.P. Tony pitched me more of the shithouse-crazy Steven Hawking antagonist angle. This handicapped evil genius blamed Uncle Sam for the tragic loss of his parents in a U.N. bombing raid over Kosovo (or was it Mogadishu?), and his vitriolic hatred of all things American had terribly and irrevocably reached the boiling point. Using his diabolical manipulation of the Internet, Hawking would create chaos on a scale the U.S. had never witnessed before (okay, maybe in <u>Armageddon</u>). Planes and public trains would crash. All electricity would be cut off. The ATM's in Beverly Hills would seize up, giving way to fierce rioting by the Fendi and Coach-obsessed.

As Tony's sales job neared climax, Joel Slyberg, one of the big honchos in Motion Picture, dropped by. With a quick, moist handshake, Slyberg bullied into the booth beside me, pressing me into an awkward studio exec sandwich.

"So what do you think, Tommy boy? Great project or what?"

"John. My name's John."

"Duh. Who said it wasn't? <u>Romeo Is Bleeding</u>, one my personal favs, by the way. Cheers on that. Great stuff."

Peter Medak had directed <u>Romeo Is Bleeding</u> -- not <u>Romeo Must Die</u> -- back in '93, which was apparently the last time Slyberg had treated himself to an Altoid. Each concussive syllable Jackson Pollock'd my glasses with salty halitosis. Big-time Richard Nixon vibe, this guy, unctuous and slightly reptilian and entirely unashamed to let his freak flag fly in either department.

Slyberg picked up the hard sell, pitching twice as fast as Tony, and together, with Brooklyn mentally limping along behind, they gangbanged me into considering the project.

* * * * *

I got the script. Tony had not been lying. It totally sucked donkey balls.

I know, I know, <u>EVERY SCREENWRITER IN HISTORY</u> says that the moment they're sent a rewrite, savoring some fleeting sense of superiority while passing judgment from high atop a cineast's ivory tower. The same century-old "*can you believe some fucktard actually got <u>paid</u> to write this shit*?!?" that young writers enjoy putting on blast to build themselves up.

But no, dude, really -- this time it *was* an epic shitting of the bed, officially and without dispute. Now it became crystal clear why they'd been so aggressively courting a promising up-and-comer like me. The project was pretty much a boondoggle at this stage, so they needed a scribe with the skill set to actually crack it, but they didn't want to pay the monster quote usually

294

accompanying such chops. Insulting? Not at all. These jobs can be manna from Heaven for new writers, giving them precious opportunities to climb the film biz food chain.

The operative words being "*can be*". The flipside is the ever-present risk of taking a hollow-point to the head.

My first thought after reading the pages? Someone's gonna take a hollow-point to the head on this project... and I'd prefer it wasn't me.

Here's the thing. New gigs are all strawberries and cheesecake -- until the money changes hands. That's when all the ego and judging and snarky writer shit comes to a screeching halt. Because now it's on you, brother, you're responsible. Those shitty previous drafts? Totally on your watch now -- as if they were *your* brainchildren and this was *your* passion project to begin with. Other writers? *What other writers*? Hell, you may as well have written those pre-existing pages yourself, because once the check's cut you become the only writer ever involved.

Take the gig, inherit all its bad ideas plus find your ass on the hook for the new Academy Award-quality stuff they're expecting you to dial in after, say, a week or so "working your magic".

In a matter of twenty-four hours -- just enough time to Blitzkrieg your text plan bragging all over Hell and back about the crazy money you'll make -- a difficult rewrite job can turn into your own private Afghanistan.

And suddenly *you're* the cocky fucktard getting paid to write this shit... with your neck squarely in the noose.

* * * * *

Day of our first story meeting it was Africa hot. Air
conditioning was strictly sci-fi when they designed the
'66 Bug, meaning my drive into the studio was like
having Vidal Sassoon point his favorite hair-dryer in my
face for five miles straight.

Further suffering followed. The Front Gate nobodied
me into a monster parking garage anchoring the
furthest possible corner of the lot. Believe me, I'm the
last guy into any sense of entitlement. I clearly think of
myself as the original Working Class Hero; a blue-collar
kid made good, no frills or fru-pampering necessary.
That said, during the writer's surgically brief
honeymoon period (i.e. before you start turning in
pages), you're usually hooked up with a spot next to the
office that first meeting -- the same glorious treatment
I'd gotten round one in the commissary.

Round two? No such luck. Underground it was a full
thirty degrees hotter, so within microseconds of
parking, it looked like I'd been doused with a fire bucket
of hyena piss. My pits appeared to be bleeding out. My
hair was matted flat against my skull, except for one
monstrous cowlick which had somehow remained
bone-dry and was now pulling a <u>Kingpin</u> all over the
fuckin' place.

Fuck it, I scolded myself. That's what I got for "keeping
it real" instead of driving a Mercedes, Hummer or Lexus.
After that, I quit thinking altogether; conserving my
remaining bodily fluids for the parched half-acre crawl
between myself and the Executive Building. When I got
there, I planned to promptly beg hands-and-knees for a
lukewarm Crystal Geyser.

296

* * * * *

Giorgio, the world-renown Euro director, was running the Industry-standard thirty minutes late. This forced all the players to sit there making mindless Hollywood small talk ("That film was *awful*, a big budget version of <u>The Apple Dumpling Gang</u>." "Yeah, but did you see the opening weekend?!?") to help kill the time.

The line-up was VP Tony, studio-friendly butt-frencher Brooklyn, and Giorgio's development "peeps" -- co-producer M. Antoinette and recent MFA grad Simonette, their company reader. Simonette was attractive in that perky B-cup blonde, paint-by-numbers, D-girl-next-door kinda way. Alarmingly, she was costumed in the full-on Catholic Schoolgirl Outfit of a baby-faced high-school sophomore despite being at least 25 years old.

I shit you not, Dear Reader, as the ghost of Dalton Trumbo is my witness, this was no "maybe" or "sort of looks like" horny extrapolation on my part; this was standard-issue Pontiff design straight off Central Casting wardrobe racks -- white bobby socks, plaid skirt, telltale tuft of white panty pointedly peeking out. The whole nine, as it were. It couldn't have been staged or wardrobed any better.

For years, I'd heard rumors and shit-talking about the Director's proclivity for, shall we say, *extremely* youthful girls (I'll admit, the word "pedophile" had popped up now and again), but until you're face-to-plaid-skirt-and-tuft-of-white-panties with it, well, it just seemed like workaday hatering. Now, however, my take would require some serious re-evaluation.

Inappropriate? Outrageous? Fucked up and just plain creepy? *Obviously*. But I'd had a few deals by then, so I surfed it with the same stiff upper lip as everybody else

297

in room. That poor D-Girl could've been wearing a John Gacy clown costume and I wouldn't have said a word. My mind was already focused on far bigger concerns.

Because on top of it all, the VP's office was a broiling Zip-loc of stagnant studio air -- giving even that scalding parking garage a run for its money. Maddeningly, nobody else seemed the slightest bit uncomfortable, all five as cool as cucumber spa treatments. I alone appeared to be feeling it, my only prayer for cool oxygen a tiny open window behind Tony's desk where the most fragile of breezes was fighting to take shape.

WHAAAAMMM! Office door bursts open and the great Giorgio himself power-waddles in... the whole dumpy, unshaven, über anti-climactic 5' 7" of him. Not only short, but *beaucoup tub o' lard,* this guy, chubby yellow-and-black striped sweatshirt making him a dead ringer for some bumble-bee dirigible flying in the Rose Bowl Parade.

"My apologeez," The G-Man's accent seemed wildly exaggerated, a Robin Williams mock-up, no doubt intended to humor or hoodwink gullible Americans. Which was sorta odd since he'd owned a home in L.A. for twenty years and spent a good chunk of his time here. "I had zee most important meeting, zee MOST important. But alaz, I am here now."

Fuck me. This was the legendary director?!? The cinematic genius who'd made a film so incredible I'd worshipped it most my adult life, seen it *fifteen times* and owned it in every possible format from VHS to Laser Disc to DVD?

Believe in Bad Omens, Dear Reader? Those itsy-bitsy Karmic signposts popping up to give us fair warning, if only we could puzzle out what they were warning us *about*?

First thing Giorgio did when he came in -- *the very first thing* -- was to bee-line (pun intended) straight for that solitary open window and SLAM IT CLOSED as hard as his pudgy little arms would allow.

Those embryonic stirrings of cool air? Gone. Kaput. *Fini.* The humidity inside compressed and my ears popped as if he'd sealed the top hatch of a WWII submarine.

That's when I knew, in the deepest hollows of my hopeful screenwriting bones, that my initial prediction was right -- somebody *was* going to take a bullet on this project.

And that somebody looked and suspiciously sounded a lot like me.

That meet-and-greet halitosis shower in the Studio commissary, the broiling drive, the broasting subterranean garage, the naughty, pedophile-approved schoolgirl outfit... red flags had been *everywhere*, screaming for me to hit the Eject before it was too late. But big, eager, cash-starved dummy that I was, it had taken Giorgio's guillotine window slam before the light bulb finally snapped on. There was no exit now, no way out. I was taking the ride whether I liked it or not.

I am Jack's colon bracing for non-consensual insertion.

First forty minutes, Giorgio boldly leapt into the fray, surgically diagnosing the project's many ills. The famous director spoke with great authority about what was, what might evolve and what should never be.

299

Regrettably, none of these self-assured freestylings had much to do with the actual project we were working on.

This wasn't my first trip to crazy town. I quickly I.D.'d these as the nonsensical ramblings (a.k.a. "brainstorming") of a producer who hadn't read *a single page* of the scripts -- sadly, not nearly as uncommon as you might think. Between the punishing demands of five-star film festivals (with ample, buttery buffets, evidently), AFI Achievement awards and 20th Anniversary DVD Director's commentaries to record (enunciated in textbook English, as it would turn out), it was clear the bold-faced log line atop studio coverage was probably as far as he'd gotten... fingers crossed.

For a young writer like myself, really starting to feel my oats and find my "A" Game, this was whiplash of the worst sort.

Over the previous ten months, I'd written an animated feature for Jeffery Katzenberg and saved a greenlit movie for Joel Silver. These gentlemen were legit bad-asses, the Seal Team Six of studio production slates. Being great producers, they knew their projects inside and out, and from the instant they hired you it was lock-and-load time. Showboating or pretending was certainly not part of either man's development process. Their business was *making movies*, and anything that got in the way of that was simply wasted time.

So I'd enjoyed this mind-boggling, twelve-month winning streak of working with the very best of the very best, *Hollywood legends, for Chris'sake*, and Giorgio had seemed perfect to provide the punctuation mark on my magical trifecta. On IMDB and in the popular imagination, Giorgio was right up there, one of the big dogs. But in the room, well, he was just... big. I'd gone off to see the Wizard and instead found an ordinary little munchkin hiding behind a tawdry Technicolor screen.

Nonetheless, gamely and with the greatest respect, I attempted to point things back towards dry land. You know, get down to business, jumpstart some concrete discussion of the shit-ton of salvage work ahead. Last I'd heard, this was a hundred-and-fifty million dollar movie, and sooner or later we'd need to get under the hood and see what's up.

Turned out, I was the sole inhabitant of Reality Check Island. *Nobody else was with me.* They feigned complete enthrallment, listening to Giorgio with a rapt attention usually reserved for foreign heads of state and Mayo Clinic chest cutters. Whenever I dared address story, I was ignored or daggered with hateful looks. At one point I think somebody actually (GASP!) hushed me!

Meanwhile, completely unencumbered by logic, the famous European auteur kept barreling ahead full throttle...

"Our Hero is chasing zee bad guy Hawking, chasing him everywherez. He gets tipped off to Hawking's hideout and drivez there! Zee S.W.A.T. Team kicks zee door down, and *voila!* Stephen Hawking is already gone, having gotten away by secondz!" Big-time theatrical pause here. "Zee authoritiez search zee place and everywhere zey find zis <u>monkey hair</u>. That's right. *Monkey hair.* And zey ask zemselves, 'What ziz all zeez monkey hairz?'"

Pitches it again. Same <u>exact</u> beat. Hero tipped off to Hawking's (second) hideout... S.W.A.T. busts the door down (a second time)... and guess what, they've just missed Hawking (twice now) "by mere secondz"! And, of course (everybody join in!), "Zey ask zemselves, _'What ziz all zeez monkey hairz?'_"

By now I'm physically wincing, knowing G-Man's got nothing, that he'll never land it, and that I'd be flying solo on fixes from today on. Finally, a full eternity later, the chubby lil' bumble bee rounded third and came digging for home --

"And later, what you find out is, because Stephen Hawking is messed up..." lightning fast, Giorgio HUNCHED HIMSELF OVER in grotesque imitation, flapping a "paralyzed" arm like a chicken wing and making the most bizarre "retard face" of all-time, "Hawking has <u>A</u> <u>SUPER</u>-<u>INTELLIGENT</u> <u>MONKEY</u> as zis assistant who runz around doing everything for him!!!"

I was so stunned, swear to God, I almost lost the handle on a fart. The VP's full-blown sauna went silent as the deepest vacuum of outer space. One thousand one... one thousand two... one thousand three...

Brooklyn was first to venture out into this potentially career-killing abyss.

"Oh, Giorgio," the star-fucker blurted out. "_You're giving me chills!_"

* * * * *

After that, everything trap-doored straight into Screenwriter Hell.

That traditional writer's "honeymoon period"? The frequent calls, the ultra-supportive studio meetings with back-slapping, fist-bumping execs stressing how much they "love you for this", "what a great fit" you are, how they "couldn't conceive of a more perfect writer" for the project?

Not so much.

From urgent first week discussions of flying me to Cannes to work with Giorgio while attending the festival, my stock plummeted to his V.P. M. Antoinette busting a cap in my ass the nanosecond my first *ten pages* were turned in.

Giorgio's hatchet gal had all the warmth of an Eighteenth Century hangman. Nothing I did was right, nothing I suggested pleased her. She'd approve an outline, then skull-fuck me like a Tijuana hooker the instant I'd executed her pages verbatim. Whatever tack I took, however I reworked the scenes or reimagined the characters *at her request*, M. Antoinette still forcibly entered me from behind.

Yet when it came to helping with fixes -- to lighting a candle instead of cursing the developmental darkness -- Ms. Congeniality played possum. She'd assume the vague, mumbling persona of a 1950's French Existentialist and her English vocab would violently contract by at least 50,000 words.

Whatever larger political agenda was afoot -- or how it pertained to me or the work I'd been hired to do -- was kept strictly classified. Even V.P. Tony punked out, taking shelter behind the Studio playbook (*Rule #2641 -- Keep writer completely in the dark at all times*). Gamely, I figured with a down-low "heads up" or "hey brother, watch your six" I could get my bearings and surf whatever meat grinder I'd stumbled into. Thing was, Tony wasn't inclined to give me either. My former Cobb salad crime partner left me twisting, steering clear of the potential blast radius at any cost. Even when asked point blank, man-to-man, all he'd give me was this sad little tap dance of slightly embarrassed obfuscation.

On any studio project, the Director becomes the most important player. Every professional writer knows this (or should know it) and it's only logical, nuts-and-bolts common sense. Should the movie ultimately get greenlit, it's the Director who'll be out there in the Real World someplace actually making the Studio's $100 million dollar movie. It's no exaggeration to say he or she becomes your commanding general (think MacArthur or Patton), the brave soul tasked with slogging through production's bloodiest trenches and most brutal psychological battles while *still* being able to find the creative presence of mind to wrestle a quality motion picture safely into the can.

Once physical production begins, the Director becomes your go-to-guy or gal. All your chips are riding on them now, and you've got no choice but to back them 100%, come Hell or high water. Sometimes a Director's *sheer force of will alone* is the only thing separating a potential hit from a $100 million-plus sinkhole into which, first thing Monday after a disastrous opening weekend, Hollywood will begin bulldozing dozens of once-promising careers.

...Which is all fine and well and which I perfectly understood. The Director is *El Jefe*. "He's the Duke, he's A-Number One!" Got it. Couldn't have said it better myself. There was just one catch --

We *weren't* out there making the movie yet.

We were an easy thousand miles from that, adrift on barren storytelling plains without a single usable page. Traditionally, this is the point of genesis where Studio, Director and Writer come together and -- all monkey hairz aside -- lock down the very best version of what they want their movie to become.

(Crickets chirping. Long beat.)

Don't they?

$$* * * * *$$

Per my earliest, darkest suspicions, I took a bullet to the
head. That summer became my screenwriting
Afghanistan, a savage studio killing fields where naive
young recruits like myself got IED'd into oblivion.

I spent two exhausted, terror-stricken months slaving
and worrying my balls off trying to fix the movie. The
Studio sunk their spurs into me day and night, insisting
that if I wanted "my script" to become next summer's
epic tent-pole blockbuster, then it needed to be airtight
by Sept. 1. -- a paltry eight weeks way. Remember, we're
talking a Page One on a $150 million dollar, donkey
balls-sucking movie which, at it's structural center, had
heavily-armed S.W.A.T. teams discovering empty
apartments filled with monkey hairz. In civilian terms,
this gig had the same level of difficulty as, say, trying to
fit a B-1 bomber inside a ribbed condom with a
blindfold on.

Sadistic? Disingenuous? Dangling the keys to eternal
riches and quick success before a kid like that? Ya
think? But being a good soldier, young and cocksure,
they knew I'd rise to the bait. How could I not? How
could any writer who loved movies not?

Passing the buck, I began riding *myself* twelve-plus
hours a day. My level of commitment, already extreme,
was promptly redoubled. If all the knobs were already
on ten, I dimed them to Spinal Tap's mythic eleven.
Fresh-faced kid I was, I was determined *not to let these
nice people who believed in me down!* Even if that meant
grinding my sense of self-worth into hamburger.

"If I can just fix this thing," I kept telling myself, *"I'll be given the keys to Willy Wonka's Chocolate Factory! Only this time, it'll be filled with J-Lo butted hotties, cold cash and crazy cars! My penis will grow another three inches! My parents will become even <u>prouder</u> of me!"*

Yours Truly pulled a baby-faced Martin Sheen/<u>Apocalypse</u> opening -- bloodied, pickled in grain alcohol, wearing nothing but skid-marked bikini briefs as I went spiraling into the abyss. I started barking wild-eyed at friends over Knicks scores, making uncouth dietary demands at Abbott's Pizza (*"More fat, Tommy! More fat goddamn you!"*) and became a MASSIVE DICKHEAD to generally anyone within my kill zone.

How nutty did I get playing the Good Soldier? Given *my* personality? I was given hook-up passes to the <u>Gladiator</u> premiere (<u>sitting in Ridley Scott's section, no less</u>!) that I passed on because... you're never gonna believe this... I felt *guilty* about not working instead. Yeah, still viciously kicking my own ass over this one. I literally sat down and had a serious talk with myself, deciding I couldn't take *three hours off* to see the greatest blockbuster of its era, that year's Best Picture winner, while sitting next to its director and producer. That's who I was back then -- the drink the Kool-Aid, take-one-for-the-team working-class Boy Wonder.

That now-legendary premiere featured <u>Perfect 10</u> models in skimpy togas and REAL FUCKIN' TIGERS! Wasn't there. Didn't see 'em. Got the starry-eyed recap from hungover pals the next day.

During that summer, a new phrase was worming its way into the mainstream, one I hadn't gotten the memo on -- "panic attack". Only years later would I realize I'd sucked up five or six of 'em during those two months.

"I wanted a mission, and for my sins, they gave me one. Brought it up to me like room service. And when it was over, I'd never want another..."

Exactly eight weeks later, I submitted my draft. V.P. Tony high-fived me like we were the Showtime-era Lakers, specifically praising my ideas for carrying the cat-and-mouse of the film, a thorn in the Studio's side since the project first began.

That was the only feedback I ever got. Ever. It was also the last I heard from Tony, Brooklyn, Giorgio, M. Antoinette or pedophile poster girl Simonette.

Ludicrous? Counterproductive? A ridonculous waste of time? That's just how some studio deals play out. Ninety-nine percent of the time when things go sideways you *never* find out what was actually going on. They feed you a fat paycheck then Medivac you in-country under withering crossfire to perform the bloodiest triage surgery. Whether or not you make it back out alive isn't high on their list of priorities. Your ass is expendable. That's why they pay disproportionately well -- think of cold cash as the numbing cream screenwriters apply after being violently crapped back out the other side.

* * * * *

Ricocheting from shithouse to penthouse and back again happens a good deal in this town -- which means, of course, you weren't really part of the penthouse crowd to begin with.

But you know what hurt worse than what Studio X put me through?

How I treated *myself.*

307

As a young writer under heavy fire, I'd made a tragicomic decision -- to take it all <u>personally</u>. With any perspective at all, I would've realized I was the only person involved doing that. Think Brooklyn and the studio guys lost sleep over it? Think Giorgio lost his appetite for buttery film festival crumpets? Think Simonette quit having her Catholic schoolgirl outfits dry cleaned? Fuck, no, they did not. *It was just business.* Within a month of fading me out, they'd hired the next in a long daisy-chain of writers to follow. It was me alone, the self-anointed Good Soldier, who chose to internalize the less compassionate parts of the process. By treating business as personal, I'd made myself into the emotional patsy.

Which points to a razor's edge all good writers must learn to walk. If you're too trusting and open, you'll be disemboweled by the rewrite process; if you're too cynical and hardboiled, your pages will lack heart and suck dick, agonizingly obvious to everyone from your employers to your agent or manager.

This later take can be lethal. No matter how much "heat" you may have, get a reputation for mailing shit in and going through the motions, folks will simply quit hiring you at some point. But the former can be equally debilitating as well, manhandling your mental toughness and spiritually bringing you to your knees.

So exactly where *should* a good-hearted writer neck-deep in dark forest stand?

My professional take is to work from a place of personal pride -- <u>*care even if nobody else seems to*</u>. Kick ass and write well because <u>you're</u> concerned about how it turns out. If nothing else, it builds character; further strengthening craft while developing coping skills you can lean on moving forward.

308

Every time you crack a story problem or devise a fix for something having eluded five or six previous writers and/or creatives, you deepen your knowledge base, acquire an awesome new weapon for your growing arsenal. When it comes to structural mechanics, many of these strategies can be repurposed for future writing gigs or spec scripts whenever similar issues arise... and you'll continue perfecting variations on them throughout your career.

Ultimately, my friends, you'll discover that money alone isn't enough of a motivation. Sure, you'll bask big time in that blissful shockwave of first getting paid to write. It's *fuckin' awesome*, no doubt. But once the street sweeper sucks up the victory parade confetti, there's still gonna be a shit-ton of hard work to do. This is where the happy distractions fade, dollar signs cease to matter and the proverbial rubber meets the unforgiving road.

One thing I've found time and again is that when you legitimately care, daring to invest your best self in a project, it really helps take the edge off an otherwise thankless ordeal.

GREEN ENVELOPES

Say you take everything *Tough Love* preaches to heart. Do all the right things. Spend a year or two seriously woodshedding. Build up your craft, cobble your skill set together. Find a good read who gives constructive feedback. Continue working your ass off without throwing a pity party every time you get a pass -- which will happen a lot more often than not.

One day thereafter, if you're *very, very lucky*, everything breaks your way and all the stars align, you may actually get a movie made.

It may come from an entirely original script or it may happen by rewriting an existing project. Either one will work just fine. Super Bowl rings are rare, and whether you're starting or coming off the bench, that Championship bling sparkles with the same intensity.

Movie wraps, picture's locked, release date is set and the advanced studio or company hype begins corkscrewing through cyberspace. After a thousand-plus thankless hours shackled to your computer and a lifetime's worth of harrowing ups and downs, the shit is finally and irrevocably <u>real</u>. Fantasy has become reality. Doubt is no longer relevant. You stand proudly atop screenwriting's Mt. Everest in plain view for all to see.

Now just one seemingly small thing stands between you and that off-the-hook Hollywood premiere, triumphant four-color French one-sheet and Two-Disc Special Edition BluRay with your name about 1/8 inch high in blurred factory laser print --

Writers Guild of America Arbitration.

Arbitration is the final, critical step to getting proper creative credit and insuring your financial participation in the film's profits for generations to come. Every writer involved in any film falling under Writers Guild jurisdiction goes through this process whenever there is the slightest question or disagreement about the film's appropriate authorship -- about who deserves on-screen credit and who does not.

Grab a Sharpie, fellas, and jot this part down -- there is nothing more important for a screenwriter than winning Arbitration and getting credit on a film they've written. NOTHING. I wish you could see the take no prisoners, blood in my eyes expression I'm wearing while writing this. Never have I been more dialed-in about any subject in my life.

Rightly winning a WGA Arbitration means everything.

Why is this such an urgent, vital and serious point? Why does it have me game-faced and white-knuckling my MacBook here in Volcano Tea some fifteen years after my first experience with it?

Because winning an Arbitration on a film you wrote radically changes your life forever -- both as a professional writer and a human being.

Not only does getting screen credit slam dunk your inner-film geek fantasy of getting a movie produced with your name on it, it throws wide the doors of opportunity on *dozens of future projects* that haven't even happened yet. It launches you onto a far superior career path involving better material and a much bigger quote. Being produced makes you real in this town, gives you a track record, a resumé, makes your ideas seem far more potent and inspired than they did before your movie came out. It gets you meetings with producers and execs who wouldn't see you before, didn't even know you were alive. It puts you in consideration for projects you'd previously only read about on wannabe forums and IMDb Pro.

Getting credit is a massive upgrade, from Southwest to Virgin Atlantic First Class, elevating you from some desperate, keening, hopeful putz to the more honorable title of "produced screenwriter".

And that's just for starters. Wait 'til you hear about the pay bump that accompanies such a promotion.

Yet, despite Arbitration's do-or-die, make-or-break importance in a writer's life, almost nothing about the mechanics of *how it works and why* seems easily accessible. During my lazy and indifferent Googling, I have yet to find a source that truly gives you the pro-style, boots on the ground 411. Surprisingly, even many longtime Guild members find themselves in the dark when suddenly thrown into the process.

Does it really matter why nobody's bothered to hip you to this info before? Not so much. Just thank your lucky stars you found *Tough Love* and I'm here to hook your ass up.

Worldwide, tens of millions of movie lovers have long shared the same erroneous assumption -- that you write a movie, your name magically pops up on the big screen, and you stroll off into your wonderful new life wearing a form-fitting bodysuit made of thousand-dollar bills.

Nothing could be further from the truth.

For pushing twenty years, writers have been stacked onto projects like cordwood, the more the merrier it seems sometimes. The closest thing comparable is Major League Baseball, where a different relief pitcher is brought in for damned-near every new batter, righty or lefty, sometimes for just a single pitch.

Does this largely counterintuitive, assembly line approach -- deliberately herding too many cooks into an already crowded kitchen instead of giving a writer or two time to thoroughly plumb the depth of the material -- make for a better end-product? Apparently not. Take a cursory glance at the past decade's theatrical releases and the myriad of multi-authored "go scripts" being bounced around town even as I write this. I would humbly submit that the vast majority of their results speak for themselves.

Development, despite being capricious and deeply flawed, "is what it is" -- as fully entrenched as the Insurance lobby and the NRA and not going away any time soon. Which means you'll need to learn to negotiate the ins-and-outs of the system during your career regardless of your personal feelings about it.

Be smart. <u>Expect multiple writers on most any legitimate film</u>. This has become the rule, not the exception. In today's Hollywood, having just one writer is an extreme rarity reserved for the hallowed few who have earned the privilege via A) writing quality, critically acclaimed projects B) writing projects packing proven box-office punch despite critical scorn or C) self-financing and/or vanity projects a.k.a. being able to raise the money themselves.

If you're fortunate enough to be solely credited or not involved in contesting screen credit, count your blessings, my friends. Just remember a logjam of writers will most likely be involved the next time you manage to get a movie made.

There are a truckload of films produced each year which have between, say, three and five writers. What's the problem, you wonder? Fuck it. Go Santa Claus. Give 'em *all* credit! Let everybody share in Hollywood's wondrous bounty!

Personally? LOVE the concept. If it were up to me -- in some perverse parallel universe where anybody actually gave a shit what John Jarrell wants -- believe me, giving everybody screen credit and permanently installing Daylight Savings Time are my two top priorities. (That's right -- I have absolutely no problem with Red State kids trudging to school in foreboding darkness if it means more sunlight in Venice Beach.)

But shy of that extremely unpleasant world with my crazy ass at the wheel, there are a host of major problems with blanket-crediting everyone.

First of all, the WGA *Screen Credits Manual* mandates that "*screen credit for screenplay will not be shared by more than two writers, except that in unusual cases, and solely as the result of Arbitration, the names of three writers or the names of writers constituting two writing teams may be used.*"

(The wga.org website has complimentary PDF's of the *Screen Credits Manual* available for anyone to download free. I highly recommend grabbing a copy -- http://www.wga.org/uploadedFiles/writers_resources /credits/screenscredits_manual10.pdf)

Why only two writers, perhaps three at the most?

Because Arbitration's function is to determine appropriate credit for writers who have legitimately *earned it* through their participation.

Often additional writers are brought on and the entirety of their contribution is discarded the instant they get the hook; none of their work survives past their brief, senseless and sometimes lucrative tenure. Others may be hired who <u>do</u> make changes sticking all the way into the Final Shooting Script -- but as good and necessary as they are, only a handful play a substantial part in the film's final storytelling. Since the average feature can take upwards of seven years to get made, multiple writers are almost certain to be involved along the way. Inevitably, how much or how little each writer contributes -- and the *value* of the changes they make -- varies wildly across the board.

Now imagine for a moment you're the writer who *actually wrote* the majority of the finished film. The man or woman who created the movie's universe as fully realized on-screen -- the dramatic construction, the dialogue, the original scenes, characterizations and character relationships. If you're responsible for the obscene amount of heavy lifting which brought all that good stuff to life -- *which made it feel real* -- the very last thing you're gonna dig is handing out <u>free</u> <u>credit</u> to a laundry-list of strangers you've never met, don't know, don't give a shit about and who didn't add much to the finished script.

Why should complete strangers be allowed to jock-ride your success? Siphon off your rightful glory and build careers on your back? If you invented the coolest Droid or iPhone app ever, would you abruptly give the credit to some guy you don't even know? Would you devise a company-saving strategy in the corporate world, then let the nerdy V.P. two cubicles down reap all the rewards?

Fuck no. You would not. Not only is the idea stupid, it's downright un-American, flying in the face of the self-determinism red-blooded patriots like myself hold so dear.

Which segues nicely into the issue of the big league greenbacks involved.

Each writer's contract contains a <u>credit</u> <u>bonus</u> figure -- the amount of additional money you're owed above and beyond your writing fee if the project ultimately gets produced. Here's where the plot thickens -- <u>studios and production companies only pay credit bonuses to the writers who wind up with their names officially on the film</u>. **In a nutshell, no screen credit, no bonus**. Simple as that.

These bonuses can involve mad cashish, ranging anywhere from say $5,000 to well over $1,000,000. Intense right? Keep in mind, this is "passive income" -- payments you get without ever having to lift a finger or write another word. The studios just fire off a fat check with your name on it. As you might imagine, for anyone who's struggled long and hard to make their bones in this brass-knuckles business, the feeling of getting a credit bonus is near-orgasmic.

Traditionally, screenwriting deals have both a "front-end" and a "back-end". I'll use one of my own deals as an example. For a thriller I wrote, my contract was for 350/750 -- that means a $350,000 front-end against a $750,000 back-end.

The front-end is <u>guaranteed money</u> for the different writing steps you'll do -- first draft, second draft, polish, tweak, etc. This is what you're being paid to write the movie.

The back-end figure is the <u>total</u> <u>amount</u> of money you can make on the project if it gets produced. So, if your deal is 375/750 you simply <u>subtract</u> the front-end figure from the back-end to calculate your credit bonus. In this case, $750,000 minus the $375,000 you've already been paid equals an additional $<u>375,000</u> going straight into your pocket. Likewise, if your deal was 100/200, you would have a $100,000 credit bonus, and so on. Simple formula, isn't it? Subtract guaranteed writing money from the back-end figure and you get your credit bonus amount.

If you <u>share credit</u> with another writer, you get what's called a "shared credit bonus" -- fifty-percent of your sole credit bonus figure. Following my deal above, that would mean $187,500 instead of the $375,000. (Still sounds cool, no doubt, if somehow lacking the sonorous bliss of the full three-seventy-five.)

But don't forget -- you only get credit bonus money <u>if</u> you receive screen credit.

Gettin' it now? Starting to grasp why Arbitration is of such critical importance and why it's so fiercely contested? <u>Hundreds of thousands of dollars hang in the balance for every writer involved</u>, a large enough screenwriting slush fund to pay off student loans, get a nice place to live, provide for your wife and children, take care of your parents, help out your closest friends, etc.

...But you don't get a single red cent of this movie biz Monopoly money unless you emerge from WGA Credit Arbitration victorious.

For the winners, those who *do* gain credit, the good times are just beginning.

Following your fat credit bonus will come <u>residuals checks</u>. Writing residuals are passive payments from a host of ancillary markets that generate income from the movie you wrote. For example, if you wrote a theatrical feature (something exhibited in theaters) you would get residuals from every other potential source of income trickling down from there -- BluRay, DVD, VOD, network TV, premium cable, basic cable, Netflix, etc., starting in the U.S. and spreading globally to cover all the foreign markets as well.

Bet your ass it's every bit as awesome as it sounds. Every time someone buys a BluRay, you get a cut. Granted, it's pretty tiny, but it's still a cut. Every night some Coachella casualty gets stoned and couch-locks with your flick on cable or streaming via Amazon Fire, it means you'll be getting yet another slice. This glorious ritual repeats itself down each and every rung of the exhibition ladder, all the way to some kid's three-inch Hello Kitty Sidekick screen, where they're paying for it in some fashion, too.

Hopefully, the light bulb has snapped on for even the most dim-witted of *Tough Love*'s readers, and with the shock of an altar boy's first amyl nitrate popper you've realized residuals can add up to a shitload of money in their own right. Residuals from one film I wrote ended up making me more money than my fee for writing the movie in the first place. Couple hundred thousand more.

And here's the fun part, a little tidbit working writers hold dear to their caffeine-saturated hearts -- this residual cash arrives from the Writers Guild in very distinctive <u>seafoam green envelopes</u>. Not to fetishize them or anything (awkward cough), but to be precise they're 6" x 9" Pastel #24 Light Green.

No other envelope in the world looks quite the same, and when you find one of these little guys napping

inside your mailbox it means "FREE MONEY" awaits...
always a nice way to kick off the day.

The Writers Guild is responsible for collecting,
managing and protecting writers' residuals worldwide -
- a massive benefit of membership. When unscrupulous
Biz-types try and cheat a writer out of residuals,
whether hiding in some distant Mongolian outhouse or
lurking inside a Barney's Beanery corner booth, the
WGA goes irrevocably Freddy/Jason on their asses. The
Guild carries a big stick in this Industry, and they have
zero problem hounding these sub-human parasites to
the ends of the earth to see justice done and get that
money paid out. How do I know? They did it for me
once -- spending *two years* corralling one of these filthy
foreign-sales cocksuckers and shaking the $20K he
owed me out of his famously tight pockets. Thanks
again, Residuals Department!

After hearing I'd gotten credit on my first film, an old
buddy from NYU who'd become a successful TV writer
called me up. We were jawing away when he dropped
the bomb about these little green envelopes of love. I'd
been in the Business close to eight or nine years by

then, but since I'd had nothing produced I didn't know the first thing about residuals.

"Just wait," he clued me in. "One day you'll walk outside and find one of these awesome little fuckers just sitting there. It's the best feeling *ever*."

Sure enough, one cloudy Wednesday I rolled out and discovered my own tidy green envelope fattening my mailbox. And you know what? It *was* the best feeling ever. Being compensated for your writing after years of penniless struggle? Being paid for your story that multinational corporations are shrewdly marketing and making millions off of? *Goddamn right it feels good*! As satisfying as being permitted to affectionately speed-bag Kate Upton's glorious breasts or getting to cup-check those Tea Party goofballs on Capitol Hill in the collective nutsack.

But again (insert record scratch FX here)... you do NOT get residuals if you don't get screen credit in the first place.

So, yeah, now you know. Getting your blurry name on that BluRay box is pretty damned important.

* * * * *

Over the years, I've been in Arbitration three times as a writer, worked dozens of them as an Arbiter (one of the panel members who decides their outcomes) and currently sit on the WGA Screen Credits Committee working Pre-Arbitration and Policy Review Board Hearings as well as expert readings on a volunteer basis -- which is the *only* basis Guild Members serve when it comes to all things WGA-related.

Writers gain <u>nothing</u> by participating. In fact, it *costs* them a ton of time and sweat equity to help out and lend a hand. They do it because they believe deeply in the Arbitration process and want to support their fellow writers however they can, which are the exact same reasons I became involved.

The pages which follow are <u>my own personal observations and opinions</u> regarding the Arbitration process and in absolutely no way represent the Writers Guild of America or WGA policy of any kind, in any way, shape, form or fashion -- period, end of story, case closed, fat lady singing, etc. etc. *ad infinitum.*

My thoughts are simply the take of one screenwriter -- me. There's no "secret sauce" shortcuts here, no "inside scoop" or "magic bullet" loopholes to boost you into the end zone. Just the musings of a crazy old codger who grew up on baseball, Black Sabbath, apple pie and Chevrolet; some generous scribe who's been around the block a few thousand times and believes that "sharing is caring". (okay, I almost vomited writing that.)

My first experience going into Arbitration was on the Hip-Hop Kung Fu actioner <u>Romeo Must Die</u>, which ended up with a total of six screenwriters. I was extremely fortunate to be working with Joel Silver, who was gracious enough to call me and another polish writer into his trailer for a quick heads-up about what lay ahead of us.

Joel gave us the Cliff Notes on Arbitration, then took time to single out what he believed was the most critical part of the process --

<u>The statement you write to your Arbitration Committee.</u>

The set-up for Arbitration itself is pretty straightforward. Prior to a film's release, the studio or production company sends a formal <u>Notice of Tentative Writing Credit</u> to the WGA and all the project's participating writers. These tentative credits are supposed to reflect who the company actually thinks deserves credit. Unfortunately, how that's determined varies from outfit to outfit. Some studios get lazy and put down their favored writer without much understanding of the material, others actually have employees read and review the drafts trying to apply WGA standards. Either way, they both net-out at the same place -- simply providing a non-binding starting point for the official Guild determination of authorship.

If a participating writer agrees with the tentative writing credits, they don't necessarily have to do anything. If nobody involved contests them, and an Automatic Arbitration isn't triggered by one of the writers also being a production executive on the film, they will pass on to become the official credits.

(During instances in which a Production Executive participates in the writing process alongside Guild members -- say a director, co-producer, etc. -- Arbitration is <u>automatically triggered</u> to protect WGA writers from unfair influence, undue prejudice or fear of reprisals.)

But if a writer *doesn't* agree -- say they're not mentioned for credit, or disagree with the *other writers* getting credit alongside them -- they file a <u>written protest</u> with the Writers' Guild. This written notice officially begins the process of a formal Arbitration proceeding.

Once the process begins, all the relevant materials are gathered together by the WGA. This can include everything from a film's original source material (book, graphic novel, magazine article, etc.) through the drafts each writer submitted while under contract, all the way up through the end of production and ADR work (looping/dialogue replacement). <u>Writers themselves choose which of their scripts they want officially representing their work during an Arbitration</u>. This allows you and you alone to cherrypick the drafts you believe best showcase the deep and essential nature of your contributions, further insuring the fairness of the proceedings.

An insane amount of material can pile up if the scribes involved aren't judicious in their approach. Let me give you an example. If five writers submit four drafts each you already have twenty drafts to be fully gone over by an Arbitration Committee. I was standing in the Warner Bros. story department as they were preparing the materials for <u>Any Given Sunday</u>. There were in excess of <u>fifty</u> <u>drafts</u> being submitted by the various writers for arbitration -- and I'm sure that's nowhere close to a record in this town. That certainly isn't the norm, though, and not something any sane writer would aspire to.

Here's my advice. Say you wrote six drafts of a film. **You probably only need to pick the <u>one</u> <u>or</u> <u>two</u> which best cover your contributions**, marking the others as "Reference Only" so your Arbiters can peruse them if necessary to confirm smaller points of contention.

The obvious logic is that from pass to pass the script you're developing doesn't necessarily undergo massive, wholesale change. More often, these revisions are smaller in nature; patches of new dialogue, new action within existing scenes, , lightweight fixes, minor tightening, etc.

323

It's important not to overlook the fact that your Arbiters (fellow human beings and writers just like yourselves) actually have to *read* all the materials submitted. Pedantically and/or neurotically overloading them with drafts is any Guild member's prerogative, but I have yet to see it increase a writer's odds of success. Judicious choices are really the ticket IMHO, because they help maximize the <u>impact</u> of your material. Why make some diligent reader wade through six hundred pages -- potentially muddling your own argument -- if one hundred will accomplish the exact same thing?

In any case, this isn't much of a problem because the Credits Dept. helps walk each writer through the material selection process, making sure they're one-hundred percent satisfied with whatever they choose to submit.

Having successfully vetted and approved all the involved materials, the WGA now assembles an Arbitration Committee to review them, with the ultimate goal of reaching a binding, final determination of screen credit for the film in question.

<u>An Arbitration Committee</u> consists of three Guild Members, selected randomly from among approved fellow writers. Again, these Arbiters are *your peers*, all volunteers, and their names are kept anonymous to ensure fairness and protect the integrity of the process -- just as all participating writers' names are blinded to ensure against any possible prejudice or disadvantage in the panel's decision making. <u>Not everyone in the WGA qualifies to be an Arbiter, by the way</u> -- before you can apply, you must have three screen credits or five active years in the Guild. These aren't easy standards, helping make sure potential Arbiters bring hard-earned professional experience to the process.

Now here's the critical thing Joel was cool enough to point out -- once the process begins, you're given just <u>one opportunity</u> to make direct contact with the writers sitting on your panel. **This comes via your <u>Statement to the Arbitration Committee</u> -- a single letter which outlines your entire case for deserving screen credit.**

Joel straight-up told us this letter needed to be outstanding in every way. It needed to advance the smartest, strongest, most compelling argument possible on behalf of our work.

Think of your Arbiters as <u>CSI: The WGA</u>. They're going to do their homework no matter what; reading and reviewing every line of submitted material whether your letter is great, shitty, inked in magic marker or scribbled in broken Farsi. That's exactly what they signed up for, and believe me, that's precisely the job they'll do.

<u>Statement or no statement, all decisions are made based on the submitted pages</u>. The drafts themselves -- the black-and-white work spanning some one-hundred and twenty odd pages a pop -- are without question the ultimate source of evidence on any writer's behalf. This is one dynamic which never changes. The written word alone is what determines your fate.

That said, the advantage of a world-class Arbitration Statement is that it allows you the unique opportunity to laser-focus your argument in <u>the most precise possible terms</u> for these three anonymous individuals; to frame your contention in your own voice and call specific attention to claims you believe of paramount importance in backstopping your argument.

Personally, I find this to be a particularly brilliant and insightful dynamic of the Arbitration process. We are *writers*, after all, and the realm of the written word is (allegedly) where we thrive and best express ourselves. Having ample time to contemplate and engineer your very best argument puts everyone involved on equal footing. Some writers may be fantastic in the room, natural born pitchers with the eternal gift of gab -- but not so great on the page. Others can be mumbling bastards, their mouths full of marbles -- but absolute geniuses once their fingers hit the keyboard. By bringing everybody back to the black-and-white of it all -- ground zero for any screenwriter -- the blank page once more becomes the great equalizer.

A compelling letter can play a huge part in deciding who gets credit. That's what legendary producer Joel Silver was impressing upon us that fateful rainy day in his Vancouver trailer. Not only does writing an Arbitration letter provide your only <u>direct</u> testimony, it's also the only part of the process any writer actually *controls.* Everything else is decided completely independent of his or her input.

How important is writing a good letter? Joel told us Steven E. DeSouza had written such an amazing letter in The Flintstones Arbitration -- with an astounding *fifty-two writers* in the mix -- that it actually got *Joel* a million dollar bonus. How? Joel was attached as a producer alongside Steven, so when Steven won, Joel emerged victorious well. Now *that's* a great Arbitration Statement.

By now I hope you understand that writing a successful Arbitration letter may become the single most important event of any writer's career; a fortuitous launching pad from which they may scale blistering new heights, personally and professionally.

Let me urge each of you to consider this with the utmost seriousness and preparedness moving forward. Phoning it in simply will not cut it. Not if you care about your writing career.

* * * * *

What happened with my own Arbitration after that?

I went home and did exactly as Joel suggested -- I wrote the best letter of my life. I busted my ass, intellectually pushed myself. Made a comprehensive and compelling fact-based argument then supported it with precise page-numbered examples and point-by-point explanations -- all done with a maximum of brevity. I wrote with the same respect, sincerity and conviction I would if addressing the Ninth Circuit Court of Appeals (on an important case like, say, having Daylight Savings Time permanently installed).

When you're the fifth and final writer involved on a project, it's *extremely* difficult to gain screen credit. Point of fact, the further you move away from "first position" (being the first writer) the longer your odds become -- especially if you're the guy called in to save a movie just weeks before production begins.

This is only logical, right? Because as you get closer to physically shooting a script, less and less substantial changes get made out of production necessity. The movie is already "there" enough to have been greenlit. Characters have been cast and actors scheduled. Locations are locked, set pieces passed off to stunt and pyro guys for prep and planning. Major plot lines are pretty much written in stone by now, any late tweaks typically coming in the form of dialogue -- often the least impactful category carrying the least amount of weight in Arbitration.

So going in as Writer Number Five, I already knew I was at a substantial disadvantage. *Nobody* thought I could win; not my agent, my manager, nor my showbiz friends.

"Don't worry," they offered pre-emptive consolations. "People in the Business know who did what. Everyone will know who really wrote the movie."

These folks weren't unsupportive, far from it. They were simply trying to cushion a hard blow well in advance. My lawyer Joel McKuin (whom I subsequently christened "The Rock 'N Roll Attorney") was extremely helpful during this time, but even good 'ol J-Mac didn't believe I had a snowball's chance of winning.

There was something else only I knew, however. Something none of my peeps had any point of reference for. *That I'd actually done far more work than necessary to meet the Guild requirement for a screenwriting credit.*

(And F.Y.I., folks in the film industry <u>don't</u> <u>know</u> who "really" wrote the movie -- they don't have the slightest idea and could care less about your Arbitration drama. If your name isn't on IMDB or Rotten Tomatoes, for all practical purposes, you *didn't* write it. Or as author Alex Haley so profoundly put it, "History is written by the winners.")

Bravely, I holed up in the children's section of the Venice Library -- tiny-assed Tyrion-sized tables and chairs, but none of the piss-soaked bums stinking it up on siesta -- and went about creating my masterpiece. I worked on it for three full days. My argument was fairly challenging because my contributions were strewn across all four of the key areas used to determine screenplay credit as outlined by the *Screen Credits Manual* -- <u>dramatic construction, original and different</u>

328

scenes, characterization or character relationships and dialogue. In my particular case, there wasn't one big, obvious, smoking gun/slam dunk concept or category capable of meeting the required percentage on its own. The threshold for this film was being responsible for at least 33% of the Final Shooting Script.

Instead, I was asking my Arbiters to please make careful note of my smaller -- but extremely vital -- contributions in *every category* and cobble these percentages together. Of course, this would also require more work on their parts. But I trusted in my peers and the process, remaining confident that once they did the cumulative math, the grand total of what I'd contributed would put me well over the goal line.

You'll please excuse any immodesty when I say I wrote a damned good letter. Perhaps not quite Steven E. DeSouza/The Flintstones God-tier level, but hey, this was my first Arbitration. I'd kept it nice and tight and on-point, relying on laser-sighted logic to make my case. There was no whinging or whining, no grandstanding or chest-beating, and there wasn't a single line of purple prose or pedantic flab to be found across any of my fifteen single-spaced pages.

Satisfied I'd done my absolute best, and having proofread and mind-fucked my statement 'til my eyeballs bled, I braced myself and mailed it in.

Couple weeks later the phone rang. Before I'd finished "Hello?", a nice woman from the Credits Dept. told me I'd won the Arbitration and would receive a shared credit. She laid it on me *fast*, like an adult pulling a child's loose tooth -- so quickly, in fact, I didn't even have a chance to get nervous. This caller also let me know the decision had been unanimous -- in fact, I was

329

the *only* unanimous writer of the three who had emerged victorious.

I'd won Arbitration. The Movie Gods had spoken (or was it the Hard Work Gods?) Either way, I was extremely fortunate my Committee took my contentions seriously and dug deep in doing their homework. Anything less than the most thorough and dedicated expert reading on their parts would most likely have sunk my battleship.

Being the green rookie I was, I had no idea what a game-changer this would become. Like I said before, it changes lives. Even before the film came out, I got sent better projects, started working steadily and began making more money. All because of that shared credit I earned on Romeo Must Die.

Just a few months before the movie came out, my Dad and I shared a fantastic Hollywood moment at the Promenade. We'd gone to catch Any Given Sunday over the X-Mas holiday and were slogging through the trailers when one came up that sounded strangely familiar, like I'd already heard the one-liners before. Then Isaiah Washington came on-screen, running my lines clear as day and suddenly it all hit me all at once.

That's Romeo Must Die. That's my movie.

"Hey! I think that's my movie!" I blurted out.

"That's your movie? That one?" Pops was gesturing wildly at the screen.

"Yeah, *that's my movie!*"

Joel Silver had worked his magic again. RMD had a fantastic trailer, very The Matrix-like, with slick visuals and perfectly chosen music. It just totally kicked ass.

330

Then my name (*Holy shit!* *My* name!) flashed on the credit tag and my Dad and I just started laughing our asses off, like we were sharing a tank of nitrous or something.

Nobody from the studio had bothered to let me know the trailers had started running. Why would they? I mean, I was only the guy who saved the whole damned movie in two weeks, right?

But in a fitting twist of fate, going in blind made the surprise a thousand times better. You couldn't have staged it for greater impact, and having my Pops there sharing it with me was the ultimate cherry on top.

Listen, when you actually see the trailer for a film you've written it completely Fukushima's your brain. You "know" that you wrote it, that it exists, that you were paid for it, paid taxes on it, etc. Yet when confronted face-to-face the first time with the abrupt *reality* of it, well, you just sit there dumbfounded and awestruck. That illusive goal you've been scrambling after most your adulthood is now legit, to the whole world, exactly as you promised/threatened so many times while struggling to believe it 100% percent yourself. Here's hoping the heavens smile and some of you experience the exact same sensation, tripping major ballsack with loved ones the way I did that day.

Two short years after RMD, I would buy my folks a home and help finance their school for gifted students in Phoenix. Soon after that, I was able to set up my first adult investments with Merrill Lynch -- just in time for the tech market to crater and swallow 80% of them. Later, they would christen this "The Dot.Com Collapse".

Nothing quite like being an adult and coming into your own, is there?

331

The unexpected byproduct of my Arbitration experience was deciding to get involved as a WGA Arbiter myself. Truly a man after Groucho's heart, I usually avoid belonging to any club that'll have me as a member. But I was so deeply thankful for my fellow writers' diligence in giving my case fair consideration, I felt returning the favor for other Guild members would be a good thing to do.

That was twelve years ago. Without question, it's one of the best, most fulfilling decisions I've ever made. Far better and more profitable than having put my savings in the stock market.

* * * * *

Twenty-plus pages later, here's what you need to ask yourself --

Why on Earth, with everything they've ever worked towards hanging in the balance, would *any* writer decide to get sloppy or lazy or cop an attitude when writing their Arbitration letter?

They'd have to be insane, ungrateful and irrevocably egotistical enough to require electroconvulsive (a.k.a. shock) therapy, right?

Evidently, not so much. Arbiters endure letters from arrogant, way overconfident, totally-full-of-shit writers all the time. It's not uncommon in the least, simultaneously showcasing the worst of writer behavior while breathing fresh life into the age-old Industry stereotype of us as cranky lil' bitches with Napoleon complexes and the world's tiniest dicks... present company excepted, of course.

Why, Dear Readers? *Why Would You Do This*?

332

Some of the letters I've read working Arbitrations simply defy explanation. Self-absorbed goofballs shuckin' and jivin' like their credit is already in the bag, the process some pro-forma victory lap, some light-hearted coronation, and they already *know* they're getting credit because, well, they *are* special and they, like, *totally* deserve it, dude.

Once I received a <u>single</u> <u>paragraph</u> Statement to the Committee which basically said -- "*Well, I was talking to some of the other writers, and we all agreed we're going to get credit anyway, but thanks for taking time to read this...*"

Swear to God, I thought that long-awaited aneurysm was microseconds away.

News flash. <u>Arbitration is an extremely solemn and serious proceeding, a right that several generations of screenwriters before you had to fight tooth and nail to gain and work hard over the past sixty years to maintain</u>. Your fellow Guild members serving on committees approach this with a maximum of purpose and integrity. So when you shine it on and disrespect the process you're doing yourself no favor in your Arbiters' eyes.

(Quick drop, Snoop V.O. -- "*When you diss Dre you diss yourself.*")

Luckily for half-smart jokers like these, no good Arbiter is going to withhold credit because of a letter lacking class or common sense. Believe me, if they did, there'd be an army of dumb motherfuckers out there without their names on a box load of movies.

Nope, that's not how WGA Arbiters roll. Despite a writer aggressively shitting the bed on their Statement, if their work is found to meet Guild requirements, credit's given where credit's due. That's how righteous Committees can be.

However, a stranger's generosity is *never* something you should bank on and certainly nothing to put yourself at the mercy of. Making your case to a Committee is no different than presenting yourself in any other aspect of life; whether it's meeting a prospective landlord, interviewing for your dream job or asking some big-booty hottie out on a date.

Reality check -- Do you really want to risk planting a seed of distaste in any of these peoples' minds before they actually see your work? Potentially poison the well before you've even left the starting gate?

Bet your ass *I* don't. So why would *you* recklessly hamstring your chances before your peers have read a single word? We aren't talking about sucking up or being a self-immolating ass-kiss here (God knows, there's a psychic penalty for that shit, too). *We're talking about being polite.* Respectful. Professional. Acting like an adult, even if you're not completely sure you are one.

Keep in mind that while you're clowning and slacking, the *other writers* involved (cold-hearted killers like myself) are preparing a quick and cozy funeral for you. We're shrewd and smart and we take this process very, very seriously. We delight in constructing airtight letters which keep you from seeing screen credit. So your overconfident bravado (read: idiocy) only helps *us* secure a lifetime supply of precious green envelopes, leaving your rookie ass out in the cold.

Should this point not be Carl Zeiss Super-Speed sharp, let me sledgehammer it home one last time --

Arbitration is full-contact, cutthroat and ultra-competitive, with monster dollars and pro careers at stake. No quarter is asked, none given. Fellow participants -- your *de facto* opponents -- will go to any lengths possible to out perform and/or outmaneuver you and win. Further, this is exactly as it should be, Darwinian fitness at its finest atop of the screenwriting food chain.

Which begs one question -- "*Why would John so selflessly share his fifteen years of hard-won experience on both sides of the Arbitration aisle with us? We're hardly worthy and he doesn't seem like that sweet a guy.*"

'Been asking that myself. Absolutely no idea. *Nobody else* cared enough to give you a leg up -- Not *How To Write A Screenplay In Ten Seconds*, not *Selling Scripts For Dummies*, and especially not those mega-pretentious tea and gluten-free crumpet $3,000 McFee-style "getaways". While they're busy extolling "The Odyssey" and spewing trite platitudes like, "*To find the truth, get your own heart to pound while you write*" (yep, real quote), I'm keeping it street and trying to get your ass paid.

The brass-knuckles reality is that, besides Blake Snyder, none of these other bullshitters have been in Arbitration. They don't know the first fucking thing about it.

Believe me, from the moment *Tough Love* hits cybershelves, I fully anticipate what I'm sharing to be re-branded and re-presented (read: stolen and poorly camouflaged) by these same cottage industry charlatans. This is the Information Age. How long until low-grade, back-alley knock-offs such as *How to Win Arbitration in Ten Seconds* and *Arbitrationlogue* start popping up like fake Armani sunglasses?

Alas, concerned readers, don't sweat it -- the Rock 'N Roll Attorney promises my pockets will be nicely padded with summary plagiarism and IP judgments while I'm busy writing the sequel -- *Tough Shit Screenwriting II: More Bad News.*

Meantime, I'd like you to exit Instagram, shutter your 4Chan/h window, quit Snapchatting pics of your naked buttocks and, if at all possible, pay close attention to the vital instructions which follow.

* * * * *

When Arbitration begins, the WGA sends you a list of the materials involved for your personal review. Both company and Guild-verified, these are the official drafts participating writers can review and select from to represent their work in the case.

It's at this precise instant, chambering a sawed-off, speed-loading your Sig and duct-taping a KA-BAR behind your calves, that I urge every writer alive to hit "pause" and ask themselves one critical question --

Do you honestly believe you deserve screen credit on this film?

Fellas, I'm not looking for a knee-jerk "*Fuck yeah!*" or "*Nobody's gonna bust a nut in my backside!*". This is serious business, worthy of objective, selfless, adult consideration.

Why? Because if you don't honestly believe, down to the marrow, that you're able to make a compelling case -- to *prove* your work meets the required threshold -- you're just setting yourself up for an inevitable beat-down.

Despite the sheer tonnage of uninformed bullshit I've heard people talk on the subject (two decades worth, to be precise) there is <u>no</u> <u>such</u> <u>thing</u> as "getting lucky" in Arbitration. There ain't a single damned thing capricious or random or blindly-by-the-seat-of-your-pants about it.

Any claims we make are vetted by <u>three</u> <u>different</u> <u>screenwriters</u> who go over every last page of material as many times as they feel necessary to make the right decision. Drafts are worked over near-forensically -- marked up, broken down, multi-color highlighted within an inch of their lives. In this age of digital *everything*, Arbiters still work hardcopy page-in-hand, like a pack of wild-eyed Jesuit monks. Many a time I've served on Arbitration committees where I wanted to <u>physically</u> place opposing pages side-by-side to see who's who and what's what... and that's exactly what I did. Yanked the brads, plucked the pages and put 'em in a police line-up, side-by-side. Doesn't get more illuminating than that.

Think execs, producers and prospective buyers can be relentless when it comes to making sense of material? Imagine what an experienced *one of your own* is like when entrusted with this level of responsibility. How meticulously do you think a tight-assed stickler for detail like <u>me</u> would get into it? Get *off* on it?

Yeah. You'd have better "luck" trying to foist a Nigerian Ponzi scheme on Barry Diller or David Geffen.

Consider this fair warning, my friends. Your Committee Members take their duties *personally*; they well understand that this process informs their own livelihoods as well, and they sure as hell didn't volunteer precious time to do a half-assed job or give some lazy goofball a free pass.

337

Don't get it twisted. **I am absolutely NOT trying to discourage anyone who believes they have a legitimate shot at getting screen credit from entering Arbitration** . Having already heard my own trip, you know I'm a huge fan of going for the gold whenever justified. Lock and load, brother. This is simply me pumping the brakes, trying to insert some reasonable checks and balances into the mix before you go stormtrooping impulsively into the deepest end of the pool without the firepower to back your play.

Brutal as getting one-hundred percent real with yourself can be, it's absolutely critical. Obviously, every screenwriter in recorded human history wants credit on *everything* they've ever written. Put my name down on that list, too. But since life doesn't work that way, an accurate, objective appraisal of your contributions is required to have any real shot moving forward.

You may have seen <u>Live Free, Die Hard</u>. Decent movie, right? I was one of the many, many writers on it. If I remember correctly, there were something like fifteen of us who did drafts in one form or another over an eight-plus year period. That's a monstrous, heaping stack of WGA Arbitration material -- dozens of scripts to juggle, a bottomless pit of pages to work through, plus source material.

While breaking down the Final Shooting Script, I found essentially the same overriding structure my work had first put into place. Same beats, same dynamics, all dead-to-rights in black and white. This framework sure as hell hadn't existed *before* my drafts, and the studio execs had specifically praised it back when I first submitted my pages.

First came that ugly, indignant rush of blood to the head. *Bastards! Trying to steal <u>my</u> work? How DARE* *you?* All this was said aloud in my snootiest "Pardon me, do you have any Grey Poupon?" voice, even though I was locked in my office alone. The drums of war began to pound. Cannon were loaded, horses mounted, the Officers armed with muskets and sabers -- *Goddamnit, men, don't fire until you see the whites of their eyes!*

Then I started reading more closely.

The movie had evolved in a multitude of ways. Most the characters were reimagined and given new backstories, which meant reworking the majority of the film's dialogue. Specific elements which at first blush appeared taken sideways or lifted straight across -- legit smoking guns you could get a warrant for -- revealed themselves as vague and inconclusive under closer scrutiny. Since I'd had my hands on the wheel, the film had been reconceived to the point of becoming a Bruce Willis/Die Hard vehicle. Which, I had to admit, was a damned good idea (Christ, why didn't they think that up on *my* watch?).

Apart from perhaps the flow of the overriding structure -- which wasn't anywhere near the required threshold on its own -- what became plain as day was that I hadn't contributed enough to the final script. There was no way around it. Whatever my specific efforts once upon a time, they obviously hadn't stuck in any deeper, lasting fashion. I didn't have a case. Meaning I didn't deserve credit.

Was it a let down? Ya think? What'd I do? Manned-up and did the right thing -- I walked away. Didn't even bother contesting it.

Believe for a second I didn't want a savory chunk of those blockbuster Die Hard residuals? My own vulgar slush fund to piss away on Botoxed strippers, You-

Certainly-Fooled-The-Hell-Out-Of-Me! transsexuals and my own full-time masseuse, pedicurist and chauffeur? *Bet your ass I wanted it*! Screw the hard work of writing, who *wouldn't* rather climb into their freak full-time and never worry about paying the rent again?

Not meant to be. This go 'round I simply hadn't earned it. *C'est la guerre.* And to my credit, I was smart enough not to waste eighty-some hours of my life constructing a desperate, grasping Arbitration Statement I knew was totally full of shit.

<u>Facing a similar situation, my friends, I highly recommend you do the same</u>. If you don't have the goods, <u>own</u> it -- don't bother trying to bluff anybody, least of all yourself. Because once three of your diligent peers put your pages under the lamp, they're going to find out exactly what's what.

* * * * *

Let's assume you've followed *Tough Love's* advice. Given all the involved materials a meticulous, open-minded review. Now egoless and coming from a place of complete equanimity, you find yourself more convinced than ever you may be entitled to screen credit.

Love it. Let's roll up our sleeves and get down to it.

Here's the single most important thing to remember when facing Arbitration --

The sole purpose of your Statement to the Arbitration Committee is to prove beyond doubt that your lasting contributions to the Final Shooting Script have met or exceeded the threshold required to assign you screen credit.

340

Translation? The facts, bro, just the facts.

Writing a statement is your turn on the witness stand, the one and only opportunity to give direct testimony on your own behalf. Emotional content means nothing -- anger and indignance even less. Name-dropping will have experienced Arbiters laughing themselves off couches and treadmills. Your Committee is comprised of fellow writers, many of whom have built careers working with some of the biggest stars, directors and producers in the business. Do you really think name-dropping Kevin Hart, Kevin James or Taylor Lautner thirty-five times is going to wow them?

The facts, bro, just the facts. Try and keep it on the reals. Keep your Statement professional and on-point at all times.

When constructing your case, Step One should always be reviewing the *Screen Credits Manual* (or *Television Credits Manual* as appropriate). Section II discusses the Credit Determination Procedure step-by-step, and specifically outlines what every writer needs to pay attention to. This includes what to do when you first receive Tentative Notice of Credit, how the Selection of Arbiters and Verification of Materials works, and what type of content you're allowed -- or not allowed -- to include in your Statement.

Case in point. Participants aren't permitted to mention the contingent compensation at stake -- a.k.a. the amount of their credit bonus. Hard to imagine *any* self-respecting adult trying to ply their peers' guilt by writing "*If you don't give me credit I'll lose $300,000 and my kids will starve*", but this Business tends to distill folks down to their worst ingredients, and I'm sure a mortifying number of numbnuts have still given it a shot.

341

You're also prohibited from seeding information into your statement which pertains to the development process itself. The SCM kindly offers one example -- *"the fact that a project was 'greenlit' after a certain draft is irrelevant in determining credit"* (top p. 10). See how this works? Anything outside the writing doesn't count. So that's a resounding NO to any starfucking writers out there -- taking a Saturday call from the Studio Head, having a bromance with the Director or doing fat lines with the Lead 'til dawn don't play a factor.

I suggest reading through Section II with eyes wide open. A working knowledge of rules procedure can make all the difference.

You can see that the WGA has steadfastly focused on making this process as fair and equal as humanly possible, eliminating any and all factors extraneous to the real matter at hand -- whether or not you deserve screenplay credit. This is precisely the way every writer should want it. Backstage shenanigans and hometown calls may play a very real part in the rest of Hollywood, but within the Guild there remains a strict adherence to certain principles. IMHO every writer should be groveling on their knees thanking whatever Gods they worship for this. *Can you imagine what getting credit would be like if it played by the rest of Butt Town's rules?* Can you say *B-L-O-O-D-B-A-T-H*?

Next up is Section III -- the big daddy of the SCM. These are the money pages, my friends. They cover official Guild Policy on Credits in exacting detail. Specifically, Section III.B explains the rules used for determining credit and reviews the various types of credits writers may receive on a film (i.e. "Story by", "Adaptation by", "Screen Story by", etc.). The instructions here should help you decide exactly which credit you're seeking and why. After fully educating yourself on the subject, chose whichever seems most appropriate for the depth and scope of the written evidence your drafts provide.

May I humbly point you towards the most logical starting place? The <u>key elements</u> Arbiters look at in determining screenplay credit, all conveniently laid out by the <u>SCM,</u> Section III.4.C --

-- <u>Dramatic Construction</u>

-- <u>Original and Different Scenes</u>

-- <u>Characterizations or Character Relationships</u>

-- <u>Dialogue</u>

These are the dynamics at the epicenter of *everything* credit related. Pay particular attention to p. 21 as it explains the subjective nature of how contributions are considered and decisions are ultimately reached by your Committee. Focus on Section III like you're studying for the New York Bar Exam. Pour over the material like your writing life depends on it -- because it does.

Point of fact -- there is <u>no</u> <u>such</u> <u>thing</u> as over-preparation when it comes to Arbitration.

Common sense should tell you no two cases are the same and no set formula or plug-and-play paradigm exists to work from. That said, the variety of successful arguments to be made is limited only by a writer's imagination. Strange as it sounds, try and get loose, let your hands go and *have fun with it.* Go after its creation with the same alacrity and spirit of invention you might an über cool new spec idea.

Broad strokes and general contentions are <u>not</u> what you're going for; they lack any lasting impact in proceedings this involved and complex. **What's of paramount importance is coming up with <u>explicit examples</u> and <u>specific page and/or scene numbers</u> to back up your every claim of authorship.**

Believe a critical scene in the Final Script originated with you? *Prove it.* Point your Arbiters to the <u>exact draft</u> <u>and</u> <u>page</u> where they can find it. Invent a crucial character, only to have it not-so-slyly renamed and camouflaged by subsequent writers hoping to hijack authorship? *Prove it's yours.* This ain't the time for subtlety. Hit your Committee with full-on forensic evidence.

The *Screen Credits Manual* comes out and openly greenlights getting surgical with it -- "*The statement may include breakdowns and illustrative comparisons between the final shooting script and earlier work... which would help the Arbitration Committee to evaluate the writer's contribution...*"

With this in mind, all that remains is devising your specific approach and tailoring it to the strengths of your particular argument.

Years back, I remember a case where a writer submitted an incredibly detailed spreadsheet breakdown for the Final Script. I'm talking N.A.S.A. level stuff here, customized Excel box-grid dutifully assigning credit for scenes, dialogue, etc. to the column of whichever participating writer the author felt deserved it. It was extremely visual, professional and well-thought-out by any standard.

The punchline? *The vast majority of their claims of authorship didn't actually originate in their drafts.* That's right, even a cursory reading of the involved materials made this obvious. Whether it was disingenuous sleight of hand or a case of passion run amok which blinded their objectivity, God only knows.

But like I said, the spreadsheet *was* excellent. So first-rate, in fact, that by flipping its conclusions inside-out it became a checklist confirming *two other writers'* contributions instead. **By not being accurate and/or honest this writer had inadvertently detailed a perfect case for their opponents' arguments instead.**

Whatever your argument, however you choose to construct your Arbitration Statement, please be very, very careful. Taking credit for things we didn't create or material that didn't legitimately originate with us -- whether by mistake or pre-meditation -- is highly unlikely to slip by an experienced Committee. When they catch it, it'll cost your case big time.

* * * * *

This seems the perfect place to shift focus onto what you should specifically <u>avoid</u> when writing your letter. Many writers can be extra stupid and extra stubborn when it comes to making cases (ever been in a pro story meeting or writer's room?), so please consider this my official *Tough Love*-approved **Do Not List for Credit Arbitration Statements** --

1) <u>Do Not Take Anything For Granted</u>.

In any discipline, looking past your opponents is a fatal error, fraught with as much danger for screenwriters as NFL quarterbacks, Congressional candidates and Olympic boxers (What? Another sports analogy?).

Say you've literally written 99.9% of a movie. Doesn't matter. You *still* need to make an outstanding argument on your own behalf. Nothing in Arbitration is "self-evident". There are no "done deals" or "sure things", and you never, EVER pull your starters, no matter how big a lead you may think you have. You have but <u>one</u> concern, my friends -- permanently putting this sucker to bed and inking that credit in the record books, once and for all.

If you've ever watched the UFC (guess what, delicate males, women like it, too!) you've probably seen that once a fighter hurts his opponent, they jump on 'em full-tilt, hitting them with *everything* including the kitchen sink. It's the <u>ref's job</u> to stop the fight if it's gone too far; let him worry about that. You keep wind-milling punches until the guy wearing the black UFC polo waves you off, just like you see on those Hi-Def $60 PPV's.

In place of Muy Thai, Dirty Boxing and Brazilian Ju-Jitsu, WGA members use cold, hard facts, unerring points of reference and iron-clad logic. These are *our* weapons. Before stepping into the Arbitration Octagon, be sure you've skillfully armed yourself and fine-tuned your contentions appropriately. Daydream ahead to any victory parades and you'll wake up flat on your back, staring cross-eyed at a blurry Herb Dean as he finishes counting you out.

2) <u>Don't Go Into Arbitration Thinking You're Going To "Get Lucky" -- You Will Not</u>.

Seen this tragic miscalculation a million times. Half-smart writers who've heard the system is a crap-shoot or coin-flip, that blindfolded monkeys throw darts at a board and no-talent, brain-dead writers waltz out with credits they don't deserve. Dum-dums like this approach the process like some cheap Boardwalk shell game, buying in because, well, some lucky bastard's gotta win, right?

Would anyone take the MCAT's this way? The California Supplemental Exam for Architecture? Counting on blind luck to pull you through?

Straight away, let me take a gigantic, milky piss on this type of non-thinking. The WGA is <u>not</u> your local liquor store, Arbitration is <u>not</u> the fuckin' Lottery, and that "somebody" who wins sure as hell will <u>not</u> be you.

Blind luck ain't invited to this party. Veteran writers (One, Two, <u>Three</u> of 'em!) review every page, a veteran Consultant and the Credits Dept. backstopping them should the slightest question about procedure or application arise. Oh, wait. Did I mention nobody's in any hurry? Your Arbiters often have <u>two</u> <u>full</u> <u>weeks</u> to devote to coming to their conclusions -- and can get even more time simply by requesting it.

Comes down to it, you wanna act the Judge Judy low-life expecting some vague miracle to lurch into your lap -- no problem, knock yourself out. You are *precisely* the type of dork big boy writers get massive jollies debunking, out-writing and blow-torching to crispy smithereens. Come prepared, son, or prepare to get wiped the fuck out.

This has been a friendly Public Service Announcement from hardcore veteran screenwriters everywhere who can't wait to kick your ass and take all the glory -- and the loot -- for themselves!

3) <u>Do Not Go Into Arbitration Unless You Honestly Believe, From The Very Bottom Of Your Heart, You Deserve Screen Credit</u>.

I already hit this pretty hard a few pages back ("Do you honestly believe you deserve screen credit on this film?"), suffice to say I'm a big believer in taking a long, hard look at the Final Shooting Script to assess what kind of credit -- if any -- you might have a case for. Personally, I create a mock-up "stress test" for myself, stringing together the empirical evidence on my behalf and seeing what kind of weight it'll carry. Bottom line, if I can't convince *myself* at this juncture, I don't have any chance of sneaking it by three eagle-eyed Arbiters like myself.

Finding your name in the mix on an arbitration in itself doesn't mean that much. Projects hire an ever-growing assortment of writers these days. Having *worked on* a project is very different from being one of its primary *authors*. Just because you remodeled the kitchen or tiled the bathroom floor doesn't make you Frank Gehry. Legit veterans understand this and have no problem with it.

Who the fuck doesn't dig free money? Pulling down an unexpected production bonus would be awesome for any of us. But as my laser-engraved epitaph will put on blast from my The Man With The Iron Fists II cremation urn -- **"They ain't givin' that money away"**. Nowhere is that more true than when involved in the fiery crucible of Arbitration.

Credit Arbitration is hard. Emotionally exhausting. It's a crazy amount of work and a constant irritant; like a chainsaw lodged in the side of your skull for a month or two. You're held hostage on a emotional rollercoaster ride full of steep twists and turns, and rarely (if ever) are you able to clear your mind of the proceedings forever looming over you.

Being entitled to credit is not a given. First you must earn authorship on the page, then you must provide proof of that authorship to your peers. As writers, sometimes we see what we want to see -- especially with emotions running high and real money at stake. Regardless, I'd urge you not to put yourself through the meat grinder without an honest, objective belief in your cause -- and the rock-solid heavyweight facts to back it up.

4) <u>Do Not Cop An Attitude</u> (a.k.a. <u>Do Not Be A Douchebag</u>).

We're all writers here. We get it. You're pissed. Even being asked to spend time making a case for what is so obviously your work feels like a terrible injustice, perhaps even an outrage! Anyone without a brain injury who isn't deaf as a post and blind as a bat can see <u>YOU</u> <u>WROTE</u> <u>THE</u> <u>FUCKING</u> <u>MOVIE</u>! Why should *you* have to prove *anything* to *anyone*?

Belching up bile that way make you feel better? Awesome, dude. Now table that silly egotistical bullshit and get a grip on yourself. As Frank Hackett/Robert Duvall says in <u>Network</u> -- "Your indignation is duly noted; you can always resign tomorrow."

Life ain't fair, bitches -- Hollywood even less so. The only "justice" you'll ever see in this godforsaken Business is the justice you fight for and win convincingly. My take is pretty straightforward. If you deserve credit, you've got nothing to worry about. Trust in your abilities, have faith in your accumulated contributions, then focus all that energy constructively on the task at hand -- <u>writing the very best, most persuasive letter possible to carry the day</u>.

Crop-dusting your Committee members with bombastic contentions and diva-like declarations is pointless. It's the Arbitration equivalent of road rage. Ask anybody in L.A. how helpful *that* approach is when it comes to working things out with strangers.

349

My advice? **Keep any and all emotion out of the mix when writing your statement**. Suck it up. Be professional. Insulate your panel from any residual toxicity or insecurity you're dealing with, difficult as that may be. <u>Remember, it wasn't your Arbiters who sent the Notice of Tentative Credit to the Guild</u> -- your old pals the <u>studios</u> came up with those crackerjack suggestions all by their lonesome. The only reason your peers are involved is to ensure everyone -- especially you -- gets a fair hearing now that it exists.

What impresses Arbiters are well-constructed arguments, written with precision, logic and equanimity. You be *that guy* -- let the other writers become the chowder-heads poisoning the well before anybody's even picked up a draft.

Best of luck, fellas. Break a leg out there. Shitcan the attitude. Do your homework. Construct your most compelling case. Write the strongest statement possible.

After that, let the chips fall where they may... and may the Movie Gods be with you.

Policy Review Boards

The results of any WGA Arbitration are definitive and legally binding. Whether you're pumped about the outcome or more pissed off than Michael Douglas in <u>Falling Down</u>, the decision is final.

Let me repeat that for the legions of screenwriters who go stone-deaf whenever this subject comes up --

The decision of your Arbitration Committee is final.

A number of adult professionals have just spent a wicked amount of time and effort researching the matter and determining who rightly deserves screen credit. They've worked the hard math, searched their souls and written out their decisions with specific examples of how they came to their conclusions. Your three peers -- with continual support and oversight from the Credits Dept., plenty of astute checks and balances and the steadfast guidance of their Arbitration Consultant -- have, at long last, landed on what they feel is a fair and just decision.

That ain't gonna change simply 'cause *you* don't like it.

<u>No writer likes losing</u>. Just as no Presidential hopeful, Miss America contestant, pro snowboarder or ambulance-chasing attorney likes coming up short. Just as <u>NOBODY</u> <u>ON</u> <u>PLANET</u> <u>EARTH</u> likes hearing "no" and walking away empty-handed.

Losing sucks. If there's a simpler truth, I haven't heard it. Not everything in life has a happy ending. Shit sometimes breaks the other way. By a certain age, we all know the deal.

Imagine a Hell on Earth in which every spurned screenwriter losing an Arbitration can demand a new one; seek a brand new trial in a higher court with fresh hopes of winning it all next time around... simply because they don't dig the verdict.

Know what you'd have?

What we've *already* got in the larger U.S. -- utter and total chaos.

A self-propagating litigious ecosystem fueled by ego, mayhem and insanity. Credits would take years, even decades, to battle out. Movies would winnow their way down from theatrical release to Hulu loss-leader before the Supreme Court finally, retroactively, puts their noble feet down and hands down a final decree.

Of course, by then nobody will *care* who the writer was.

Thank Christ WGA Arbitration doesn't have that problem. Our process is a civilized nod towards sanity and propriety; a reasonable solution for unreasonable people during increasingly unreasonable times in an entirely unreasonable business. <u>Arbitration *is* the professional screenwriter's Supreme Court</u>. There is nothing higher. There are no Mulligans or takebacks or trying to weasel one's way out of its findings. The buck irrefutably stops here.

Which underscores my contention that you want to do it right to the very best of your abilities the first time. Because it'll also be the *only* time.

Sometimes though, as you might expect, the spurned and disgruntled writer simply can't let go. Their immediate impulse is to fight on, seek more favorable justice somewhere else, worthwhile or not.

So they appeal.

Section II D.7 of the *Screen Credits Manual* (p. 13) explicitly outlines the mechanics for appealing an Arbitration. Any participating writer can request a <u>Policy Review Board Hearing</u> (PRB) within twenty-four hours of the decision. But here's the thing --

<u>You can only request a PRB based on procedural grounds</u>. Nothing having to do with creative content or individual writers' contributions to the Final Shooting Script is considered.

Plain English? **<u>Policy Review Boards don't exist to reverse decisions made in Arbitration</u>.** This is

352

probably the number one most commonly misunderstood element of the entire Arbitration process. Members of a Policy Review Board do not make any judgments based on the written material. Point of fact, they're not even allowed to *see* the written material. All your PRB takes into consideration is whether or not there was any serious deviation from Guild policy in determining credit. Hence the name, "POLICY REVIEW Board".

Other than simply hating the verdict, what are the grounds for such an appeal?

>A) Dereliction of duty on the part of the Arbitration Committee or any of its members.

>B) The use of undue influence upon the Arbitration Committee or any of its members.

>C) The misinterpretation, misapplication or violation of Guild policy; or

>D) Availability of important literary or source material, for valid reasons not previously available to the Arbitration Committee.

In my experience, the two most common types of appeals are based on either A or C, or sometimes both -- dereliction of duty and misinterpretation of Guild policy.

Ready for the straight dope, rookies? In my years serving on the WGA Screen Credits Committee, I've seen just one PRB overturned and a new Arbitration ordered. *One.* I'm being exceedingly polite when I say winning these appeals is extremely difficult and requires an extraordinary set of circumstances taking place to even get the conversation started.

Take "A" -- dereliction of duty. Know what that's code for? Straight-up accusing one (or more) of your Arbiters of not reading all the materials. That's right, boldly insinuating that a fellow professional writer, approved by the Guild, who <u>volunteered</u> their time with zero compensation (save the complimentary M&M's or stale KitKat chucked into the mountain of drafts messengered by the Credits Dept.) suddenly up and decided they didn't want to read stuff. In particular, your stuff.

What's the motive here? I'm pretty bright, explain it to me. *Why in the hell would someone willingly volunteer, then not do what they willingly volunteered for?* <u>Especially when they can beg off and be replaced simply by calling the Guild</u>? Shit comes up, scheduling conflicts arise. So be it. You call the Credits Dept. and ask them to find someone else. Done. That simple.

Better still, how do you prove this? How do you *prove* that someone willfully did not read everything, or at least not thoroughly enough for your liking? Have a nice long think on that while I move on to "C".

Grounds for appeal "C" -- Misinterpretation or misapplication. The implication being that one (or more) of your Committee members either didn't understand what they were reading or somehow mistakenly misapplied your contributions to other writers instead. Entirely possible, right? It surely must have happened on some rare occasion or the rule itself wouldn't exist. But again, you're going to need explicit proof of such an accusation, some way to show an Arbiter couldn't wrap their head around your pages, was lacking mental comprehension and/or somehow went AWOL and decided to wholesale credit your work to your opponents -- and that's a very high standard indeed.

Starting to grasp why PRB appeals are so difficult to win? **They revolve around policy and procedure -- nothing pertaining to writing or the creative process or "who came up with what" plays any part in the proceedings.** I would argue that prevailing in a PRB is a thousand times harder than winning a credit arbitration in the first place, for precisely the reasons stated above.

Readers, in all seriousness, if after reviewing your Arbiters' decision letters you still feel there's an argument to make regarding any of the grounds for appeal, then by all means -- request a Policy Review Board immediately. Firsthand, I can testify these claims are investigated by the WGA with the upmost solemnity and sincerity, and that you'll be given every opportunity to make your case.

However, if we're keeping it really, really, *really* real here (*Tough Love's* mandate from Word One) and what it essentially boils down to is your being mad as hell you didn't get the credit you'd hoped for... and now you're winging it in hopes of scoring a fresh Arb with much smarter and more sympathetic Committee Members, well... you'll simply be rubbing salt in your own wound.

I suppose the reason I feel so strongly about all this (strongly enough to ink this in when I'd much rather be out trolling the Venice Beach for Euro tourist girls with crippling Daddy Complexes) is that 99.9% of the PRB's I see are simply screenwriters pissed off they didn't get screen credit.

They're just angry. There aren't any underlying policy or procedural issues. Outraged and impassioned and ready to tear some anonymous motherfucker's head off for cockblocking their success. This particular dream didn't come true, and, like any screenwriter, they aren't

355

taking it sitting down. Perfectly understandable. Being a fighter and refusing to take "No" for an answer is part and parcel who we *are*. Screenwriters are nothing without that level of resolve, right? Our careers wouldn't have lasted long enough to find our ways into an Arbitration in the first place.

Becoming irrational, however, is something different and entirely beside the point -- it won't offer anything in the way of solutions or solace.

* * * * *

Once you wade through a writer's bombastic *pro forma* Notice of Appeal, know what the most common, hackneyed and epically lame rationale damn-near every writer who loses an Arbitration drags into their Policy Review Board Hearing?

"*ANY IDIOT WITH HALF A BRAIN WHO READS MY DRAFT CAN SEE I WROTE THE MOVIE*!"

Yep. Writers come right out and say exactly that during their hearings. Boiled down all it translates to is -- "*I wanted to win.*"

Like I said, brothers and sisters, losing sucks, I'm right there with you. Hell, if I were king, even writers nowhere *near* the project would get credit. But "I wanted to win" is not reason enough for the Writers' Guild of America to overturn a honorable decision reached by your hardworking peers.

As fate would have it, while I was selflessly pounding away on *Tough Love* to ensure my readers had a fighting chance to live out their dreams (end shameless self-aggrandizement), a heavyweight writer of some renown requested a Policy Review Board Hearing. They hadn't received credit as the third or fourth writer out on a project, vehemently disagreed with the decision and wanted their day in court.

Can you guess what the essence of their argument was?

"*ANY IDIOT WITH HALF A BRAIN WHO READS MY DRAFT CAN SEE I WROTE THE MOVIE*!"

That's all they were packing. Strictly paint by numbers. This is a long-time Guild member we're talking about -- not some F.O.B. Floridian goofball with a fanboy site. An accomplished veteran who knew better.

Still, for thirty-plus minutes Mrs. Big Name Writer proceeded to go old-school blowhard; raving and bitching and carping about how the decision was an egregious miscarriage of justice, inconceivable really, and how the Guild better get their shit together, The Revolution Will Not Be Televised, etc. etc. *ad nauseam*. You'd think they were lecturing about the First Amendment or Civil Rights or some goddamn thing -- not a million-dollar VOD movie she was already getting producer and director credit on.

Yet, despite the incessant bluster, Mrs. Big Name Writer failed to produce the slightest hint of impropriety having occurred during their Arbitration. They generated a shit-ton of heat, but not the faintest sliver of light.

What were we just talking about? *Policy Review Boards only consider policy and procedure. Nothing pertaining to writing or the creative process plays any part in the proceedings.* By the way, this isn't some high-level C.I.A. state secret or disingenuous disclaimer buried in the fine print -- it's in easy-to-read black and white on the pages of your free *Screen Credits Manual* for the entire world to see.

PRB's do not exist to reverse decisions made in Arbitration.

But that's precisely what Mrs. Big Name Writer wanted anyway.

She felt entitled to another shot -- at the expense of fellow Guild members, of course, their lesser-known, not-so-famous peers. Yet they couldn't make a single accusation against the credit stick.

Big Name came in with nothing and (all together now) they left with nothing. Funny how that works, isn't it? Five bucks and a bowel-thrusting "*I wanted to win*" will get you little more than a Red Velvet cupcake 'round here... and you may have to wait behind a tour bus of German and Japanese tourists just to get that. It certainly ain't gonna sway a Policy Review Board.

Rabid Arb Haters

Hating on Arbitration is as fashionable in Hollywood as hating on LeBron James was before he won back-to-back titles. Mercifully, LeBron had a prescribed pathway to shed his detractors. Arbitration, I fear, will never enjoy such good fortune.

Any way you slice it, people love to publicly crap all over the credit process, apparently without knowing the slightest fuckin' thing about it.

Have they had a movie produced?

No.

Have they ever been in an Arbitration?

358

No.

Do they understand the actual mechanics of how it works?

No.

Do they have even the most remote or tangential personal experience with the world of Arbitration *at all*?

Not so much.

Then by what possible rationale do they feel entitled to rant against something they know <u>nothing</u> about?

Would they lecture the Secretary of State about nuclear arms deployment in the Far East? Would they posture and browbeat the guys in Radiohead about their song-writing methods? Would they suggest new bypass methods to a chest surgeon at the Cleveland Clinic? Not unless they wanted to be ridiculed by a billion bloggers or so. And yet here they are, bullhorn flush against their ass lips in coffee houses and on forum boards nationwide going on about the WGA.

I suppose Emmy-winner Ian Maitland, by far the coolest professor I had at NYU Film, pretty much nailed it when he confided --

"There's no expert like someone who's never done it."

During the past couple years, there was a pathetic public dust up by someone who didn't get credit on a film. They lambasted the Guild, claiming the system was sloppy and broken, blah, blah, blah. Attempting to hijack the moral high-ground this way was completely absurd, of course, because the writer knew full well the

Guild wouldn't -- and *couldn't* -- stoop to their level and get into a pissing contest. <u>Legally, the WGA can't make public any details of what takes place in a private Arbitration hearing</u>. They're sworn to professional silence to protect the integrity of the process and all the individuals involved.

Bad losers talking shit and lying publicly doesn't really bother me that much. Welcome to Main Street U.S.A. Post Bush stealing the election, it seems there's a dishonest dickhead lurking around every corner. The mind-blowing part was <u>THE INDIGNANT, OUTRAGED HORDE OF ANONYMOUS ARB HATERS</u> blindly caterwauling into forum boards in defense of the writer. One snide crack at the Writers Guild rained down after another from disgruntled and/or failed wannabes everywhere. Their verdict was unanimous -- Arbitration was an abomination, an epic clusterfuck that simply did not work.

Skimming through these preposterous diatribes, a brilliant line from <u>Heathers</u> stuck in my head -- "Thank you, Miss Fleming, call me when the shuttle lands."

Where <u>any</u> of these people involved in this writer's Arbitration? Was a single one of them physically in the room at any time during the PRB?

No, of course not, it isn't allowed. They'd never get past the front desk.

<u>So how in the name of Christ do they know fuck-all about what went down in this case</u>?

They don't. Which is precisely my point. People can bark and bitch and have big authoritative-sounding opinions 'til they're blue in the face, but buttonhole them about it, they'll have no choice but to admit they don't know dick.

Maximum number of people involved in an Arbitration that goes all the way to a Policy Review Board? Twelve. <u>TWELVE</u> <u>FUCKIN'</u> <u>PEOPLE</u>. Three Arbiters, one Credit Consultant, two WGA Credit Dept. Coordinators, three writer/peers sitting on your Review Board, and however many writers are involved (let's say three, which is about average).

Yet I saw nearly a hundred strongly negative posts in one forum alone. That equates with a hundred silly chuckle-heads who know *nothing* about the specifics of the case, all deciding to preach straight out of their ignorant butt cracks. The evidence supporting their outraged, armchair hating? The editorial hearsay of one losing writer and whatever urban legends they've accumulated about the WGA over the years.

See the disconnect? **You fucktards have no idea what you're talking about.** If you weren't in the room and personally involved you aren't qualified to have an opinion. Further, if you haven't participated as writer and/or Arbiter before, you don't have an appropriate frame of reference, making it impossible for you to even participate in the larger conversation.

Yet like every other gaseous simpleton out in Kim & Kanye-land, you're perfectly willing to barf disinformation and conjecture at a venerable sixty year-old process you couldn't explain the mechanics of if I put a loaded AK-47 to your head.

<u>And what about the writers in the case who did earn credit in the eyes of their peers</u>? Just because they didn't throw a self-serving public pout, does that mean their take is any less valid? And if it's as tragically

broken as some suggest, why aren't they complaining as well? Seems to have worked just fine from where they're standing.

General Rule of Thumb For Intelligent, Thinking Adults Worldwide-- Try and actually know *something* in regards to whatever the fuck you're braying about. You will be called on it by people who *do* know -- like me, just for starters.

Let's put this matter beddy-bye and cut straight to the chase --

WGA Credit Arbitration is no different than Democracy in the United States -- imperfect, occasionally flawed, far from ideal, but still the best goddamned system, by a country mile, the world has ever seen.

Or, put conversely, it's the absolute worst system for determining credits out there... except all the other systems.

Yep, the ball can take funny bounces. Seemingly "unfair" results have emerged from Arbitrations, many nearly-impossible to grasp by anyone outside the proceedings. Nonetheless, the system works year-in and year-out, and thousands of professional screenwriters will be happy to back that up -- winners and losers both.

Before the Writers Guild took a stand in the 1940's, producers could literally award writing credit to anyone they pleased. *Anyone.* They could put their mistress's name on screen, their poodle's, the pool guy, whomever the fuck they wanted. In fact, this same absurd dynamic gave birth to the term "son-in-law credit". Check out the books The Hollywood Writers Wars and West of

<u>Eden - Writers in Hollywood 1928-1940</u> (both out of print, ironically) if you want an eyeful of how fucked up things were for screenwriters back then. You'll barely be able to believe what you read.

Self-government and gaining control of whom rightfully receives screen credit was a victory of unimaginable proportions for writers. For the first time in Hollywood history, it brought fairness and objectivity to the process, making a very public statement about a writer's contribution having legitimate value which deserved to be taken and treated seriously. Understand that without the bold efforts of those brave souls preceding us, none of the benefits today's candy-assed screenwriters take for granted would have been possible. There would be no rightful screen credit. No pension plan. No health care. No green envelopes.

There would be nothing except whatever trifling crumbs studios and producers chose to bestow upon us.

If you believe the Guild, given birth by those enduring these levels of injustice and entrusted with the solemn imperative of protecting writers' rights forever after, would install -- and then stand by -- an unfair system detrimental *to its own writers*, then you've gotten it pretty twisted. Time to Google some shit and educate yourself. In short -- call me when the fuckin' shuttle lands.

But listen, the last thing I want to seem is close-minded (waits for laughter to die down). So in all fairness to disgruntled writers and embittered lurkers everywhere, go ahead, give it a twirl -- present the WGA membership with a prescriptive, working alternative. If you can singlehandedly lick sixty years of peer/professional engineering from the safety of your cubicle or while playing Genius at the Apple Store, knock yourself out. I feel confident speaking for thousands of Guild members when I say we'd absolutely *love* to see it.

Meantime, you'll pardon us if we don't bet the farm or hold our collective breath.

One last point before my private nurse doles out my prescribed "happy pills" and I finally simmer the fuck down -- **Never believe for a moment that the studios, production companies, directors, producers or anyone else has your back over your own Guild**. They've never had it and never will. Working as a screenwriter is just another subset of labor vs. management, however genteel, more civilized or more glamorous it might seem.

Comes time for negotiations over future media and *your* resulting residuals? The money that feeds you and your family? Keeps you going through rough patches and career dry spells? That's when you'll see exactly what I mean.

Just Some Friendly, Non-Consensual Insertion

Completely out of the blue, a long-time producer friend of mine called. Yashir was 100% Persian but spoke with a disarming Texan drawl, mind-fucking a ton of folks the first time they sat down together. Five or six years earlier he'd hired me to rewrite a film his company was developing.

"Great news, John," Yashir greeted me. "Alien Zombie Munchers has a shot at getting made."

This was the project I'd worked on; a fun, campy, low-budget homage to '50's monster movie drive-in fare that involved cannibalistic zombies. It'd been a blast to work on, certainly a poor man's <u>The Thing</u>, but done very self-aware and tongue-in-cheek.

"Fantastic," my voice waffled with surprise. The odds of cobwebbed projects finding their way into production were sadistically low. Theoretically, it's always a possibility, but long shots rarely pan out. When a project fades to black, smart writers learn to walk away, hunt for a new gig and simply get on with their lives -- it's the only way to stay sane. "Shoulda-coulda-woulda" is a psychic black hole that, when indulged, can swallow a writer whole.

Goddamn, I thought, you've gotta love this business. Most days it was violently trying to stove your head in, but once a blue moon it sent golden ducats cascading into your lap like some Karmic slot machine.

"Yeah, it *is* fantastic, John. Here's the thing..."

Whoops. Producorial curveball dead ahead. I'd opened the floodgates of hope and relief too soon.

"The money guys have given me an *extremely* tight budget, absurdly low. Frankly, given the films I've made, it's a fuckin' insult." You could sense Yashir warming to the sound of his own pitch now.

"Bummer, Yash... But I'm not sure how that involves me."

"Well, not sure if you remember, but way back when this thing first started, you had a tiny production bonus coming if <u>Alien Zombie Munchers</u> ever got made."

Bet your ass I remembered. Screenwriters *never* forget potential paydays, however remote or unlikely. We're neurotic shut-ins, after all, without much to focus on except Final Draft upgrades and, you know, other tiny concerns like OUR DAY-IN, DAY-OUT, HAND-TO-MOUTH SURVIVAL.

"Yeah, something like $22,500, right?

"Exactly. Twenty-two five."

Yashir's awkward throat-clearing gave way to the pained braying of a lost puppy. "But I really can't afford to pay that now, John. Not with this dogshit cable budget they've saddled me with." Conspiratorially, his voice lowered. "Off the record, the whole thing's touch and go. Having to shell out that much could keep us from making the movie *at all*."

"Really? Doesn't sound good."

"No, but hey, count your lucky stars -- I'm calling with a golden parachute," My old friend artificially brightened now, like he'd tucked back a hit of hospital-grade helium. "I convinced the Network financiers to approve an offer of $5,000 for you up front -- *whether the picture actually gets made or not.* Manna from heaven, baby, am I right? This whole shitty deal is hanging by a thread, Alien-style odds of survival, but I'm still making sure you get paid! You know how crazy making a fuckin' movie is. Nothing's ever real until you're standing on set with film flying through the gate -- and even then sometimes it's not real!"

Outside my window, I could see my stony cap-and-stem neighbor (a descendant and heir of Matisse, I shit you not, currently posing as a Venice *artiste*) encouraging her pit bull to tear down a tall, fragrant trellis of jasmine. Fuckin' rich punks. I made quick mental note to plant a size twelve Sketcher up in her butt the instant the call finished.

366

"Hold it, Yash. Did you say *five thousand dollars*???"

"Pretty sweet, huh?" but my utter disbelief had thrown him. "But hey, John, buddy, like I said, if we can't make something work, it might deep-six the whole fuckin' project. I'm doing the best I can here under pretty shitty circumstances."

Couple quick things about my old friend Yash --

He'd invented one of the most popular franchises in the history of cinema, which means, of course, *of all-time... ever... on Planet Earth.* One helluva accomplishment and no small feat. For pushing two decades, his creation had dominated multiplexes, generating beaucoup bucks for all involved. Yash personally made *millions* each year in royalties and licensing fees, quite literally whether he got out of bed or not.

Further, as much as I legitimately like Yashir (to this day we're still friends), he's a shameless, unrepentant, unapologetic penny-pinching son of a bitch. That's not a slam or insult in the slightest, just a simple statement of fact. Ask anyone who knows and loves him, hell, ask Yashir *himself* -- they'll all tell you the same thing. Nothing personal about it, that's just Yash's trip, how he came hardwired from the factory. In my experience, it's also a trait shared by most successful producers.

So while having a certain theatrical quality (he did make movies, after all), Yashir's fairy tale of being some white knight dispatched with a save-the-day offer of $5K -- less than 25% of what I was already owed contractually -- from these mysteriously tight-fisted "money men" fell a little, shall we say, flat. Like a cold pancake frisbeed from atop the Chrysler Building. Not a word of this bollocks did I believe.

Pleading poverty would never be one of Yash's strong suits. He spent more maintaining his pool each month than my entire bonus. Hell, the wily bastard probably had that much in large-faced Franklins stashed inside the ashtray of his twelve-cylinder Lamborghini.

But much like Lesson Number Two in <u>Scarface</u>, "*Don't get high on your own supply*" is the mantra of anybody on the money-end of moviemaking. None of them want to pay for *anything* they absolutely, positively, one-hundred percent don't have to... and many times they'll *still* fight shelling out until the Courts force them to.

Simple reason for this? Whatever they save goes directly into their pockets.

Fuckin' hell, New Line tried to screw Peter Jackson out of profits from <u>The Lord of The Rings</u> despite making a couple <u>billion</u> worldwide. Why *wouldn't* any producer worth their salt have a go over $22.5K with some friendly unknown? I mean, he kind of *has to*, doesn't he? Nature of the beast.

"Tell you what, Yash," I offered. "We go back. You hired me during a pretty rough period in my career, and I'll never forget that. I certainly don't want to hold up your movie. How 'bout we split the difference? Say $11,000 -- half the bonus -- and I'll sign whatever you want and walk away."

Right about now you might be wondering -- *what in the fuck was I thinking*? Giving up REAL MONEY that could help pay for any number of things to a very rich man who couldn't possibly spend his evergreen fortune?

Truthfully? I was being a nice guy; a stupid, thankless and potentially lethal take I go out of my way to warn others against. But I was overjoyed to learn I'd be seeing *any* money from Alien Zombie Munchers, had another writing gig and, anyway you sliced it, Yashir *had* hired me during some lean times, helping keep my drive for screenwriting glory alive.

One good turn deserved another, right?

"Eleven thousand?" Yash's dissatisfaction inflated with an onrush of dead air. My generosity obviously wasn't as heart-warming as I'd expected. You'd think I'd just crapped in his KooKooRoo.

"Five's the ceiling, John. That's all I'm authorized to offer. If by some Act of God this thing still gets off the ground, I'd rather let you roll the dice in Arbitration."

I was good with that and told him so, without a second's hesitation. Trying to be cool was one thing; allowing a multi-millionaire to slap his dong across my face something else entirely.

There wasn't an ounce of hostility or anger on either of our parts. We politely small-talked it home and wrapped up the call. This was business after all, not personal, and both being professionals we understood that.

Many moons would pass before I'd hear Yashir's voice again.

* * * * *

Months flew by. I spec'd a teenage Deliverance which, to my great dismay, flatlined. Perhaps that beat where the .357-strapped Homecoming Queen stripped the wheelchair-bound Principal buck naked and ordered him to "quack like a dirty, filthy duck" had pushed things a bridge too far. It had been a tricky beat, I must admit. But in the absence of honest feedback (strangely, none was forthcoming from potential buyers) I could never know for sure.

After a brief ass-whipping playing Boardwalk hoops, I staggered home to discover a manila envelope perched python-like on my front porch. The telltale blue-and-white WGA logo was plainly visible on front.

It contained a Tentative Notice of Credit for <u>Alien Zombie Munchers</u>.

Sure, I was surprised. Especially since nobody had bothered to tell me it'd <u>already</u> <u>been</u> <u>shot</u>. Why bother? I mean, I was only one of the *writers*. One of those invisible inconveniences who *made the whole thing up*.

Good news. The letter inside informed me I was sharing credit with two other writers.

Guess the dogshit budget hadn't handcuffed Yashir after all. I wondered what had finally pushed the picture over the top -- that fortuitous Act of God he'd ranted about needing or the paltry cash savings of trying to hose me out of my production bonus.

Neither of which mattered now. It was what it was. I was getting fair credit and my ol' buddy Yash was on the hook for the full freight -- $22,500.

As if it could be that easy.

You must've sensed a pattern by now, Dear Reader. *Nothing* in this diabolical business ever ends that cleanly or with that little struggle.

Next day, I bike home from the most morally abhorrent "coffee date" in human history -- a buxom Child Psychologist happily admitting she nuked Malibu toddlers with anti-depressants whenever their

370

divorcing, dysfunctional parents felt they "couldn't cope" with them anymore (*Holla Main Street, Santa Monica!*).

What should I find but a <u>second</u> manila python on the porch.

That's right. Envelope Number Two.

This one had a "new-and-improved" Tentative Notice of Credit -- one without my name on it.

What fresh manner of Hell was this? I'd seen some dirty, wild shit before, sure, but could Yashir's company even *do* that?

Eager to find out, I called his attorney's number straight off the notice.

The gentleman explained that, regrettably, Yashir had "made an error" -- my name had slipped through "accidentally". Although Yash was sorry for the misunderstanding, he couldn't in good conscience recommend me for credit. It was a "matter of principle", I was told -- he simply didn't believe I'd earned it. Too much time had passed and too many writers had been involved.

Sure -- which totally explains why he'd tried to buy me out in the first place.

Pissed off? Quite the opposite. In all honesty, I started grinning like an idiot.

Tomorrow it would be back to the Venice Library and those tiny-assed Tyrion-sized tables in the children's section -- full-speed ahead into Arbitration.

* * * * *

Yashir didn't understand Arbitration, didn't get what it was about. In all fairness, *why would he?* He was a producer. It would be tantamount to asking me to take the Master Sommelier Diploma Exam. It's not my field. I don't drink wine. What the fuck would I know about it?

Cosmetic concerns like how many years had passed or how many writers had been cycled through mean nothing when it comes to screen credit. Personal preference and/or personality don't play a part. Arbitration is an exercise in screenwriting forensics -- the only thing that counts is what's on the page. As I pointed out earlier, all that matters is the material actually used; what's down in black and white for the whole wide world to see. This is the one inviolate truth about the Arbitration process which never changes.

Had my unctuous buddy Yash taken a second to survey the material, he would have realized what I'd already known long before he'd tried to buy me out --

My drafts had created several crucial devices which informed every single scene of the Final Shooting Script. Without what I'd personally invented, there *was no script* as he knew it. Yashir could churn-and-burn through an army of word-slingers and it wouldn't make any damned difference at all.

Let me illustrate this dynamic with specifics. Who knows? Maybe it'll prove helpful during your own Arbitration some day.

The project was a riff on John Carpenter's The Thing (and Agatha Christie's Ten Little Indians before that) scripted on a much smaller scale. Out of financial necessity, low and no-budget films need to stay self-contained with one main location usually doing most the heavy lifting. From studio-level <u>Aliens</u> to Indie-made <u>Reservoir Dogs</u>, "hotboxing" your world, keeping it small and cut off from the universe at large, is a tried-and-true genre standard. Not only does this keep physical production costs down, it also helps alleviate endless potential logic problems.

Every project has pesky questions you'll eventually be called upon to answer, like "*Why don't they just call for help?*" Hotboxing backstops you with credible answers. Because they're in deep space, light years from Earth, that's why. Because they just robbed a bank and they can't risk leaving their hideout. Because a big storm's a comin', cutting off all phone and radio communications for a hundred miles. Most any potential plausibility killer can be put neatly to bed by simply keeping your characters locked down.

This particular project was set in a bus station besieged by an approaching winter storm (what? you've heard that one before?). The protagonist, Striker, escapes from a prison transport and takes shelter inside the terminal, holding the waiting passengers hostage. The twist is that one -- or maybe more -- of these folks are actually people-munching alien zombies who recently crashed their flying saucer.

It ain't Dostoyevsky, I know. But for the most part, big budget or small, these familiar paradigms are the very life's blood of genre fare. Even something as awesome as Fukasaku's <u>Battle Royale</u> (shameless ripped off and sodomized by <u>The Hunger Games</u>) remains full-blooded genre to the core. What really decides the perception of something being considered "B-Movie" or not is the <u>execution</u> of this type of material. <u>Blood Simple</u> is a classic example of taking stock elements and set-ups and elevating them beyond their modest, derivative genre means. Fully aware of the cringe factor from piggybacking words like "cannibal", "aliens" and "zombies" together, our project was designed as Eisenhower-era cheesy, ironic fun from the start.

So... Striker takes over the bus terminal. His plan is simply to surf the situation, survive the aliens, ride the storm out, then disappear into the sunset.

Dramatic? Satisfying? Not so much, right? Sure, it's a classic set-up, so there's plenty of potential. But built in at the core is a mind-numbing level of passivity. I mean, seriously, what's the Striker character gonna *do* for ninety minutes? Drink root beer floats and read <u>Highlights</u>?

Further, the film lacked a Female Protagonist. That's right. Frame one, the picture was a sausage fest. I'm not sure they'd even scripted in a woman's bathroom. Granted, Carpenter's <u>The Thing</u> is one of few modern films which doesn't have a single woman in it. That said, we didn't have John Carpenter, this wasn't 1982 and flying estrogen-free simply wasn't marketable, especially for a cable movie. Besides that, for any writer, having a solid female character is *always* preferable from a myriad of creative standpoints. Most obvious of which is giving you the raw material for a lot more scenes with the protagonist.

Passive protagonist. No Female lead. Straightaway, my rewrites focused on dealing with these two script killers.

Step One, I changed the bus terminal into a small rural airport. Doesn't seem particularly earth-shattering, does it? At least not until you consider that it ultimately provides Striker with something completely non-existent in earlier drafts -- a viable plan for and means of <u>escape</u>, by aircraft.

374

By clearly defining Striker's goal as escape (as quickly as possible, mind you), he's no longer sitting on his ass, hoping to get lucky and avoid annihilation. This one bold stroke has now created the primary motivation for his character to become proactive above and beyond just routine survival.

First, Striker will need to search the airport (proactive). During the search, he'll now discover an old hangar with a broken-down ski plane inside (proactive). Being broken, Striker will have to repair it (proactive). Other passengers will discover what he's up to and Striker will have to turn back a revolt (proactive). The rest of the plot plays out similarly.

By answering that essential Screenwriting 101 question *"what does your character want to win, gain, get or achieve during the course of the screenplay"*, all the action, motivations, characters and pretty much *the entirety of the storyline itself* begins revolving around Striker, the aircraft and the possibility of escape.

Before you know it, the film has become aggressively repopulated with new scenes supporting this refashioned infrastructure. Wholly original scenes that you've created and now get credit for. By inventing a serviceable Female Protagonist, you've essentially doubled your money in this department. Henceforth, there are all sorts of emotional avenues to explore between her and Striker; character traits to examine, backstories which can emerge, the suppressed stirrings of personal chemistry -- none of which existed before your pages.

The plain fact is that one right idea can become of monumental importance, redefining the very marrow of any project. That's how powerful one "simple" revision or "little" change can turn out to be.

At the very core, being a writer is about *making choices* -- choices which best inform the project and give you the most storytelling options. This is a perfect example of how a great choice can pay long-term narrative dividends far beyond what anyone might expect.

My pages' big payoff came in classic cinematic fashion -- the ruthlessly self-interested Striker appearing to abandon the Female Protagonist before suddenly sacrificing himself to ensure her survival instead. This was critical because it served as Striker's defining moment; neatly landing his character arc and allowing for a successful resolution as the film's worthy protagonist.

For this particular Arbitration, the WGA Credits Manual stated "*for a second writer to share screen credit, the contribution to the screenplay must consist of changes of a substantial and original nature that go to the root of the drama, characterization and content of a screenplay and constitute substantially more than the contribution of the first writer.*"

It also mandated that "*A writer may receive credit for a contribution to any or all of the above listed items... in addition, a change in one portion of the script may be so significant that the entire screenplay is affected by it.*"

My money points -- having created a proactive lead who's motivation informed all the subsequent action and inventing the film's first viable female protagonist -- went directly to the heart of these instructions. Providing more than enough of a platform to build my case for shared credit.

* * * * *

Couple weeks after all the statements were submitted, the Guild called. The Arbitration panel ruled to give me shared credit on <u>Alien Zombie Munchers</u>.

Much more fun than that? Yashir's follow-up call.

My slippery pal clearly hadn't conceived of me winning. It'd never crossed his mind, a complete and utter impossibility. Homeboy was still trying to plead poverty when I needled him with my sweetheart offer of a beggarly $11K to walk away.

"I know, I know," Yash's voice was tinged with shell shock. "But given all that time and all those drafts and stuff..."

Crocodile tears flowing freely, yes, he admitted wishing he'd taken my deal (hint, hint). On my end of the phone, I was Mt. Rushmore, giving him nothing. If he paid me the full $22,500, Yash pleaded further, that would mean he personally made less than $20,000 on the entire movie!

Highly doubtful. But with the movie finished and the cable network no longer on the hook, there was no debating one thing -- my bonus would have to come directly out of Yash's own pocket.

I am Jack's balls being laughed off.

"Yash, to be fair, you're the guy who suggested I 'roll the dice in Arbitration'."

Death row appeals exhausted, he finally gave it up.

"Wow, John. What are we gonna to do about this?

(Thought bubble -- *What's this "we" shit, paleface?*)

377

"Well, Yash," I told him. "I think you'd better send the Rock 'N' Roll Attorney a check for twenty-two five. That's what we're going to do."

"*Really?*"

"Really."

Like I said, this was <u>business</u>, not personal. Nobody understood that better than the two of us. Our exchange was totally cool and collegial. This is a guy I like. <u>Still</u> like. In fact, I'd venture to say we respected each other even more after the smoke cleared.

My take? There'd probably never been any "pre-emptive offer", no mysterious "money guys". Yashir was just doing what smart producers do. A) Writers are generally hard up for cash. B) I'm a writer. C) Why *not* take a shot at getting me to snap up the chump bait, allowing him to cement the all-important Chain of Title for a bargain-basement $5K? It's the same play *anyone* in his position would make, including myself. Don't forget, he also charges the <u>financiers</u> a sale price for the script -- *de facto* double-dipping -- so how much he'd *already* cleared *on top of* what he might save from me is anybody's guess.

And that, Dear Readers, is how the film business rich get even richer.

End of the day, Yashir had taken his shot -- rolled his own dice -- and come up empty. Like a true pro, he took his lumps, manned up and sent me a check.

Of course, this being Hollywood, you always have to be careful what you wish for.

Not long after that, <u>Alien Zombie Munchers</u> was released -- and I was shaken by how hard I'd fought to

378

get my name permanently etched on a pretty crummy movie.

What Would Big John Say?

There's a disturbing new trend taking shape in Arbitration today -- screenwriters are starting to hire so-called "Arbitration Consultants" to write their Statements to the Committee for them.

They can pay upwards of $10,000 for the privilege.

Even crazier? These self-proclaimed "specialists" still get the $10K whether you win or not.

Neck deep in *Tough Love* by now, I expect you can predict my take on this.

IMHO if a professional writer is paying someone else to write their Statement they're equal parts fool and fishhead. *You're a writer, goddamnit!* Pro enough to have worked on a produced film and gotten into credit arbitration. So why in the name of the Old Gods and the New (holla *Game of Thrones!*) would you put your future in the hands of a hired gun who's nowhere near as well-equipped as you are to undertake the challenge???

There's no logic to this. It simply doesn't track.

Each Arbitration is fundamentally different and unique from the bottom up. This isn't like hiring a strip mall C.P.A. to total tax receipts and file a 1040 EZ. There's no certification program for this stuff. You can't PayPal the University of Phoenix or (God Forbid) UCLA Extension and grab an Associates Degree in "Writing Successful Statements to the WGA Arbitration Committee".

<u>Arbitration statements are strictly cut to order, hand-tailored Savile Row</u>. Nobody can possibly explain the intricacies of story and plot, the motives behind surgical restructuring and character recalibration with the clarity of a working writer who developed the material hands-on. These elements go to the very heart of any movie's authorship, and the ability to appropriately illustrate them resides in nobody's brain and soul but your own.

An Industry crime partner of mine recently regaled me with tales of an Important Writer involved a huge arbitration -- big stuff, millions of dollars hanging in the balance. This writer's swank Downtown law firm assigned a junior attorney to his case, billing out twenty-plus hours attempting to ensure the right result. They pored over statements, coordinated with the Guild, badgered them to do XYZ, etc. Several opposing writers contended that Important Writer's statement was at least partially written by someone on his O.J.-style Dream Team -- which didn't matter because there's currently nothing on the books saying this is illegal.

After all that white-shoe weaponry and those big-league resources were brought to bear, know what happened?

Important Writer still lost.

They didn't get credit. All that extra cheddar vanished into thin air.

Like I said, technically there's nothing "wrong" about paying for it (intentional double entendre), giving someone else cash to ink in your Statement. Hell, you could have your mommy write the sumbitch while breastfeeding you, I suppose. But many writers and Guild staff members would *love* to see a rules change regarding this. Unfortunately, for the time being, it's within the boundaries of fair play.

But that's really not the point, is it?

Why would a writer talented enough to become an A-Lister to begin with allow *somebody else* to take the game-winning shot? Someone with nowhere near the same level of skill and talent which got the writer where they are in the first place? Someone without one iota of the writer's *organic knowledge* of the material having fashioned it firsthand?

Can you imagine Larry Bird or Michael Jordan begging *somebody else* to shoot their free throws for them? Ted Williams or Derek Jeter pleading for a pinch hitter? Try and visualize Picasso asking a complete stranger to color in his Blue Woman, or Van Gogh passing his brush to a passerby for fear of fucking up his sunflowers. <u>ARE</u> <u>YOU</u> <u>INSANE</u>? What tragically confused fucktard would ever put the future of their creative careers in *anybody's* hands other than their own?

When the stadium lights are up bright, clock ticking, crowd deafening and the pressure on, some folks want the ball in their hands and some do not. Magic, Bird, Jordan, they *always* wanted the ball. They *called* for it. Resolute faith in their own abilities nurtured what would become legendary self-confidence.

Screenwriters aren't the slightest bit different. To get wherever you are now, or wherever you hope to go, requires trusting *your* instincts, having faith in your ability to create fascinating scenes and characters, unique and entertaining voices and points of view, *from completely out of thin air*, nobody else in the cockpit beside you. That's the gig in a nutshell. Space monkey, solo shot.

So don't waste time psyching yourself out. Just climb into the cage and swing the bat harder than you ever thought possible.

My professional opinion? Lifetime 3-0 in Arbitration, Arbiter on dozens of films, Screen Credits Committee member who regularly works PRB's and expert readings for the Guild?

<u>Do Not Hire A "Consultant" Of Any Kind To Work On Your Arbitration Statement</u>.

You won't be improving your odds. <u>You</u> are the participating writer. Nobody is better suited to the task at hand. You and you alone have the best chance of constructing a winning case. This is plain, empirical fact.

Know what happens when someone botches the money shot, Dear Reader? They spluge all over themselves. Don't be the hapless goober with chud sluicing down his leg, the idiot with his asshole stretched wide as a manhole cover from farming out their case and allowing some other joker to flush it away.

Bear in mind, there's nothing written in this book I wouldn't say directly to anyone's face. Some paid parasitic "consultant" has a problem with my take, please, have 'em hit me up -- <u>toughlovescreenwriting@gmail.com</u>. Happy to meet whenever they want, wherever they feel most confident (their Therapist's office, Life Coach or Rabbi's house) so I can commence slapping the Silly Putty out their mouths.

(Make sure they put, "*I'M RIDICULOUSLY FULL OF SHIT AND DESPERATELY NEED AN ASS-WHOOPIN'*" in the Subject line to bypass the Spam filter.)

Enough already. This last rant exhausted me. Suffice to say, this is one of those situations where perhaps the most critical question any screenwriter can ask themselves is this --

What would Big John Milius say?

Think the bad-ass who scripted Magnum Force, Apocalypse Now and Conan The Barbarian (among many others) would bitch out and hire a stand-in? Go ahead, holmes. Ask him. My money says you'll be playing Tootsie Pop with his Desert Eagle when you do.

* * * * *

Hollywood is nothing if not dripping with irony.

While writing this very chapter I was drawn into a surprise Arbitration over a film I'd saved. Scout's honor, no bullshit. That's just the way my luck runs.

Why was it a "surprise"? Well, because only two of us wrote the film and the Notice of Tentative Credit gave us shared screenplay credit, with my name in second position. Even though I'd done extensive M*A*S*H trauma surgery to make sense of the script and save the day in record time, I figured fine, fun job, happy to have the work, shared credit is no problem.

In fact, I called to notify the Credits Dept. it was all good. I was cool with everything and didn't expect either of us to contest the Tentative Notice.

"I don't think there's an issue," I said confidently. "Pretty sure the other writer feels the same way."

"Actually, John," the woman in Credits tip-toed forward. "The other writer's attorney just faxed us. They're protesting. They want sole credit."

383

Long beat. Quiet hiss of me crapping myself. In utter disbelief.

Other Writer knew what was what -- what *they'd* written and what *I'd* written. Which draft turned a deeply flawed and unproducable *idea for a movie* -- grammar-free and written in ALL CAPS -- into something <u>real</u>; a film with legit characters and dialogue and a legit plot which could be physically shot and then shown to a paying audience without a riot over refunds taking place.

Day and night, our drafts. Red light, green light. Not even the hipster craft service kid refilling the M&M's would argue it.

Giving Other Writer complete benefit of the doubt, I emailed and asked if they knew what their attorney was up to. Perhaps it was a simple mistake, I shrugged, some officious gaffe he hadn't been in the loop on. With mega-politeness (which doesn't really suit me), I expressed surprise at the protest, explained my being fine with shared credit, but made it clear that, hey, if they wanted to punch it out in Arbitration I was good with that, too (sound familiar?). You wanna buck, homie, then buck. Getting into a dogfight seemed totally unnecessary, but ultimately it was their call.

No response. Never heard back. Not so much as a subject-line "Fuck you!" or a quick, dismissive "Who is this?"

Hmmm. Does that mean "*Thanks for your miraculous overhauling and salvation of my movie in a comically-tight thirty day window*" is completely out of the question?

Yours Truly was so busy being magnanimous -- rare as an Asian schoolgirl who doesn't adore Hello Kitty -- that I hadn't noticed the bloody meat clever coming straight for my throat.

To the mattresses we went. No Children's Section this time. Home office, Stalingrad-style. Get some mileage out of that mortgage. I got WAY fired up. Perhaps TOO fired up, if bloody gums and acid reflux is any fair measure. This Arbitration I vowed to bury. Get jungle with it. Human sacrifices, heads on pikes. "*To crush my enemies, see them driven before me, and hear the lamentation of their women*," per the Big John/Oliver Stone recipe for crisis resolution.

I'd been assembling my thoughts about the Arbitration process for *Tough Love* and now, abruptly, I was applying them directly to my own statement. Practicing what I planned to preach, so to speak. What a trip, right? What better way to battle-test my shit than under fresh enemy fire?

My letter was hardcore -- I used a bazooka of logic to blow up an ant hill. The decision came down. I'd won shared credit, exactly as I'd agreed to without complaint. But this time there was one subtle difference.

Now I was in <u>first</u> position.

Per the *Screen Credits Manual*, the writer considered to have made the biggest contribution is placed in first position. Subtle thing, no doubt. Super nerdy writer stuff. Won't get you laid. Most movie lovers eyeballing one-sheets from the popcorn line will go their entire lives without knowing the order of writers' names has any greater significance.

Not important. *I know.* My peers know. And so does Other Writer. The guy who tried Pearl Harboring my ass for a sole credit they knew they didn't deserve.

* * * * *

As *Tough Love's* assorted war stories make plain, for working screenwriters, "the price of freedom is eternal vigilance". It's incumbent upon you to fight boldly for anything you've rightly earned. Much like writing itself, you're on your own. Nobody else can be expected to take an interest, give you a heads-up or offer any air support. The outcome rests solely upon your performance alone.

You won't prevail in Arbitration because you think you "deserve it", believe you're a bad-ass or consider yourself "special" somehow. Self-delusion and rationalization has assured the defeat of many a self-important scribe.

You'll triumph because you did the work, were able to showcase objective evidence of that and then comprehensively back it up with a compelling, point-by-point case underscoring your contention.

By following the advice I've shared in this chapter, you'll find yourself much better positioned when your day in Arbitration finally arrives. **None of it guarantees you'll win**. Not in the slightest. What it does provide, however, is some piece of mind; the inner-confidence of knowing you took the very best shot possible.

There are two kinds of screenwriters in the world -- those who get green envelopes and those who don't. Hope you earn your own residuals some day soon.

HOW COULD ANYBODY GET SO LOW?

ZEENA
What's the boss been razzing you about?

STAN
I was just asking him about that guy that does the geek business.

ZEENA
That's always a sore point in a carnival.

STAN
Why?

ZEENA
The geek is one of our biggest draws, but a lot of performers won't work a show that carries one.

STAN
I can't understand how anybody could get so low.

ZEENA
(with rueful sympathy -- as one who knows)
It can happen.

-- Jules Furthman/Nightmare Alley (1947)

Back in the chapter "This Writer's First, Glorious Payday..." I kinda skipped over the six months between my first script flat-lining and my second being optioned by legendary producer Larry Turman.

This was done in service of expediency -- that jam-packed story had already made my point, and I didn't feel like ass-cramming yet *another* quasi-fascinating digression into it. God Knows, whenever a writer themselves feels they're running long, well, you know it's time to holster the sucker.

But in truth, those missing six months were the most brutal of my young life.

Between taking all those meetings, having my hopes obliterated at the goal line, then taking shelter with Mike in our Venice Beach studio to hammer out a second screenplay *a lot* of crazy shit happened.

When I'd motored the VW into Butt Town, I was armed with nothing save $200 and an old friend's futon to crash on. My buddy Vern lived on N. Orange Grove, right behind Domiano's, with legendary Canter's Deli directly across the street. Being a good guy, he agreed to put me up for a month -- but the clock was ticking because we both knew any longer could push way past our respective pain thresholds and damage the friendship. My only industry connection was Suzanne, the agent Mike had ensnared at the Portland Marriott. So that was it, the full extent of what I had backstopping me -- Suzanne's phone number, my buddy Vern's couch, barely enough cash to survive two weeks, and last, but not least, my turtled, quaking, terrified cock.

From Day One, job hunting was a Mongolian clusterfuck. This was Winter '91. After twelve years sleepwalking under Reagan/Bush a deep recession had taken hold. Young, strong, eager and willing, I still couldn't find work *anywhere*. Believe it or not, I even applied to serve hot meals to the homeless at a soup kitchen. Tedious late-night work, sure, but eight bucks an hour. To my wide-eyed astonishment, I didn't get the job. The guy checked out my resume and said, "One look at this, I know you won't be around long."

388

Whether he meant Butt Town would cornhole and crap me out like so many other F.O.B. film students, or because I was a cinch to "make it" he never did make clear... but I have a pretty good idea which way he was leaning. Having extinguished any meager hope of my employment, the guy abruptly switched tacks and started asking me what movies I liked.

My desperation began a slow burn. I followed a tip about Industry temp work to an agency up on Sunset -- a dark building of dirty '60's glass you can see dry-humping the Strip from all over town. When I walked into the offices, there were already thirty-plus people waiting ahead of me. Like I said, times were brass-knuckles tough, and a whole generation of film biz wanna-bes like Yours Truly were on the full-time hustle, looking for *anything* to help keep us in the game and allow us just one more day to try and chase down our dreams.

Finally, over an hour later, it was interview time. The agency's Grand Poobah was a corpulent fifty-plus pretending he was thirty, with an expensive peroxide job matching his piss-yellow Lacoste tennis sweater. When I sat down, he pulled a nasty stink-face like my dress shirt was sewn with dogshit. Let's call this gentleman "Myles" just to be polite.

Myles took a cursory glance at my resume (NYU, white-shoe Wall St. paralegal) and mashed it into a messy pile of 'em like a cashed cigarette. Right away you could tell the daily swarm of faceless young hopefuls disgusted him. *Who the fuck did we think we were, coming to Hollywood like this? Didn't we know our defeats were imminent? That millions far better than us had already come and gone, leaving empty-handed and broken... sometimes even worse?*

389

Obviously, Myles didn't say that aloud, largely because he didn't have to -- his embittered eyes did all the scolding. They mocked and belittled you every time you spoke. Sicker still was how much he loved lording his miniscule sliver of power over the struggling less-fortunate like myself. Fucker got his jollies from it, taking a gleeful victory-crap on any poor kid who found themselves at his mercy.

Your allotted ten minute "interview" was, in fact, Myles's chance to heap further humiliation upon you. His Majesty badgered you into admitting that, yes, you probably should've thought things through better, shouldn't you, and that given the astronomical odds against success your ambition could more accurately be considered a tragic miscalculation.

This fuckin' guy was like some sadistic, central-casting San Quentin C.O. playing God with the prisoners, his life a permanent Community Theater call-back for Borgnine's Sgt. "Fatso" Judson in <u>From Here to Eternity</u>. Those whom Fatso favored would eat. Those whom Fatso did not went back to The Hole without so much as a moldy biscuit to nurse on.

Thick-skulled and hardboiled as I already was at twenty-three, it was still profoundly demoralizing. Yet because I was desperate enough to sit there and take it, politely lock-jawed while he psychologically buggered me six ways to Sunday, Myles ultimately took pity on me and tossed me a crumb.

My reward? A three-day gig serving as the temporary piss boy in the CAA mailroom. Twelve hours per, I was on sore feet delivering big specs and swag bags, and after Uncle Sam finished reaming my check, I hit the bricks with $183.50.

And Sgt. Fatso Myles? He had plenty more fresh meat to bugger and mind-fuck, and I never heard from the fat bastard again.

* * * * *

It's *astonishing* how sharp your memories remain of times you were face-down and out for the count. I couldn't tell you what I did with the entirety of 2012, but these twenty-plus year-old beat-downs come flooding back to me in color-saturated Hi-Def 1080p.

Particularly vivid among them is hitting a Beverly Center ATM to access what remained of my N.Y. bank account. Inside, my life savings -- a whopping $15. Not to further carbon date myself, but back in '91 some banks still allowed you to withdraw $10 at a time. However, this go 'round after feeding in my card, I discovered ChemBank had *just* changed over to the new $20 minimum policy, like, that same week.

Twenty dollars. Minimum. I only had $15. That meant I couldn't get my beggarly, Dickensian mitts around my last fifteen lousy bucks! *Fuck me.* By now, I fully assumed I bore the invisible mark of Cain. Forget black clouds, I'd somehow become a walking Indian burial ground. I mean, not *everything* can break against you, can it? At least that's what I kept asking myself over my nightly diet of forty-nine-cent Value Menu burritos.

My last production gig before moving to L.A. was as grip/gaffer on a Coca-Cola print campaign. It took place during a storybook summer in Seattle. The crew was super cool and stony, and some most excellent times were had by all. As a special gift on the job's final day, the photographer gave everybody heavy duty Eddie Bauer survival parkas. Really top-drawer jackets, filled with goose-down, waterproof Gortex shells, the works.

391

Riding high on red wine and surrounded by my new friends at the wrap party, I never could've guessed how valuable a gift that jacket would become. Saying it saved my near-homeless balls from freezing off more than once that winter is a criminal undersell.

Eddie Bauer's a cool company. They have a very generous policy of giving full refunds for anything you return, no hassles, no matter what the condition. In the brutal aftermath of my ATM blue-balling, I'd simply exhausted my options. I didn't have a cent. So it was up the third floor Beverly Center escalators looking for Eddie Bauer I went.

Returning that jacket for its $200 value stung bad, Lucy yanking the football from under Charlie Brown then snap-kicking him in the Reese's Pieces, that bad. The Eddie Bauer Register Girl's sad look didn't help any. It was pity, not sympathy -- perhaps even disgust. Didn't matter. By that point (just three hours after I'd awoken) I'd taken so many kill shots I was numb anyway. I pocketed the two hundy and, feeling like the greasiest sub-human loser in L.A., reentered my Tuesday no longer wearing a coat.

Next stop on my Slide of Shame Tour? Waiting tables at a schmancy new place on Beverly Blvd.

Owners of the wildly successful Authentic Cafe tried opening a breakfast annex a few doors down, something to appeal to the Industry crowd. To this day, I have no idea how I heard about it, but they needed waiters so I hauled-ass over. Finally, a little daylight. The manager hired me on the spot.

Thank you, Dear Baby Jesus! Now I could stay in L.A., get my feet back under me, start strategizing my way through this Byzantine slaughterhouse of a business. If nothing else, perhaps I wouldn't have to sell off my clothing one piece at a time anymore.

Here's an old joke. Ever hear it before?

"Know how to make God laugh?"

"Tell Him your plans."

Baby Jesus hadn't bothered hipping me to one tiny little glitch in my new game plan. Being brand-spanking-new, *not a single fucking soul* came into the restaurant for breakfast. Nobody even knew the place was there. The owners launched from a dead-stop. There was no advertising, and they weren't using Authentic's menu, so there wasn't any carry-over from their regulars. The coup de grace came via "location, location, location" -- it was situated in a notorious Beverly Blvd. black hole where flagging Gelato shops and other small businesses crawled off to die.

First day on the job, the whole debacle snapped into sharp focus for me. You waited on maybe five customers max across an eight hour shift, meaning you spent most your time cleaning, stocking, etc. but not actually making any money. I believe the most I ever took home from one full day -- not joking in the slightest -- was $15. I got one free meal per shift. Past that, the new job was *costing* my broke ass money.

My co-workers didn't offer much solace. Über-trendoid and aggressively young Hollywood, my coming from N.Y.C. -- boasting both vicious wit and blue-collar work ethic alongside my surgically-attached Yankees pro-style -- didn't exactly fire-start any love fests. They essentially viewed me as *The Unclean*, beyond even the bottom rung of the L.A. caste system. Aardvark'd up like the cast of <u>Reality Bites</u>, they would glower at my flannel shirt and Swiss-cheesed 501's and keep a safe distance lest my lack of attitude and affectation should somehow infect them.

During one of my shifts, somebody left a copy of *Variety* behind. Wiping down the table, I did something I've never done before or since -- I picked it up and flipped to the classifieds. Spotlit bottom left-hand corner was a boxed ad seeking production assistants (P.A.'s) for the American Film Market (AFM). Fuck, I figured. Exactly what I'm looking for. All it said was to fax in your resume and they'd get back to you.

After work, I walked a couple sun-baked acres to Kinko's and fired it off. It cost $2 of the $18 I had left. Two weeks later, crickets, nobody had called. Great move asshole, I remember riding myself. Two more precious dollars down the toilet. Good money I could have used to finance two last Burrito Supremes!

* * * * *

Alas, Dear Reader, even now I was still *miles* from rock bottom. My epic shame spiral hadn't even finished the First Act.

Somehow I picked up a bizarre mystery rash carpeting the full expanse of my groin. (Sweet visual, right? How's that for "thinking in pictures"?) No, this didn't arrive via sleazy, unprotected intercourse with the acid-washed army of Paula Abduls cruising Gorky's or the Hollywood Athletic Club. If only it had been anywhere *near* that sexy. Nope. Simply stepped out of the shower one day and there it was. Guess it's a gift. All my life, I've been real lucky that way.

Given how broke I was, going to a "normal" doctor was out. So I hit the White Pages (remember those?) and lucked into a free public health clinic maybe half a mile down Beverly.

My buddy Vern's mom was taking him out to lunch just as I started off. They insisted I grab a ride with them, would <u>not</u> take no for an answer. Like a colossal dumb-ass, I had them drop me off right in front of THE FREE CLINIC.

There was a real ugly, confused moment as they realized where we'd stopped. The clinic signage may as well have been a diseased male crotch bordered in flashing red neon. Perfect Mel Brooks timing, both their heads swiveled to eyeball me in backseat.

"You're going *here*?"

"Yeah. Uh, yes."

"*Why*? Isn't it filthy in there?"

I lost it, went completely ape-shit. "<u>*WHY? BECAUSE SOME VICIOUS ALIEN RASH IS BURROWING THROUGH MY BALLS AND IF I DON'T EASE MR. SALTY'S SUFFERING QUICK I'M GOING TO GO POSTAL*</u>!!!"

Quiet whisper, back in real life, I outright lied -- "My parents wanted me to grab a quick physical, uh, you know, make sure I'm tip-top while I'm out here." Punctuation came courtesy this creepy Peter Lorre <u>M</u> laugh I'd never heard escape my own mouth before.

They were nice people and good friends but they just didn't get it. Their middle-class minds were unable to wrap themselves around the plain fact I was broke... penniless... busted... fuck it, POOR. I was smart. Came from great parents. I'd gone to NYU. They *knew* me. More importantly from their perspective, *I was white.*

395

So how in God's name could I be going to a (gross!) free clinic? Big time 404 Error. Does not compute.

"Thanks for the ride!" I bolted out for the clinic. Body lice from other fire-crotched, poverty-stricken patients like myself seemed a small price if it meant escaping cross-examination in the confines of their leathery new Saab.

Fifteen minutes later, a very clean doctor gave me some cream for my mystery rash. Mercifully, before my one month ended and Vern sent me packing, neither he nor his mother ever mentioned our trip to the Free Clinic again.

* * * * *

Next came a cafe night shift I'll carry with me in IMAX 3-D until the pyramids turn into Pop Rocks.

During that first burst of studio meetings, when everything was coming up strawberries and cheesecake and the sky seemed the limit, I'd met Nick Grillo at Paramount. Nick was a long-time vet working with Mace Neufeld on Tom Clancy blockbusters like The Hunt For Red October. A baby writer blinded by the Hollywood sign couldn't have run into a nicer guy. An ex-pat New Yorker in the very best sense, with that brass-tacks Back East sense of humor in spades, Nick went out of his way to be enthusiastic. Nobody knew better that my odds of survival were long and ugly, but Nick didn't dwell on that, doing a good deed purely out of kindness and making it all seem possible *anyway*, which is something I've remained eternally grateful for. When you're spread-eagled and hemorrhaging in this town, encouragement from anyone real like Nick can easily be the difference between continuing to believe in

yourself or throwing in the towel, folding up and
blowing away.

So this one miserable night I'm working the cafe's front
counter, when who walks in but Nick and his wife.

Hit by an avalanche of shame, my heart just froze. Last
time I'd seen this kind soul, I was some promising up-
and-comer surveying limitless horizons while strolling
the Paramount lot. Now here I was, just *three months
later*, slinging day-old croissants in a filthy apron, my
fast start D.O.A. and only days (perhaps hours) away
from taking a knee and begging the folks for a plane
ticket back home.

What did I do? Dropped straight to the floor. No shit.
<u>Right</u> <u>down</u> <u>to</u> <u>the</u> <u>cruddy</u> <u>ground</u> -- co-workers wide-
eyed -- and fucking *crawled* on hands and knees into the
back so he wouldn't see me. Forget about as a writer, <u>as
a man</u> I refused to endure the humiliation of who I was
right then, of proving Nick's confidence false and myself
just another might've-been who'd already burned
through whatever potential he'd once possessed.

In reality, Nick may not have even remembered me, and
being the supportive sweetheart he was, he certainly
wouldn't have cared or looked down at me if he did. But
see, it wasn't really about Nick -- *I* simply didn't have
strength enough to take the blow if he'd seen me and
recognized my face.

So I hid out in the stock room, stacking trash bags and
fighting like hell to choke back a chestful of self-
loathing. If I hadn't been so goddamn angry -- at myself,
at Hollywood, at my shitty luck -- I definitely would
have started crying.

* * * * *

397

The cafe manager called me into his office not a week later. He was an alright guy, smart, if painfully effeminate from my manly-man point of view.

"Hello John, how you doing?"

"Great. What's up?"

He gave it to me straight, no helmet, no pads.

"I'm afraid I'm going to have to let you go."

Surprised? Sure, a little. But to be entirely honest, I wasn't shocked. When you spew something like 10,000 words a day like I did at twenty-three (rest easy, these days I'm down to a thrifty eight thousand), *by definition* you're bound to talk a lot of shit. A metric ton of it. Political correctness? Never been my forte. So I figured I'd unwittingly tap-danced over some invisible line, enraged my nose-pierced co-workers or pissed off a customer with some smarmy, offhand comment I perceived as proof positive of my comedic genius. And, hey, I was fine with that. ·Everyone's a mixed bag and that was just, well, me. Nothing shy of an elective full-frontal lobotomy could ever change it.

Besides that, I wasn't making any money. So I really didn't give a shit.

"I totally get it," I reassured him. "No problem, I'm already in the acceptance phase. I'm fired, I no longer work here, I no longer have a job. But before I leave, could you please just tell me what I did?"

"Well..." the manager edged into a deeper state of contemplation. "You're never late... always on time...

"Yep..."

"And you always work really hard...

"Okay..."

"You're honest. You've never stolen from me..."

"No, I have not." By now my face must've looked wildly perplexed. "So then what is it?   What did I do wrong?"

"Well... it's just a *feeling* I get.

"*A feeling?*"

The manager pushed my final $45 paycheck across.

"That's right. A feeling you're not a good fit here."

Just so we're clear, the final verdict was... "suspicion of not fitting in"? I'd have given the guy way more credit for simply busting out the old <u>Sesame Street</u> song -- "*One of these things is not like the others, one of these things just doesn't belong...*"

* * * * *

Glacially, though, the worm began to turn. Days before leaving, my buddy Vern played me an answering machine message. It was the folks from the American Film Market. They wanted me to come in and interview.

Never has a man crapped himself more completely or energetically than I did. Somehow I could sense this lowly P.A. job might be that sliver of daylight I'd long prayed for, my way out of anally-abusive temp agencies, mystery rashes, watery Top Ramen and fifteen-dollar shifts in breakfast hash hell.

AFM is the once-yearly Ringling Brothers of film acquisition, financing and foreign sales in Los Angeles.

Pretty much anything involving the Biz outside the majors goes down there. Upwards of ten thousand people attend this sprawling event over a single week -- filmmakers, distributors, attorneys, financiers, production-company-paid-for-prostitutes and the most aggressively sleazed-out middle-aged hucksters with the most fucked up hairlines anywhere. Picture an Armenian foreign sales agent with a Woody Harrelson/Bill Murray/<u>Kingpin</u> Finale hairdo two-fisting a garlic sandwich and it'll be like an Instagram feed straight from the lobby.

In short, it's an all-bets-are-off orgy of the global entertainment business. Films are screened, palms are greased, deals are closed, metaphorical cocks are sucked. To keep everything running smoothly and cover the monstrous logistics, the AFM's producer hires a strong-backed young P.A. staff responsible for everything from moving furniture and setting up company rooms, to cork-boarding Pakistani movie posters and shooing anorexic hookers away from the pool.

Walter was the producer running the show. This would be their first year at the Lowe's Hotel, and he wanted to showcase the market at its very best. I met with him in AFM's Santa Monica offices and from the moment we shook hands I was <u>on</u> -- think the crazed monkeys going bonkers to open <u>28 Days Later</u>. I yanked out all the stops, did my whole dog and pony show and got Walter and his staff laughing -- basically by being <u>the exact same me</u> that all those L.A. haters had previous hated.

You can guess what happened next. My crazy white ass O-B-L-I-T-E-R-A-T-E-D that interview. Fuckin' destroyed it. Having endured a prolonged Hollywood Sign-sized beating, it was finally my time to shine. All the marbles were on the table, all the stadium lights cranked up bright, and believe me when I say I made the utmost of the opportunity.

Walter literally had to halt me mid-routine and say, "John, that's it. You've got it. <u>You've got the job</u>." Very kindly, he hired me right there in the room.

Work started in three weeks. My pay would average $750 per, all 1099 income -- no taxes taken out. Mike had moved down from Oregon, and my new gig meant we could finally get a place together. Establish a beachhead from whence we could organize our bold counter-strike at pernicious heart of Butt Town.

...And to think it all came down to a discarded *Daily Variety* and two-dollar fax.

What if the customer hadn't left it? What if I'd ignored the Trades like I always did? What if I wasn't in the mood for the sun-stroking I got trudging to Kinko's that day?

Blind luck or fate? I'll let you decide. But for the truly serious among you, take heed and hang in there, 'cause it'd be a shame to split before seeing your lucky three-pointer finally splash through the twine.

During the three days they ran the *Variety* ad, four hundred applications had come in. They'd already hired nineteen P.A.'s. I was the last, lucky number twenty.

Months later, wolf no longer at my door (for a while, at least), I asked Walter why he'd selected my application for callback out of the four hundred-some choking his fax machine.

Know what he said?

"When I saw you went to NYU Film I said to myself, 'Now I bet this kid can move desks and follow instructions without fucking it up too much'."

Fifty-grand in student loans, and to this day it's still the only job I've gotten from going to film school.

* * * * *

Alas, Dear Reader, despite going all superhero and shit in grabbing that AFM gig, I still had one last, demoralizing mouthful of chud yet to swallow.

After exiting my buddy Vern's place on N. Orange Grove, it would still take a couple weeks for the film market to gear up and those first fat paychecks to start rolling in. This required my securing a brief stay in some final, surgical stopgap before Mike and I could rent that fabled Venice beach studio mentioned earlier and safely barricade ourselves inside.

Only one soul I knew in L.A. had such accommodations. My only *other* friend in sunny So. Cal -- a filthy rich former classmate named Noah.

Noah and I had gone to NYU together. He was archetypal silver spoon/private school Manhattan playing opposite my fresh-off-the-turnip truck West Coast kid in Birkenstocks. Opposites attract, I suppose, and we hit it off, had some good times. Regretfully, and I say this in the warmest, most respectful way possible, my big city friend didn't have an artistic bone in his body.

Filmmaking just wasn't Noah's trip. Hey, there's certainly no crime in that. Brutal truth be told, *millions* of Americans would be far better off acknowledging they don't have any discernable or verifiable artistic

402

gifts and go on about their lives. If shit doesn't fit, you must acquit. Not everybody can -- or should be -- a rock star, have a signature cologne, sex tape or reality show. In the same fashion, not everybody is meant to get an overall TV deal or sell a splashy Hollywood spec. Bukowski was light years ahead of the curve when he famously quipped -- "Dedication without talent is useless."

God bless, I say. Do something meaningful instead. Find something else you truly love. There are so many healthier, more productive and more (trust me) relaxed, fun-filled and satisfying lives to lead out there. Just grab yourself one. Mindlessly trying to brute-force a square peg into a round hole never leads anywhere good.

Regardless, Noah not becoming the next Coppola or Scorsese wasn't much of a problem, because he possessed a permanent ace in the hole.

My classmate came from money.

When I say money, I mean MAD MONEY. Late '80's Gordon Gekko/Michael Douglas/Wall Street money. A Cézanne hung over Dad's dining room table. Yes, a real one. Saw it with my own two eyes. And with family connects in The Biz, Noah was pre-ordained for a cushy Development job on some evergreen studio lot -- preferably a short drive to the beach, if at all possible.

Meanwhile, back at NYU, I did a lot of heavy lifting helping Noah get his projects finished. Gave him a hand with stuff like the shooting, the editing, the directing, or sometimes the whole damned idea in the first place. No big deal, right? Who wouldn't hook up a friend in need? That's what bro's are for.

HARD CUT TO: Winter '91, Me, L.A., leaving Vern's and desperate for a temp crash pad. Noah took my call and, hearing of my plight, graciously allowed me a brief stay. To be precise, he had accommodations befitting someone such as myself -- out on his Beverly Hills sunporch.

Many nice post-war places in B.H. have these Forties-style glassed-in sunporches. Decoratively fronting the home, they're ideal for sunbathing house plants or their owners without the blue-collar indignity of actually having to go outside. Of course, they're also drafty, half-assed So. Cal add-ons without a stitch of insulation that don't meet code.

By now it was late February. That particular year (more great luck) kicked off as one, long, ceaseless tropical monsoon. For those chest-beating East Coast souls who insist So. Cal can't possibly get cold, I would urge an icy winter's visit without jacket to forever cork such foolhardy claims.

My first sleepover on the borrowed sun porch, inside borrowed sleeping bag, shivering my youthful nuts off, I kept reminding myself that it wasn't that bad. It was far better than the Bug's backseat, and within two short weeks I would finally have an apartment, and warm bed, of my own. Further, I could always crawl into Noah's guest bathroom for a brief respite should I lose all feeling in my extremities.

First morning of AFM and my new job, I awoke to a torrential downpour. Drenched palm trees were being whiplashed around like props in a black-and-white Howard Hawks film. Only thing missing was an Old Peg-Legged Fisherman Character bellowing "STORM'S A COMIN'!" while fighting to batten down the hatches.

I'd be shivering and soaked to the bone before I could reach the driver's seat. Clocking in at the film market looking like some waterlogged homeless guy certainly wouldn't inspire confidence in Walter, my new employer, in a job I absolutely had to have. And what if my first day involved working outside? Then what the fuck would I do?

Which dovetails with sadistic brilliance back to that <u>waterproof Eddie Bauer survival parka</u> -- the one I'd been forced to hobo-hock back at Beverly Center. The instant I flashed on it, a hate-filled, red-hot thought bubble began smarting over my head.

Out of options and out of time, I crawled hands-and-knees into the furthest recesses of Noah's vast closet looking for anything I could use. Dug past pinstriped Hugo Boss and Yves St. Laurent power suits, a Crayola box of Dolce & Gabbana ties and enough wingtips and Italian loafers to satiate a 70's Filipino despot.

Buried in the furthest bowels of Noah's stash lay a forgotten olive drab army jacket all by its lonesome. Dejected and disused, it was as wrinkled, sad and stained as a Dickensian washer woman's ass cheeks. Counting my blessings, I grabbed it and hurried out the door.

* * * * *

Day One was an exhausting twelve hours, but the hard work felt good and with it came a sharp glimmer of triumph. Brute force of will alone, I was blowing topsoil out both nostrils and re-emerging from Butt Town's premature burial plot. Navigating the flooded boulevards back to Beverly Hills, my former swagger started showing signs of life. I began Iago-ing myself with promises that someday, my-oh-my, all these sorry

405

fuckers who'd left me for dead were going to pay! *How DARE they*! Didn't they understand I was destined to become the greatest screenwriter of my generation? That I planned to write and direct my epic first feature by twenty-five, precisely as my hero Orson Welles had?

Soaked like some cartoon sewer rat, I walked into Noah's place. My erstwhile classmate lorded a look from his RGB projection screen. Steadily his eyes narrowed.

"John, why are you wearing that jacket?"

Is that any way for old pals to greet each other? I wondered. No "hello"? No "How was your first day"? Not even "Wassup, bitch"? 'Suppose that meant "Jesus, buddy, dry yourself off before you catch pneumonia!" was totally off the menu.

"Noah, hey, bro" I tip-toed forward. "Raining like hell this morning and I didn't have a jacket. Found this on the floor of your closet and figured it'd be okay to borrow it. Don't worry, man. I'll get it dry-cleaned for you."

"Borrowing my jacket is not the issue," Noah scolded, catapulting a spoonful of butter pecan Haagen-Das into his mouth. "It's that you don't have *your own* jacket in the first place. I mean, what are you? Some Penn Station panhandler? *Who the fuck doesn't have their own jacket*?"

Sure, Dear Readers... (Long beat. Deep sigh.) I could've self-righteously stormed the moral high ground, sandblasted him with my best Che Guevara, played the Steinbeck/say-hello-to-the-Okie card -- which, by any reasonable standard, I had full justification to do. Perhaps I might've shamed him with woeful tales of my

406

relentless hardships and sufferings, drawn a four-color pie graph to illustrate precisely how emasculating it'd been begging some pubescent Eddie Bauer salesgirl to buy back my toasty-warm survival parka solely to keep subsisting on synthetic Mexican food?

But to what end, my friends?

Ask yourselves this -- Would *whatever* I had to say in that grim instant change the take of a guy with a fuckin' Cézanne hanging back at Dad's house?

(*Geez, John, when you put it that way...*)

Besides, my only dream right then was to make a shivering retreat to that drafty sun porch and my soggy sleeping bag so I could pass the fuck out.

"Yeah, you're right. My bad, bro. Guess I didn't think it through." This hangdog *mea culpa* was all Noah really wanted anyway, more compelling proof of his manifest rightness, and I considered it a miniscule price to pay.

Good ol' Noah -- same guy I fireman-carried through film school -- returned to watching <u>Twin Peaks</u>. Carefully hanging his jacket in the outer entry, Yours Truly went to cop some thankful zzz's.

* * * * *

Two weeks later, Mike and I finally scored that perfect beach pad mentioned in "<u>This Writer's First, Glorious Payday</u>..."

Our new bodybuilder/screenwriter landlord Lamar was majorly 'roided and Gold's Gym'd to the Nth degree. He rightfully prided himself on an ability to discern a great Pinot noir and refused to shithouse himself with anything shy of the most outstanding bud Venice, CA had to offer.

Did I mention his pot was *outstanding*? This was The Chronic-era L.A., where you often went jaw-to-jaw with real bangers and ballers to safely procure The Kind, which, ultimately, is all Lamar (God Bless his Southern Californian soul) would deign to smoke. Many an afternoon, the tantalizing orbit of his top-floor/ocean-view landlord's digs would tractor Mike or I (or both of us) inside to do frosty bong rips and marvel over sunsets with the synthetic hues of Starburst Fruit Chews.

It was here, stoned to the gills, our young minds completely jellified, Lamar explained why he had just purchased a black baby Vietnamese sow pig for himself. Shrewdly each Saturday, Lamar would play Pied Piper -- trolling that adorable little black-haired fucker up and down the Boardwalk, fine-assed girls of every delectable size, shape and flavor immediately smitten by baby pig's innate cuteness and powerless not to follow along in Lamar's parade. Never in my entire life have I seen one man get so much Baywatch-quality pussy with a grift that goddamned obvious. But there was no denying its towering brilliance, and Mike and I spent much of our first week engaged in passionate debate over whether to buy our own Vietnamese pig or not.

...But all that's for a different book entirely.

What really matters is that we'd actually done it. We'd survived separate emotional Vietnams and rallied ourselves to claw free of Hollywood's merciless jungles. Now we lived at the beach -- not just any beach, motherfucker, Venice Beach in SOUTHERN CALIFORNIA! -- with a hilarious-but-lethal former

Special Forces bartender pal on the first floor who comped us enough vodka tonics and fried calamari to make life pretty damned good, that year and the next.

Indeed, the worm had turned. From that first morning awakening in our new digs things grew brighter, seemed more possible than ever. Never again would my friend or I face demonic depths so dark and harrowing. Moving forward, of course, we simply exchanged one dictator for another -- encountering a million more/different problems along our climbs. But next time around they'd be of a somewhat higher class and miles beyond the bedrock lows of early '91.

And *that's* the story of those missing six months, the most brutal of my young life, which led to knuckling-down and writing that second goddamn script, the one I vowed would be so fuckin' good some stranger -- legendary producer Larry Turman, as it thankfully turned out -- would be *forced* to give me money for it. They simply wouldn't be able to stop themselves.

Couple final points of interest --

It was while shivering out on wealthy Noah's drafty sunporch (or in his warm breakfast nook while he was out buying a new wardrobe for his pre-ordained studio development job) that I began seriously notecarding and beat-sheeting out that very same script, the first one I would sell. Honestly, I began the process as a final act of defiance, a bloody-but-unbowed "fuck you" to the army of Film Biz darkness aligned against me before I was swallowed whole and forcibly shat back out into some mundane suburban oblivion. Who knew this Spartan decision to go out like a soldier would actually become the First Act of a twenty year screenwriting career?

409

Whatever happened to the pitiless, mind-buggering Sgt. "Fatso" Myles and his holier-than-thou temp agency? Happy to say, haven't the slightest fuckin' idea. Years later, however, during the nationwide release of my first major film, a seven-by-four-foot JUMBO POSTER was shellacked into the bus stop <u>directly</u> <u>outside</u> his Sunset temp agency's front door. Of course, Fatso couldn't possibly have known one of his faceless young former hopefuls had written it, but that was entirely besides the point. The Universe had stepped in to bestow a certain measure of Karmic justice (as said Universe is wont to do now and again), and like a man unaware there's bird shit sluicing down his back, Myles was still trumped by it whether he would ever comprehend that or not.

And Nick Grillo, the gold-hearted producer who'd taken an interest and been so supportive during my blackest hours? Glad you asked. Eight years later I found myself sitting across from Nick again -- this time during a beachfront Shutters brunch while discussing a script of mine his company was financing through HBO.

And no -- Nick didn't remember seeing me slinging hash at that long-closed cafe that night. Believe me, I asked him about it.

* * * * *

I'll be damned if that story didn't metastasize into one mammoth-assed stroll down memory lane. Even longer than the one I'd just finished bragging about having the good sense to quit when I starting writing this.

I expect the key question is why risk egregious oversharing by revisiting these wounded tales in the first place? Face accusations of chest-beating, ego-boosting and/or mean-spirited showboating? (None of which I have much energy for anymore, by the way.)

I mean, on a personal level, this saga has long-since been bloody water flushed under what became an extremely lucrative and fulfilling bridge. Things worked out far better than I could've imagined, hell, better than I could've even *scripted*. Beyond that, on any global scale, we're ultimately talking about some pretty high-class problems. It's not like I didn't have arms or legs, was growing subsistence crops atop a nuclear dump site, or found myself hounded by Central American *juntas* because of my fervent political beliefs -- although being a baby-faced twenty-three at the time, it certainly did *feel* as bad as all those things. I was a college-educated white kid trying to sell a screenplay. Cry me a fuckin' river. So here's a quick nod to keeping all things relative and in perspective.

That said, as Bob Marley so wonderfully sang, "Every man think his burden is the heaviest", and any of us can only speak best about what we've experienced firsthand.

So I suppose the real takeaway here is to put up your dukes, stick by your guns, and make the brave and terrifying promise to yourself never to fold, no matter how bad a beating you take.

During one of Michael Jordan's six championship runs (yep, MJ again), there was an interview where he shared some advice his father had given him during a tough game. I'm poorly paraphrasing, it was far more artful than this, but it was something to the effect of -- "If you're gonna go down, son, make sure you don't go down with any bullets left in your gun."

Undoubtedly, your own struggle will involve an entirely different set of malicious faces, perceived slights and harrowing "we'll laugh like hell about all this later" specifics. Much of it may go down via email moving forward, with you fighting to inhabit a city thousands of miles from Butt Town's pitiless, puckering sphincter before finally taking your medicine and moving out West to seek a title shot.

In any case, you <u>will</u> have your own screenwriting crosses to bear, and the battles you face will be fierce. As Tyler Durden so wisely prophesized, "Our great war is a spiritual war" -- and to that I would add the overtly psychological as well.

FADE OUT / FADE IN

Alas, *Tough Love's* finale approaches. We've reached that point late Third Act where, like any decent screenwriter, I drop the landing gear and try to put this sucker squarely on the runway, dovetailing everything together and tying up loose ends with a tidy little bow.

There's an ancient rude, crude and ridiculously insensitive joke I'd like to share from the prehistoric dark ages of politically incorrect humor; an era many younger readers may not have experienced firsthand. Regardless, just know that such a period did exist and it didn't bring about the end of the world -- and that for lack of a better contemporary example capable of making my point, I'm going to tell you this abrasive, impolite and potentially offensive joke anyways.

Brace yourselves, delicate Millennial vegan souls, it goes something like this --

Q. "How can you tell the Polish girl on a film set?"

A. "She's fucking the *writer*."

The more Industry experience you accumulate, believe me, the harder you'll find yourself laughing.

Being the writer is the least sexy link in the film biz food chain. We're the least exotic bunch of pale-faced hobos, horribly miscast in Planet Earth's most glamorous profession. Blade to balls, come nut cuttin' time, nobody *really* wants to be us. Everybody *says* they do, sure, but with no real skin in the game it's just boorish small talk. If someone really wants to write, my experience says they'll be somewhere (wait for it) *writing* -- not trolling Urth Cafe in Hollywood's stock

413

screenwriter costume (MacAir, leather satchel, cruelty-free latte) pissing and moaning about other people's deals alongside fellow poseurs and procrastinators.

Power? Prestige? Not part of the job description. Ninety-nine-point-nine percent of the time screenwriters don't have any real say in the feature world. Despite being absolutely essential to the process -- there is literally <u>no movie</u> without us -- we're more often viewed as neurotic, fussy piss-pants; needy, thin-skinned brainiacs forever on the verge of a simpering shit-fit should any changes meet with our bookish displeasure.

This isn't entirely without merit. Stereotypes come from somewhere, and having seen my own fair share of overpaid twats, I fully understand the instinct to bury a baseball bat in their junk. <u>But keep in mind the vast majority of writers aren't like this</u>. They work their butts off, shrugging back absurd demands and relentless pressurization time and again to give every project the very best they've got.

Still, like the lonely NFL field goal kicker, oversized helmet and sad little chinstrap, we stand apart from the full squad, even in victory. If we make the game-winning kick (i.e. save the movie or make it work) we don't feel jubilation, we experience *relief.* If we're lucky, really, really lucky, the coaches might pound on our helmet once or give us a curt pat on the ass. But God Forbid we shank one and miss in their eyes, failing to thread those pages cleanly through the uprights, because we'll be goated and savaged with every misfortune the franchise (read: project) has ever faced. Such base unfairness hits hard, hits low and hurts like hell; some of the best writers out there internalize these psychological slings and arrows long after such an experience, no matter what the movie's ultimate fate, win, lose or draw.

Basically, it's like the old song says. One truly is the loneliest number that you'll ever do.

Generations of producers and execs across Hollywood's hundred-year timeline have viewed writers as necessary evils; overhyped pariahs, lazy and criminally overpaid -- despite the hit movies or killer drafts they created to purchase their credibility. Many of the worst offenders share the not-so-secret belief that *they* could do every bit as good a job writing the script themselves. Far from some idle boast, such fond sentiments spring from their deepest Hollywood heart of hearts, and when filtered this way screenwriting becomes 98% snake-oil and 2% great ideas somebody *gave the writer* instead of the other way around.

All of which, I suppose, begs a simple question -- "Why *don't* they write it?"

Free country, last time I checked. Nothing's stopping our ever-critical employers from taking a crack at it. Why don't they just strap it on, fire up their MacBooks and take the law into their own hands? Create the lasting characters, the suspenseful twists and surprising turns and a multitude of other unforgettable moments which indelibly nestle themselves into an audiences' minds long after the multiplex closes?

Bottom line?

Because they can't.

If they could do what we do, they'd do it. Nothing would make the number-crunchers happier than ditching the writer altogether, saving on those pesky WGA health and pension payments and creatively repurposing that same cheddar back into company pockets. You may remember the most recent stab at this, "reality television", which purportedly heralded the "death of the writer". You may also recall how that corporate pipe dream netted out -- with reality TV being scripted within an inch of its gutter-surfing life like any other show.

And yet...

Despite the complete insanity of all this... the intermittent bouts of screenwriting madness testified to throughout *Tough Love's* martini-dry pages... the senseless ego and arrogance and misguided hostility... the legion of needless slights (real or imagined) taken on the chin rightly or wrongly... and, perhaps saddest of all, the sheer level of <u>counterproductivity</u> -- the myopic, heart-breaking *waste of energy* that if only reallocated from the politics of control into a <u>bettering of the scripts themselves</u> might yield a whole new standard of collegial accomplishment...

Despite all these harrowing obstacles, if we can just focus and persist, continue navigating creative curveball after minefield after trapdoor, forever dancing tippy-toe along the razor's edge of self-immolation... then we ultimately earn the privilege of participating in something unquestionably unique.

Making a career for ourselves writing movies or television.

Getting paid to do what we love.

Getting <u>paid</u> to <u>write</u>.

Getting paid to cook up a fresh batch of the coolest or craziest or funniest shit ever. Being permitted to add our own modest names alongside the treasured greats from hallowed eras prior; those fiercely dedicated screenwriting strangers who battled their ways up our same paths, faced tougher versions of our same struggles -- both within and without -- and *still* managed to triumph, igniting our imaginations and informing them with a deep, keening passion for the brave words so necessary beneath it all.

Some may claim all this comes at too high a price. That it's too painful, too punishing. That, success or failure, it summons forth the worst possible versions of people and leaves none save the morally adrift in its wake.

They would not be wrong.

I've seen many close friends, good people who would've been a great credit to this business, run screaming for their lives into careers with at least *some* semblance of normalcy or civility; with some *rules*, for Chris'sake. Given the staggering extent of bad energy in this business, it's hard to argue their logic and leaves little to say except you're sorry to see decent people like them go.

Whenever this subject comes up, like clockwork my buddy Larry (the Martial Arts guy) loves to quote Jack playing the Joker in Tim Burton's <u>Batman</u> --

"Decent people shouldn't live here. They'd be happier somewhere else."

Maybe he's right. Who knows? Ultimately, this is but one of many heavy decisions writers hearing Hollywood's siren call will need to come to grips with for themselves.

Personally, I've found that after you win the Heavyweight Championship of the World you don't remember the beating so much as the fact you're finally wearing the jeweled belt.

* * * * *

Some years ago, shooting the shit at a friend's place, I was thunderstruck by an abrupt epiphany. Fresh in mind was a widescreen '70's classic I'd watched 'til dawn the night before, and all at once I was waylaid by a delayed avalanche of understanding -- the movie's text could be read as the perfect metaphor for any screenwriter's journey.

Which film was the source of this inspiration?

Close Encounters of The Third Kind.

And no, for the last time, I was not on mushrooms.

Probably not a title you were expecting. Me neither. But let me pitch it to you exactly as I did my friend back then, and see if it doesn't make a helluva lot more sense.

* * * * *

Played by Richard Dreyfuss, Roy Neary is an archetypal middle-American family man; three kids, henpecking wife, suburban mortgage, the whole life sentence in spades.

Out on a late night service call, Roy has a spectacular close encounter with a UFO. Despite its strangeness and potential danger, it doesn't scare him -- instead, Roy becomes completely fascinated by this unique vision.

The average guy would've hauled-ass home and hid under his bed. Not Roy. He immediately chases after it

418

and parks on a bluff where other people have also gathered to watch these UFOs. They share a mind-blowing experience as the alien crafts treat them to a once-in-a-lifetime, otherworldly aerial display. This becomes a life-altering event for Roy and many of the others who witness it.

Roy tries to share this with his wife, wanting his partner to experience the same magic. But when he returns to the bluff the UFOs are long gone, and his wife doesn't believe a word of the story he's told her. First thing next morning, Roy is fired for having gone AWOL from his job to follow the alien spacecrafts.

Days pass and Roy becomes increasingly preoccupied with daydreams of a flat-topped mountain he can't seem to shake. Shaving cream, mashed potatoes, modeling clay and ultimately wheelbarrows of wet sod and soil are fashioned into crude sculptures of this mountain as Roy struggles to physically represent the vision haunting him.

The cost of Roy's obsession is steep. Henpecking wife grows furious, kids become unsettled and upset by his behavior. Soon Roy's family abandons him altogether, unable to cope with his gnawing need to get to the bottom of whatever's happening to him. Deep in his heart, Roy knows the UFOs and the mountain *mean something*, and his dream, his quest, now becomes finding out exactly what that something is -- no matter what the level of personal sacrifice.

Alone save the enormous sod mountain consuming his erstwhile family room, Roy chances onto the TV news story about Devil's Tower, Wyoming, and a nerve gas spill there. The instant Roy sees Devil's Tower on screen everything clicks and comes together -- this is the mountain he's been fighting so hard to replicate.

(Interestingly, Roy doesn't connect the dots on Devil's Tower until <u>after</u> he's been liberated from wifey and the kids. Imagine finding a take that subversive in today's family-values-at-all-costs Hollywood films.)

Roy hits the road for Wyoming. When closing in on the State Park housing Devil's Tower, we're treated to that fantastic shot of Roy's station wagon *literally* bucking the tide of fleeing vehicles -- God's Lonely Man and his modest mommy wagon corkscrewing its way forward in direct, visual opposition to hundreds of frightened others.

Roy reaches the train depot where a mob of frenzied locals are being evacuated by the U.S. Army; a mass exodus aimed at saving them from the nerve gas spill. Roy reunites with Jillian here, a woman from the bluff that night who's inexplicably drawn to the Tower after her young son's UFO abduction. Partnering up, they take Roy's station wagon off-road to get closer to Devil's Tower.

Barreling along empty roads, the couple now finds dead cows lining the gravel shoulder -- apparent victims of the same lethal gas they've been warned about. They do put on gas masks, but continue driving without hesitation. There's no alternative for these seekers now save reaching their ultimate goal and realizing whatever dream awaits them there.

Without warning, gas-masked HAZMAT soldiers surround the station wagon and take them into custody. The couple is shuttled to the U.S. Army camp at the base of Devil's Tower and questioned by the French Scientist in charge of the program. He reveals that thousands of people from all over America were drawn to the mountain by a variety of visions, but only the <u>twelve</u>

<u>most</u> <u>determined</u> of them managed to make it all the way to this final base camp.

All twelve of these seekers are given protective gas-masks and put on a helicopter for immediate evacuation, Roy and Jillian among them. But Roy doesn't believe the poisonous gas is real and -- to the other seekers' horror -- boldly rips off his mask. Nothing happens. Jillian follows his lead. She's fine as well. Roy's been right all along -- the lethal gas scare is nothing more than an Army-directed charade, an imaginary obstacle designed to scare people off and keep anyone from looking closer.

Roy and Jillian flee the Huey, joined by Larry, another one of the twelve. Together the trio begins scaling Devil's Tower. Far below in the background, we glimpse the other nine finalists being choppered back to the numbing normalcy of civilization.

Climbing the rock face is hardscrabble work. Larry fades fast, exhausted by the effort, and stops to rest while Roy and Jillian ignore their own fatigue and continue upward. A fresh Army helicopter arrives to spray knock-out gas over the terrain. Larry is put to sleep, lights out, game over. Roy and Jillian avoid the same fate by cresting the rise to safety with just seconds to spare. Out of the thousands of initial dreamers nationwide, only two now remain on the quest.

Roy and Jillian reach the "dark side of the moon" -- the opposite, hidden side of Devil's Tower. To their joyful astonishment, they find a top-secret landing strip and command center set up for communication with the UFO's. They watch awestruck as a first wave of alien crafts puts on an amazing aerial light show for the legions of welcoming scientists gathered below.

Roy is hurrying down to the command center when Jillian says she can't join him; explaining she's "just not ready yet". There's no turning back for Roy, however. He can't possibly stop this close, and they part ways with a first and final friendly kiss.

Now reaching the tarmac, Roy is left unhassled. He joins the French Scientist, swept up by the miraculous extraterrestrial drama unfolding before them.

The Alien Mothership lands. The scientists instinctively back up, many running for cover as its doors open. Not Roy. He's the only one who walks <u>towards</u> the craft, more curious and ensorcelled by its magic and majesty than ever before.

The alien life forms reveal themselves at last -- peaceful, child-like humanoids greeting those assembled. Red jumpsuited U.S. Government "travelers" ready themselves for the expected journey aboard the ship. The French Scientist successfully pitches those in charge on making a special exception to let Roy join them.

Roy takes his place in the line-up of red jumpsuits. The child-like humanoids curtly bypass the official government travelers and bee-line directly over to Roy -- taking his hands and leading him alone onto the spaceship.

Through unrelenting, uncompromising effort, and at substantial personal cost, Roy has actualized his deepest dream. He's earned the privilege of joining the aliens on an amazing journey into outer space -- surpassing even his wildest fantasies by a thousandfold.

* * * * *

See where I'm going with this? Guessed the punch line yet? Let me put it out there point-blank to ensure we're all on the same page --

If you want to be the guy or girl who gets to ride in the big fancy spaceship with the pretty colored lights you'll not only have to sacrifice, but overcome at levels you couldn't have imagined before. Moment of truth, only the most fiercely determined and intensely focused will be welcome aboard.

Not dissimilar from Roy Neary, a laundry-list of those closest to you -- friends, family, co-workers, classmates, competitors -- will fail to understand or appreciate your dedication to the screenwriting quest, the strident urgency behind it. Society at large surely won't embrace your far-fetched aspirations -- if "society" pays you any attention at all. Civilians of all stripes will gleefully inform you that choosing such a path is asinine and irresponsible -- putting your future prospects at risk, and perhaps the prospects of your future family as well.

By the way? They won't be entirely out in the weeds. Risk <u>is</u> a huge part of undertaking this journey. Perhaps no occupation is higher risk/higher yield than that of the aspiring writer in today's America. Publicly, your stock will never trade lower. Haters will commence to hate. Whenever cheap shots present themselves (slopped-up party/open bar Absolut) motherfuckers will outright dog you, straight to your face. The younger you are, the more it'll burn and, conversely, the more "chillax" others will expect you to remain. Nobody believes you're going to crack it anyway, so what harm is there in a little fun?

423

Per the lexicon of <u>Raising Arizona</u>, the world outside will become a rocky place where your seed can find no purchase.

But hey, let's not gloss over all the *other* gut-wrenching sacrifices you've signed yourself up for. Financially, you'll be open to man-sized beatings as well. Many try and juggle straight jobs and good-paying careers with writing scripts, others leave cushy gigs altogether to chase their dreams of paid full-time writing. Sometimes these brutal decisions involve orphaning health benefits, 401(K)'s and other comfy real-world perks. For young hordes of the recently graduated, this can equate with allowing their student debt to balloon wildly, largely untended and ignored.

Roy's story perfectly mirrors all this. Giving up his family, his home and (literally) every other earthly possession to fuel his ascent and grab hold of his intergalactic dream.

So yeah, <u>be one-hundred percent sure you understand what you're in for</u>. This path sure ain't no picnic. <u>You'll</u> become the nutcase in the station wagon, bucking the smug tide of fleeing vehicles to drive the wrong way. <u>You'll</u> be the goofball ignoring loud warnings that lethal gas will get you if you ignore the community's common wisdom. <u>You'll</u> be the crazy sucker bulldozing through roadblocks and farm-fencing, the wild-eyed kook staring down and shrugging off the purported Powers That Be, the dangerous, unkempt douchebag daring to discard your gas-mask and breathe deeply while Army helicopters fight to drag you back to a far less satisfying life.

Of course, if you just can hack it long enough... dodging machine gun fire and mastering the rope-a-dope... working really, really hard to get really, really *good*...

there's a chance <u>you'll</u> also become the fist-pumping bad-ass riding that alien Mothership into golden galaxies no never-had-the-courage nine-to-fiver will ever see. And the nepotistically privileged? Those pre-ordained travelers in the red government jumpsuits? No matter how many times you watch the movie, you'll notice the aliens *never* invite them aboard.

You'll be Richard Dreyfuss and all the doubters will be, well, henpecking, heart-broken Teri Garr, staring jealously into night skies for the rest of her life. You'll be you and they'll feel left behind, and never the twain shall meet. Karmically, it's even better, because you'll never have to stoop to rubbing anyone's nose in it -- they'll do the heavy lifting in that department all by themselves.

How the fuck do I know? Who the hell am I to judge?

Some crazy fucker who's lived it. Some kid who came to this nutty burg wearing Birkenstocks and crotch-rotted 501's, packing enough courage to run down my own UFO and claw my way aboard by any means necessary, no matter what the cost. Roy Neary's journey was my journey, and pretty much most of my best friends' journeys as well (Should we totally take this <u>Spartacus</u>? "I'm Roy Neary! *I'm* Roy Neary!").

Which is precisely why I wanted to share my take on <u>Close Encounters</u>. I believe it's a damned good metaphor for the nasty little gauntlet new writers have to drag themselves through. It ain't always pretty and it isn't much fun. But there's also *that spaceship* waiting on a tarmac someplace to take you for the ride of your life.

* * * * *

425

Lastly, however self-serving, disingenuous and totally uncool it may be to say this, I'm gonna say it anyway -- because it's high time somebody with legit brass between their legs put it on blast for everyone.

Screenwriters <u>are</u> special.

Americans in general are taught never, ever to say that out loud; never to imply any relative value between ourselves and our neighbors when it comes to areas of excellence, intelligence or imagination. Regardless, the blunt fact remains -- we writers have undertaken special challenges, endured special risks, absorbed a special amount of punishment and persevered with a special amount of grit, determination and (God willing) integrity along the way.

Screenwriters at all levels make a spectacular effort to scale our mountains of dreams while the majority of straights huddle in the warmth and easy shelter of the base camps and ski lodges below. We make our bones doing what most civilians can't begin to wrap their heads around and what people in other extremely creative fields can't get done -- take one hundred and twenty empty pages, blank as a newborn baby's behind, and fill them with *the right words*. Right enough so a complete stranger pays us real American dollars to possess them.

One El Coyote happy hour, I found myself in a buzzed and slightly heated debate with a junior lawyer at some hotshot L.A. firm. The question being contested? Which job was tougher -- being an attorney or being a screenwriter?

Junior's argument shot its wad posthaste, sounding vaguely rehashed from <u>The Good Wife</u> or <u>The Practice</u> or <u>Suits</u> or some other bullshit. About how hard it was

426

protecting people's rights and making the world safer and a shitload of other stuff he'd never actually do. Then it was my turn.

"Any asshole can buy their way into some half-baked Bahamian law school and end up drawing a paycheck *somewhere*..." I offered, "...and most of them do."

Next came a big show of unsatcheling my MacBook and propping it open --

"Go ahead, Clarence Darrow, write me a blockbuster."

There were endless other tacks I could've taken, of course. Asking him how many working attorneys he knew versus working screenwriters, etc. But I'd made my point, he'd totally been cool about it, and it was all good.

Verbal theatrics aside, isn't this where it all nets out? No givens, no safety nets, no sure things, screenwriters parachute into an off-the-books Black Ops mission that -- should they come up empty-handed -- does not, nor will it ever, exist.

Screenwriters are special. Fuckin' A. Whether anyone outside our field chooses to acknowledge it or not is irrelevant. If I had a dollar for every confirmed dumb-ass I've heard spouting shit on the subject, I could buy this dirty town and put it all in my shoe.

* * * * *

Three of my favorite quotes, one of which I mentioned before. Whenever projects hairpin from hot to cold, the moderately crazy metastasizes into the wholesale ridiculous and Butt Town just totally kills my buzz, I've found these gems often help keep things in perspective.

427

"Being in a minority, even a minority of one, doesn't make you mad."

-- George Orwell

"There's no expert like someone who's never done it."

-- Emmy-winner Ian Maitland, the coolest professor I had at NYU

"We have not journeyed across the centuries, across the oceans, across the mountains, across the prairies, because we are made of sugar candy."

-- the incomparable Winston Churchill

Mull 'em over. See if they speak to you with the same resonance they do me. Personally, I find they point to the very core of what screenwriting really *is* beyond blinking cursors and punching keys. Ours is a bizarre battle of wills, psychic guerilla warfare taking place on uniquely twisted creative plains. Things start off feeling like "Us against The Business"... deepen to "Us against The Unknown"... and then, finally, an evolved understanding that it's largely "Us against Ourselves" -- and has been from even before the beginning.

Do we honestly have the guts to stick by our guns in the face of such hostility towards our hopes and dreams, our vulnerable pages and ideas? To surf the inevitable ocean of frustration, coming from both within and without ourselves? To relentlessly conjure and coax the creatively spectacular from the mundane, staid and outright stupid time and time again?

Do we have the mettle? Do we have what it takes?

No easy answers, my friends, as only time will tell. But if you've gotten this far in *Tough Love*, I'll do you a solid and assume you have the makings of a contender. Clearly there's passion and desire (somehow you got your mitts on my book, right?), and obviously you possess a monster pain threshold, having endured my R. Lee Ermey routine for a couple hundred pages now. That alone proves you've got courage... or (more horrifyingly) that you're every bit as messed up as me.

Los Angeles is a city of finalists. Nobody I know came here by accident. This place provides a legit destination for those seeking *more*, yearning for a very specific success irrevocably married to self-expression. When it comes to this particular type of opportunity, no place on our big blue marble can match Hollywood's potential -- not Silicone Valley, N.Y.C., Tokyo, London or Rome.

Guess what? *You aren't going down this road by accident either.* No more than welfare mother J.K. Rowling or car-sleeping Sly Stallone with an onion skin manuscript of Rocky on his lap.

This shit is not for civilians. Not everyone should undertake this same quest. My advice? Ignore rash judgments handed down from the narcoleptic safety of average and unchallenged lives. This is *our* roll of the dice, we're all big boys and girls, and neither our oft-predicted demise nor our surprise, jaw-dropping success concerns anyone save ourselves. Friend or foe, anyone has an issue with that, tell 'em exactly what I do -- "Mind your fuckin' business. It'll make it easier for both of us."

* * * * *

I've tried to live my writing life with one simple credo in mind, a brief epiphany that struck me years ago --

429

"Never write anything you yourself would not want to read."

Sound simplistic? Self-evident? It ain't. Not by a long shot.

Pushing past the carbon-dated clichés still populating today's movies to concoct something lasting and fresh -- something <u>original</u> -- burns a massive amount of screenwriter calories. It takes serious effort not to phone it in and blindly parrot the same ol' dogshit audiences have suffered through since the beginning of time.

Let me urge you with the utmost passion not to become one of *those* writers; the "it's good enough" or "nobody'll give a shit" hack who's content aping the status quo and regurgitating freely from other, better films. In my experience, writers with such little respect for the medium end up scratching their heads, wondering why they can't get any traction while essentially flushing their vain efforts down the toilet. Get serious. Nobody real in this town wants to invest in yesterday's ideas or spend precious financing on a bad copy of a bad copy of a bad copy.

<u>Writing the same ol' shit makes you the same ol' shitty screenwriter</u>. Hollywood is predicated on the finding The Next, The Newest, the up-to-the-nanosecond über-cool shit people haven't read or seen or even conceptualized before. Making a name for yourself requires continual innovation, digging deep to surprise even the most development-hardened pros. Coming up with fresh material is *fuckin' hard*. I get it. But ultimately this is what separates the men from the boys, the wheat from the chaff, the big dogs from the yappy little ones. Nothing shy of this standard will do if you're honestly and truthfully seeking a screenwriting career.

Do yourselves a huge favor. Invest sincere care in every single line of your screenplays. Showcase how much thought and love went into your script's construction and completion. This is not some vague New Age intangible; for veteran readers this level of commitment comes across <u>on</u> the <u>page</u>. *How can it not?* When covering twenty bad-to-average, why-did-anybody-bother-writing-this screenplays a week, finally reading The Chronic buzzes you the same way watching a great film after having slogged through a dozen crappy ones does. *The great one reminds you why you loved movies in the first place.* Same exact deal with scripts. Maybe even more so.

<u>Your script needs to be that one.</u> The project which stands above and apart and gets readers re-inspired about making movies again. Boil it all down, that's what this gig is all about. Surprising strangers, and in the process surprising yourself.

* * * * *

Hollywood's brooding skies do eventually part, my friends, bathing those still standing in an intoxicating sunshine like no other. Closely-held dreams are rendered real by this radiance -- and what a rush! *Being paid to write. Even getting movies made!* Turns out there are job opportunities in the sick, wonderful world of creating motion pictures, and against what seemed the slimmest of odds you went right out and wrangled yourself one. Crazy, right? Who would've thought? Some of the folks back home might *never* fully wrap their heads around it, even while you're autographing their BluRays. And you know what's even bigger fun? Witnessing the delightful surreality of it all flashing your closest friends' faces; sweet moments of celebration which stay etched in both your minds forever.

431

From the deepest hollows of my heart, I'm pulling for every writer reading this to halo themselves with some of that same, triumphant tangerine. To taste a version of the writing life I've tasted. To get that phone call saying you got the open assignment or your spec sold. To drive onto a legendary Dream Factory lot (Warner Bros. for me, please) where your silver screen heroes made the very movies which fired up and fed your fledgling imagination. To hop a private jet bound for somewhere cameras are waiting to shoot your pages. To walk into a theater, any theater, playing *your* movie, and see your name thirty feet high, if only for an instant.

To wake up middle of the night or halt yourself middle of the day with the abrupt realization that *everything you own* was paid for by your <u>writing</u>. Writing, script by script, line by line, is what puts food in your mouth and keeps a roof overhead, offering the world unquestioned proof that you do have the mettle, did have what it took.

With this comes the real cherry on top -- *being able to live how you want to live*, highs and lows, for better or worse, year-in, year-out. How many people can say they got to choose their way of life without making some soul-stunting compromise within themselves or without? Sadly, not too many from what I've seen during my brief time on Planet Earth.

* * * * *

Guess that's it, Dear Reader. Like it or not, dig it or don't, my work here is done.

It took nearly a year to write *Tough Love*, and I plunged into it without a publishing deal or guaranteed profit of any kind. That's right, zero safety net -- exactly like writing a spec. Once finished, I found myself having to shell out eight grand just to get the book professionally vetted and indemnified.

Why risk my own hard-earned money? Violate <u>Scarface</u>'s sage edict against "getting high on my own supply"?

Because I felt this was a book that needed to be written, regardless of results, come Hell or high water, win lose or draw. The intent was purely to inspire, so I'll rest easy if it accomplishes anything close to that for future readers -- at whatever the personal financial cost.

This is commonly known as "putting your money where your mouth is".

When my long-time literary agency got *Tough Love*, they informed me it was a very, very difficult book to sell. That screenwriting was a "challenged area" and that -- despite being one of the most powerful agencies in the history of mankind -- they didn't feel they could do anything with it. Translation? My book was too small fry to expend any energy on.

Somehow this was just perfect, right? Especially given what the book itself is all about.

Who knows? Maybe they're 100% correct. Perhaps nobody outside a shithouse-crazy cabal of screenwriting shut-ins will *ever* give a damn about what's shared in these pages. I mean, isn't *everything* dealing with screenwriters considered oddball or second-class or somehow less important? "Challenged" in one metaphorical sense or another?

And yet, here it still is. And you're still reading it.

"Being in a minority, even a minority of one, doesn't make you mad."

By any and all means necessary, my friends. Work hard. Listen well. Trust your instincts. Circumvent the setbacks, stave off the self-doubt, shrug off the low blows and always, always keep your eyes on the prize. Most importantly, keep Devil's Towering your mashed potatoes and peeling off your gas mask until finally you find *yourself* aboard that schmancy spaceship with all the crazy lights.

Hey, somebody's gotta do it, right?

Why shouldn't that somebody be you?

ABOUT THE AUTHOR

An Honors Graduate of the New York University Film Program, John Jarrell sold his first screenplay at twenty-four and has been a professional screenwriter ever since. The film he wrote people are most familiar with is Romeo Must Die -- the hit Warner Bros. hip-hop/kung-fu actioner starring Aaliyah and Jet Li.

During John's career he's written films and television pilots for most of the major studios and has been fortunate enough to work with some of the finest producers and directors in Hollywood. These include -- Jeffrey Katzenberg, Neal Moritz, Joel Silver, Terence Chang & John Woo, Mike Medavoy, James Foley, Warren Littlefield, Carl Beverly and Sarah Timberman.

Among other projects, John wrote Hard-Boiled II for John Woo, scripted the animated family film Outlaws for Dreamworks and most recently co-wrote The Man With The Iron Fists II and War Dogs for NBC/Universal.

435

An active member of the Writer's Guild of America, West, John currently serves on the WGA Screen Credits Committee. He is repped by WME, McKuin, Frankel and Whitehead, LLP and managed by Ensemble Entertainment. He teaches his labor-of-love Tough Love Screenwriting Class in Los Angeles.

toughlovescreenwriting.com

Made in the USA
Monee, IL
04 March 2021

61918081R00246